Current Perspectives in Psychology

Adolescent Risk Behaviors

Why Teens Experiment and Strategies to Keep Them Safe

David A. Wolfe, Peter G. Jaffe, Claire V. Crooks

YALE UNIVERSITY PRESS   NEW HAVEN AND LONDON

Published with assistance from the Kingsley Trust Association Publication Fund
established by the Scroll and Key Society of Yale College.

Set in Adobe Garamond type by The Composing Room of Michigan, Inc.,
Grand Rapids, Michigan.

Printed in the United States of America.

Library of Congress Cataloging-in-Publication Data
Wolfe, David A. (David Allen), 1951–
Adolescent risk behaviors : why teens experiment and strategies to keep them safe /
David A. Wolfe, Peter G. Jaffe, and Claire V. Crooks.
p.   cm. — (Current perspectives in psychology)
Includes bibliographical references and index.
ISBN-13: 978-0-300-11080-7 (cloth : alk. paper)

1. Risk taking (Psychology) in adolescence—Prevention.   I. Jaffe, Peter G.
II. Crooks, Claire V.   III. Title.   IV. Series.
[DNLM: 1. Risk-Taking—Adolescent.   2. Risk Reduction Behavior—Adolescent.
3. Adolescent Behavior—psychology.   4. Counseling—methods—Adolescent.
5. Interpersonal Relations—Adolescent.   6. Health Promotion—methods—
Adolescent.   WS 462   W855a   2006]
RJ506.R57W65 2006
155.4'18—dc22
2005029945

A catalogue record for this book is available from the British Library.

10 9 8 7 6 5 4

To our families and teachers, who taught us
that relationships are the critical *Fourth R*

Contents

Series Foreword

Current Perspectives in Psychology presents the latest discoveries and developments across the spectrum of the psychological and behavioral sciences. The series explores such important topics as learning, intelligence, trauma, stress, brain development and behavior, anxiety, interpersonal relationships, education, child-rearing, divorce and marital discord, and child, adolescent, and adult development. Each book focuses on critical advances in research, theory, methods, and applications and is designed to be accessible and informative to nonspecialists and specialists alike.

The focus of this book is on adolescence and the promotion of healthy prosocial development. Problem or at-risk behaviors that often emerge in adolescence include substance use and abuse, school failure and dropping out, delinquency, crime, and violence, and unsafe sexual practices. These are referred to as at-risk behaviors because they have deleterious short- and long-term consequences for mental and physical health. In this book, Drs. David Wolfe, Peter Jaffe, and Claire Crooks examine the development of these behaviors and how they are influenced by relationships and physical, cognitive, and emotional factors that emerge over the course of development.

The authors discuss the relationships that adolescents form, with particular emphasis on how these relationships with peers and the family change over the course of young people's development. These relationships explain many of the motives and beliefs of youth that underlie choices to engage in healthy or harmful behaviors. Several pertinent and fascinating topics are addressed in relation to risk behaviors, including parental and family relations; romantic relationships; gender and ethnic differences; bullying, teasing, and harassment; lesbian, gay, and bisexual relations; gangs; and the media. In these and other areas, the authors provide the latest research findings and elaborate how these findings relate to the overall themes of adolescent development and decision making.

The excellent scholarship of this book is evident in the scope of its coverage, the authors' extensive knowledge of the relevant research, and the integration of theory, research, and practical application. The authors move from in-depth understanding of adolescent development and relationships to actions, including intervention programs and social policies, that schools, communities, and parents can take to promote positive, healthy decisions and prevent at-risk behaviors. Over the years, these authors have made enormous contributions to the research underlying this book. We are extremely fortunate to have their integration of years of experience, their unparalleled mastery of the topics, and their guidance on what practical steps we can take to improve significantly the well-being of individuals, the family, and society at large.

Alan E. Kazdin
Series Editor

Preface

Parents often regard their children's entry into adolescence with mixed feelings. They look forward to seeing their children become more mature and independent, while at the same time they worry about what their child faces over the next few years. These ambiguous—but entirely reasonable—feelings are based on recollections of their own transition into the teen years as well as horror stories from other parents and the media. The sources of anxiety center around premature sexual activity, the dangers of drugs and alcohol, and the fear of physical and emotional harm from peers and dating partners. Any illusions parents may have of putting their teen in a protective bubble are shattered by the realization of their diminished control over the multiple influences in their child's life.

This book describes how comprehensive adolescent-focused strategies can be used in the reduction and prevention of critical high-risk teen behaviors such as substance abuse, dating violence, sexual assault, and unsafe sexual practices. We feel that efforts to assist youth in making responsible choices in their relationships may play a natural—and crucial—role in promoting positive development and reducing harmful behaviors. Our team has been addressing relationship violence in its many different forms as we have worked with schools to implement prevention programs over the past decade. We also developed a model that captures the interrelationship among critical risk factors affecting healthy adolescent relationships. This model is sensitive to the nature of adolescent risk behaviors within their developmental context and examines the role of the adolescent's environment in shaping positive or health-damaging outcomes. We use this model to describe the common factors that increase or decrease adolescents' risk of engaging in health-damaging behaviors and to underscore the best principles and practices for successful prevention approaches with youth.

Much has been written about treatment and prevention programs that target particular problem behaviors associated with adolescence, such as unsafe sexual practices and drunk driving. Although

many promising programs exist, primarily those targeting sexual behavior or substance abuse, few have taken a strong developmental perspective to match strategies with adolescents' lived experience. In the
last decade, attempts have been made to involve more aspects of
youths' lives in effecting change, especially to promote positive development and to involve parents, schools, and communities. Successful
strategies seek to engage youth in making healthy choices and to an-
chor these choices in the context of their relationships with peers and
romantic partners.

A central focus of this book is to describe promising prevention
initiatives that focus on the protective benefits of healthy relationships.
We examine why current efforts that target specific, single-risk behaviors such as drug abuse are often disappointing because they lack an integrative approach that fits with adolescents' experiences and relationships. From the expansive literature on prevention of unsafe sexual
behaviors, substance abuse, and relationship violence among teens, we
argue that efforts often fail to address adolescent risk behaviors in the
context of their evolving peer and romantic relationships.

In contrast, we present a prevention strategy that shifts the focus
away from efforts aimed at single-target behaviors, which are often
driven by deficit-based explanations of adolescent problem behaviors.
The field is expanding beyond deficit views of adolescent problem behaviors toward a more comprehensive approach that considers ways to
assist youth in navigating the often difficult challenges they face during
important transitional periods. This strategy moves the field closer to a
universal model of health promotion for all youth that focuses on effective methods to encourage youth participation and healthy choices.
Throughout the book, we emphasize ways to increase the various levels of positive influence in the lives of adolescents: from the adolescents
themselves to peers, parents, teachers, and communities.

The book begins with a discussion of the nature of adolescence
and its developmentally important role in establishing health-related
behaviors that promote safety and violence prevention, healthy relationships, safe sexual practices, and prevention of substance abuse. We
focus closely on the literature related to dating violence, unsafe sexual
behaviors, and substance abuse. These topics are of importance to all
teens and are connected to one another in terms of common risk fac-

tors as well as the relationship context in which they occur. Thus, the majority of the book addresses specific prevention targets and initiatives in the areas of substance use, healthy sexuality, and healthy (nonabusive) relationships. The significance of relationships is a common theme used throughout this discussion to link the nature of these risk behaviors to healthy versus unhealthy relationships. Importantly, we take a health-promotion and prevention-science perspective rather than a clinical-intervention approach, which makes this volume more integrative and applicable to a wide professional and lay audience.

Readers will gain an understanding of the common elements underlying the expression of these risk behaviors and come to see how their prevention depends less on targeting specific problems than on promoting healthy and safe choices. The information and strategies described here are intended to benefit all adolescents and their support networks, not merely those known to face certain risks or engage in problem behaviors. Examples of ways to apply best practices at the level of the individual, parent and family, school, and community are presented throughout.

This book addresses the current lack of effective prevention programs that address teens' needs in relation to their developmental circumstances and examines the importance of investing in youth from an inclusive perspective. We take the reader beyond simply trying to reduce risk to include an understanding of adolescent problem behaviors and normal development. In the first half of the book we trace the manner in which the "rules of relating" differ for boys and girls and how these unwritten rules become prominent, and troublesome, in early adolescence. Differences in gender expectations place excessive pressure on boys and girls to conform to gender stereotypes to avoid being teased or bullied. We closely examine the dark side of the rules, including ways in which teens enforce gender expectations among their peers with abusive language and behavior, which often spills over to harassment and violence.

The book discusses typical and atypical patterns of experimentation by teens in three common and potentially dangerous risk behaviors: sex, drugs, and violence. We present a balanced understanding of today's pressures on adolescents and take a close look at the common link among risk behaviors: the relationship connection. Teens must steer their way through challenging and often frightening new situations, and an understanding of this reality provides the basis for helping them make safe and healthy choices. The first half of our study concludes with a look at the important factors influencing adolescents' harmful or unsafe choices, which sets the stage for the goals of educational, skill-based approaches to assisting adolescents in navigating these murky waters.

The second half of the book examines the principles of successful programs used by schools and communities to cultivate positive adolescent development. These groups have come to realize that the most serious and frequent adolescent health problems—such as substance abuse, sexually transmitted diseases, unintended pregnancy, motor vehicle injuries, and injuries due to violence—are potentially preventable, but only if we retool our approaches to how we educate teens about risk and personal responsibility. We also review programs that have failed to live up to their promise and extensive publicity in their search for a quick fix. We conclude with a discussion of key ingredients for partnerships with youth and educators. It is the goal of this book to engage everyone in the shared purpose of reducing harm among youth and moving this generation closer to a standard of healthy, nonviolent relationships.

Acknowledgments

We are indebted to our colleagues and families for their endless assistance in shaping the ideas expressed in this book. Ray Hughes, former learning coordinator for Safe Schools and Violence Prevention for the Thames Valley District School Board (TVDSB), has been instrumental in establishing a partnership between our research team and the classroom. Along with Debbie Townsey, a teacher with the TVDSB, Ray helped to turn our theories and principles into classroom exercises and skills that now make up the Fourth R curriculum for grade 9 physical health and education. We also thank Anna Malla and Janice Dyer for their research assistance and editorial comments that made the book more user-friendly. We had the advantage of being associated with several organizations in which talented colleagues are devoted to preventing violence against women and children and improving the lives of youth and families. Specifically, we thank our colleagues at the CAMH Centre for Prevention Science and the University of Toronto, the Centre for Children and Families in the Justice System of the London Family Court Clinic, and the Centre for Research on Violence against Women and Children at the University of Western Ontario.

We also acknowledge the hundreds of students and teachers who have enabled us to develop, pilot, and evaluate our programs. Their willingness to try new strategies and provide feedback to our team has been instrumental in the development of the Fourth R program described herein. We extend our deepest appreciation to the Royal Bank of Canada; the Royal LePage Shelter Foundation; Dr. Grant Stirling, Associate Vice-President of Development, the University of Western Ontario; and Ms. Anissa Hilbourn, Vice-President, CAMH Foundation, for their generous and ongoing support of the *Fourth R* program described in this volume.

Last but not least, we express our sincere appreciation to our families, who lent their support and allowed us to bounce many ideas off them throughout the development of the book. Everyone has his or her own view of adolescence, for better or for worse, and ours was constructed from the knowledge of our field coupled with the reality of our lives. Raising teens is always a challenge—and one that results in a better parent.

1

Valuing Adolescence

We constructed the foundation for this book 15 years ago, when the two senior authors met for the first time over lunch. David Wolfe (a recent arrival to Canada from Florida) was struggling to develop effective interventions for child-abusive parents and had begun working with the local Child Protection Agency as part of his research. Peter Jaffe was facing similar challenges in working with the police and court system's response to youth and families in crisis. Child abuse and domestic violence were recurring themes in both our research and clinical efforts and quickly became the focus of our luncheon discussion.

Jaffe was preparing an assessment for the juvenile court about a 15-year-old boy charged with the attempted murder of his stepfather. The prosecutor had made application to the court to have the charges heard in adult court because the case involved a premeditated act with a firearm. A psychological assessment for the court had been ordered to determine whether the young man belonged in the juvenile or adult system. Upon closer examination, what had appeared at first to be a violent, premeditated ambush of his stepfather when he arrived home from work was in fact the culmination of 15 years of domestic violence and child abuse. The local police department had responded to domestic violence calls at this home for many years, but the violence continued. With a growing sense of hopelessness and helplessness, the boy decided to take matters into his own hands and use the very weapon his stepfather had often used to threaten his mother.

In our view, the offense before the court was more a reflection of the community's failure to address the reality of the violence experienced in this family than it was of the adolescent's character or psychological makeup. At the time, this view was radical and could be construed as condoning youth violence. However, the assessment revealed the impact on this boy of growing up in a family war zone in which his mother frequently suffered severe physical and emotional abuse. To adapt to his family circumstances, this boy's survival and coping strategies had become increasingly desperate and ineffective. For the past three years, he had shown behavior problems in school, signs of depression and anger, poor school attendance, declining achievement, and involvement in drugs and alcohol. Rather than these problems being viewed as warning signs of possible violence in the home or other major family stressors, they were taken at face value as signs of an antisocial adolescent. There was a sense of outrage among some community members that an adolescent was capable of such an offense, and they wanted the court to impose the most severe sentence possible. The assessment, in contrast, clearly showed a normal adolescent who had faced many years of tyranny and ultimately had acted in defense of his mother, his sister, and himself. The judge decided to keep him in the juvenile system and ensure that he received the treatment and support he needed.

Many elements of this court case touched on similar themes that David Wolfe had experienced in his work with child-abusive parents in Tampa, Florida. He had been struggling with ways to intervene effectively with parents who themselves were adult survivors of abuse and had been exposed to mostly inappropriate models of child-rearing. Like the boy, these parents were before the court or child welfare system because of their violent behavior, and the judge and community were looking for solutions to "fix" the growing problem of child abuse that was emerging as a public concern in the 1970s. The search for a parental defect or mental disorder as the cause of child abuse was proving less and less fruitful. Research studies attempting to find critical differences between abusive and nonabusive parents in psychiatric symptoms or disorders were in fact revealing that this problem could not be explained on the basis of a mental disorder or individual factors alone. Evidence was pointing to major differences in family background, exposure to multiple forms of violence in childhood, and significantly impaired abilities to cope with the normal demands of child-rearing within a context of social isolation and negative relationships with others (Wolfe, 1985).

In conducting this early research, it became apparent that abusive and high-risk parents received little benefit from multiple assessments or imposed supervision aimed at determining if they could raise their children safely or not. What they required was guidance and support to manage the major stressors surrounding many aspects of their lives. Their family of origin had never provided this guidance and support, and they found themselves thrust into a largely unsympathetic and adversarial system. In contrast, their needs required concerted efforts to reverse destructive attitudes and behaviors and to manage negative emotions associated with many stressors in their lives. They needed the missing building blocks to learn the knowledge and skills necessary to foster healthy, nonabusive relationships with their partners and their children.

We shared the view that there was widespread ignorance about domestic violence and child abuse and the diverse impact of such events on child and adolescent development. Our analysis uncovered several themes, many of which have guided our subsequent work for the past quarter century:

- Children and youth reflect the lessons learned in their family of origin through their behavior, both good and bad
- Children will attempt to adapt to whatever circumstances they face, but such adaptation often comes at a huge cost to themselves and society
- Adaptation may include attempts at self-medication through drugs or alcohol, running away from home, and involvement in high-risk sexual behavior and violence
- Much of the emotional and psychological harm created by these events emerges in the context of children's future interpersonal and intimate relationships—often

marred by violence and/or victimization—which persists
across different partners and hampers their future role as
parents

   ■ A community's silence or denial of these issues leaves
vulnerable family members with no place to turn; our child
welfare and justice systems are too overburdened to provide
much more than crisis intervention

   ■ Failure to address violence in the family has both a
short-term impact on community services (such as police,
medical, education, and social services) and a long-term
and pronounced impact on community safety and well-
being

   ■ Our strongest hope rests in widespread education and
prevention that engages the entire community—from
schools to service clubs—in addressing all forms of violence and abuse and ensuring early identification and intervention

We decided to pursue a series of clinical studies to document the
nature and extent of problems associated with domestic violence and
child abuse. Women's shelters were established in many cities across
North America by the early 1980s, and the child abuse movement had
drawn attention to the effects of physical and sexual abuse on children.
These fields were still in their infancy; in particular they had not begun
to collaborate in developing services or conducting research on the impact of violence in the home. In addition, there were significant challenges involved in conducting research with high-risk families and
children (such as suitable comparison groups and access to the population), and there was substantial professional and public resistance to
recognizing the full scope of the problem. The past two decades have
shown considerable progress in overcoming many of these barriers and
establishing the necessary groundwork for sustained prevention efforts—although much remains to be done. Describing how this
change came about is the purpose of this chapter, which paves the way
for engaging youth in reducing violence and related risk behaviors over
the next generation.

Our Early Studies: The Destructive Nature of Violence in the Home

Despite challenges and resistance (much of which was unforeseen at the time), we forged partnerships with supportive agencies and professionals who shared our concerns and embarked on a long-term research effort to build the foundation for an informed strategy to prevent violence in relationships. We first examined the adjustment problems of children living in shelters for battered women, in response to growing alarm expressed by shelter staff concerning the needs of these children. Shelter directors saw benefit in such research as justification for enhancing funding for specialized childcare staff to support women and children in crisis. The timing of these early efforts coincided with growing professional and academic attention to the seriousness of violence in the family, which together created momentum for social change (Straus, Gelles, & Steinmetz, 1980). The findings from these initial collaborative efforts, discussed below, led to increased funding for shelters to develop unique assessment and intervention programs for these children as an investment in our collective future.

When we spoke to children residing in shelters with their mothers, we were struck by the extent to which they had seldom, if ever, had an opportunity to voice their fears and worries to an adult. These children most often suffered in silence because they were keeping a family secret, and at the time no one recognized the source of their emotional or behavioral problems. Even their parents underestimated the extent of conflict and violence to which their children had been exposed. In many situations, parents thought their children were sheltered from the adult violence, even though their children could often describe in detail what they heard from their bedrooms late at night or the aftermath of violent incidents they faced the next day.

In our first study, we compared a sample of 100 children residing in shelters for battered women with 100 children from the community (who had not experienced such events) on a number of indicators of emotional and behavioral adjustment. About one-third of the children exposed to violence had clinically significant adjustment problems, comparable to children seen in treatment centers, and another third had many elevated symptoms of emotional distress. Boys, in particular, exhibited a number of aggressive and disruptive behaviors that adults found worrisome and troublesome. Girls, in contrast, tended to have more internalizing symptoms such as anxiety, worry, sadness, and regulatory problems. Notably, there was tremendous variability among these children based on a host of risk and protective factors, such as their mother's health and well-being, the disruptions in their lives, and the extent and severity of the violence to which they had been exposed (interested readers are referred to Jaffe, Wolfe, & Wilson, 1990).

This early work on children exposed to violence in the home led to the piloting of psychoeducational groups to address the unique needs of these children. While helping the children cope with their circumstances and regulate their behavior, these groups also provided insight and detail into how they viewed their families, their peers, and themselves. Not only did they have current adjustment difficulties, as observed and reported by adults, in the context of group interaction they also revealed many subtle symptoms indicative of distorted beliefs about the use of violence as a conflict resolution strategy. Younger children were inclined to blame themselves for the abuse, and school-aged children were sometimes prone to blame their mothers for provoking the violence. Many showed what has since been referred to as a "victim and victimizer" view of relationships (Dodge, Pettit, & Bates, 1994b), in which abuse and power play a prominent role in how one forms relationships with peers, family members, and romantic partners. Unfortunately, counseling to address their unique problems and underlying issues was seldom available in community settings, so we undertook to develop specialized therapeutic programs to acknowledge such issues (Jaffe et al., 1990). We also worked in tandem with existing children's services to increase awareness of domestic violence, which may have been overlooked in their caseloads.

While intervention efforts were encouraging, we had to come to grips with the enormous number of children affected by violence and the futility of addressing their needs only after the fact. One of our colleagues, a school principal, pointed out that there were three to five children in the average classroom living with the aftermath of violence in their family. Communities could never hire enough therapists and police officers to deal with the enormity of the problem without stemming the tide through concerted prevention efforts. At the same time, we realized that children exposed to violence were also affected by other messages condoning violence: through the media, video games, movies, and television. In fact, the peers to whom vulnerable children most often turn were themselves desensitized to violent behavior by the impact of the broader societal message that "violence is entertainment." Similar to others studying public health issues affecting children, we concluded that our focus should not be limited to children in violent homes but rather expanded to include the broader societal influences that condone or minimize violent behavior.

In brief, these early findings confirmed that the impact of domestic violence on children was often significant, but not straightforward or consistent. An encouraging note was that the findings also implied that substantial harm to children was not necessarily inevitable or long lasting. Like other adjustment problems in childhood, recovery from exposure to violence was significantly related to positive changes in family circumstances, perceived support from family and community members, and, of course, the absence of abuse or frightening events. These early findings have been replicated and expanded in over 50 studies, which have helped to unravel the complexity of this multifaceted relationship between children's adjustment and exposure to domestic violence (see meta-analysis by Wolfe, Crooks, Lee, McIntyre-Smith, & Jaffe, 2003).

We were asked to present our research findings on violence in the home to high school students as part of our discipline's initiative to "give psychology away." We thought there was value in receiving this age group's feedback about the implications for prevention of and public awareness efforts about family violence. Over 400 students attended a half-day workshop and completed a survey asking their opinion about the role of adolescents and schools in addressing family violence. The overwhelming response showed they were in favor of public education playing a significant role in violence prevention, especially violence in family and dating relationships. Not only were the students very open to information about the subject area, many also recognized their responsibility in responding appropriately to peers facing these difficult circumstances. These initial results suggested that

violence-prevention initiatives would be welcomed by teens, who fa-
vored an approach that would make such information an integral part
of the education system (Jaffe & Reitzel, 1990).

Subsequently, we asked teens in other high schools the extent to
which they knew of peers who were coping with violence in their family or dating relationships. We also asked them to describe hypotheti-
cally how they would handle such circumstances, in an effort to understand their knowledge about resources and attitudes about this
behavior (Jaffe, Suderman, Reitzel, & Killip, 1992). This survey reinforced the fact that the majority of students was aware of family and
dating violence among peers, and moreover students were much more
likely to turn to each other for advice and support rather than adults
such as teachers, parents, and guidance counselors. These data under-
lined the importance of initiating prevention efforts directed not only
at potential victims and perpetrators but also to all teens, since they
represent the peer culture—comprised of the friends, witnesses, and
bystanders to many of these abusive events. Sadly, at best the advice
and support offered by peers was inadequate; at worst, abusive behavior was minimized, ignored, or even condoned.

At the time of these initial studies, most school boards did not
permit us to ask teens to reveal directly their own experiences of violence or abuse, out of concern for the boards' obligation to act on such
information or the possibility that it might cause undue stress on the
family. Therefore, these initial efforts approached the topic indirectly
by asking students if they believed the topic was relevant in their lives
and if they knew other students dealing with these circumstances. A
decade later this topic was more prominent in the public agenda, so we
and others were able to ask students more directly to describe their
own experiences in the past and present, provided the information was
anonymous or confidential. Parenthetically, this development reflected the rapid shift in public attitudes toward the open discussion of
domestic and other forms of personal violence and paved the way for
tighter research designs and concerted prevention efforts.

In the early 1990s, we began to work with adolescents who had
grown up in violent and abusive homes. We chose this group specifically because it offered the potential for prevention of violence in the
next generation, and very little was being done to reverse known influ-

ences. In their own words, young people explained how they were on the doorstep of adulthood and their physical maturity and growing independence put them in the role of intimate partners and potential parents. The acceleration into forthcoming adult privileges made them eager for better information about the nuances of intimate relationships and choices and more responsive to nonjudgmental information. They wanted advice on making good choices but were offered mostly warnings and punitive consequences. Given the chance to discuss their desire for positive relationships and their difficulty reconciling their own abusive experiences with their future plans, they impressed us with their insights into the challenges of adolescence.

Many of the challenges faced by these youths from abusive families were very similar to those faced by all teens but were often compounded by their lack of positive role models and feelings of apprehension and anger related to past traumatic events (Scott, Wolfe, & Wekerle, 2003). In small groups, these teens discussed issues concerning healthy and nonhealthy relationships and how their behavior and attitudes were shaped by their experiences. Most important, they recognized that despite the limitations of their past, they could learn to make healthy choices and be in charge of their own decisions. Their past family experiences did not force them into an inevitable pattern of abuse and victimization (which many believed) but did necessitate extra effort to learn alternatives to violence and self-destructive behavior. They also were attracted to an approach that did not merely focus on their problems but rather helped them recognize their choices and learn the skills for positive relationships.

In the mid-1990s, we (Wolfe, Wekerle, Scott, Straatman, & Grasley, 2004) looked for a comparison group of "normal" adolescents with no involvement in violent relationships currently or in the past as part of our evaluation of the above intervention for at-risk youth. We sought support from local high schools in conducting a study in which we asked these youth about their attitudes and behaviors concerning dating violence, their current emotional adjustment, and their past family experiences. We were interested, in particular, in the degree of association between prior child maltreatment and current involvement in a violent dating relationship. Theories linking family violence to future violence in relationships were gaining support (Riggs &

O'Leary, 1989) and were consistent with our own observations with youth from violent homes—they wanted to form positive relationships but had little understanding of what they looked or felt like.

Three important things emerged from our study of 1,400 high school students. First, to our surprise, we discovered a high rate of maltreatment in this sample of teens who had not been identified by any formal community reporting systems. Based on the norms and cutoff scores for the Childhood Trauma Questionnaire (Bernstein, Ahluvalia, Pogge, & Handelsman, 1997), about 30 percent of the sample met criteria for one or more types of maltreatment during childhood, including emotional and physical abuse and neglect, sexual abuse, and exposure to domestic violence. Although alarming, this rate is comparable to that obtained in random samples of adults (MacMillan et al., 2001) and speaks to the pervasiveness of these problems. Moreover, this subsample of youths reported levels of violence and abuse comparable to those experienced by our child protection sample (Wolfe, Scott, Wekerle, & Pittman, 2001). These prevalence rates suggest that official reporting of child maltreatment reflects only the tip of the iceberg and that a sizeable minority of youth grows up experiencing abuse and violence at home.

Second, we found that our subsample of high school youths with maltreatment backgrounds could be distinguished from their nonmaltreated peers on the basis of symptoms of distress and abusive behavior. Girls with a history of maltreatment were about nine times as likely to report symptoms of emotional distress relative to girls without such histories, including symptoms of anger, depression, anxiety, and post-traumatic stress-related problems. Boys with histories of maltreatment also reported symptoms of emotional distress, but not to the same extent as the girls. They were about three times as likely to report clinical levels of depression and post-traumatic stress as boys without a maltreatment history. Notably, only the boys from maltreating families had a significantly greater risk of using threatening behaviors or physical abuse against their dating partners. As expected, past maltreatment experiences influenced adolescent relationships and well-being, with a differential pattern for girls and boys (Wolfe et al., 2001).

Finally, we reassessed this group of students a year later to determine if changes in their symptoms of distress or their attitudes about violence in relationships mediated the connection between maltreatment and dating violence. We found we could predict the extent of violence against a dating partner a year later, for girls as well as boys, on the basis of their self-reported trauma symptoms from a year previous. Youths with maltreatment backgrounds apparently faced greater challenges in regulating their emotions and their behavior, especially in the context of peer and partner relationships that unfold in early to mid-adolescence. Attitudes and beliefs about violence in relationships were less significant in predicting abusive behavior over time, although they were highly correlated at each time point. These findings underscore the importance of trauma symptoms in understanding the association between childhood maltreatment and dating violence and highlight the need to help adolescents cope with these issues (Wolfe et al., 2004). They also remind us that the impact of child maltreatment is more than children modeling what they observed and simply repeating it in their own relationships. They have formed a view of relationships that involves power differentials and control tactics, encased in emotions of fear, anger, and mistrust. Beyond these behavioral and cognitive distortions, the impact encompasses a disruption in the child's ability to regulate emotions heightened by traumatic experiences in the family that can persist into adolescence and adulthood.

These studies that followed our discussions 25 years ago led to many valuable insights and have informed our current approach to prevention described in this book. The senior authors had the good fortune to be joined by Dr. Claire Crooks in 2001. Dr. Crooks brought extensive experience in broad-based prevention programs that emphasized active community collaboration and a firm commitment to thorough evaluation strategies. Her clinical work with traumatized and acting-out adolescents had brought her to the same conclusion: that keeping children and youth safe from abuse and harm is a necessary foundation for healthy communities. Over the past four years she assisted in developing the Fourth R curriculum, described in the latter half of this book. Together we have developed a research program that focuses on adapting, implementing, and evaluating comprehensive approaches to prevention with adolescents.

Our insights continue to be shaped by raising our own adolescents, who fill in many of the gaps left by our theories and findings.

Our adolescents remind us daily of the struggles they face with their peers, parents, teachers, and dating partners. Even in the best of circumstances, with full parental support and resources, crises are commonplace and conflict resolution skills are at a premium. We realize that adolescents, as a group, have much in common with each other despite diverse family backgrounds and experiences, and that conflict in relationships is a regular occurrence for most teens. Helping all teens navigate this critical transition period is a worthy goal, regardless of whether or not they have grown up experiencing violence. Adolescence offers an ideal opportunity for education and skills that promote healthy relationships, and the vast majority of teens are interested in learning alternatives to violence and ways of counteracting strong negative messages from their peer culture.

Building Prevention from the Ground Up: Valuing and Engaging Youth

Over the past 25 years, many books and articles on domestic violence have concluded with a discussion of the importance of prevention. However, until recently few communities fully recognized there was even something to prevent. Communities saw the deaths of men, women, and children in their own homes as isolated acts disconnected from social attitudes and beliefs about women and children. Violence against family members was viewed as an unfortunate result of family relationships, and society and its interveners, such as police, often ignored or minimized it. These lives of quiet desperation and deaths were seen as unfortunate but unavoidable, and community intervention was perceived as futile. To approach a school board and speak of preventing violence in the family would draw puzzlement or even scorn directed at what appeared to be irrelevant and inappropriate educational activities.

In contrast, today parents and civic leaders raise questions if their schools are not actively involved in such prevention efforts. Although these problems are far from resolved, we have reached a new era in which communities now recognize violence in the family as a fundamental social issue requiring major shifts in public awareness and resource allocation. It is becoming commonplace for a family violence–related death to be followed by a community outcry for a better collaborative response and enhanced prevention efforts.

As a result of efforts targeting infants and children in the first few years of life, major progress in prevention science has occurred. These initiatives have built on the growing body of literature related to infant brain development and the crucial attachment process that sets the foundation for subsequent development and future relationships (Cicchetti & Cohen, 1995; Cicchetti & Toth, 1997). Although we strongly endorse the critical importance of early childhood programs to establish positive development and reduce social and emotional adjustment problems, unfortunately adolescence still remains a poor second cousin. At the extreme, there may be concern that investing in adolescence yields fewer dividends than intervening in earlier stages of development. That is, to a large extent the die has been cast in attitudes and behavior, and intervention should be targeted primarily to those who are readily identifiable because of their acting-out behavior. There may be some truth to the view that the cost-benefit ratio of interventions is higher during adolescence, but this economic reality should not lead to abandoning the full potential of this stage of development for meaningful prevention efforts.

Positive Shifts in Understanding Adolescent Development

For many years, much of society viewed adolescents with a significant dash of suspicion, fear, and loathing. Some date the formal articulation of this view back to an early academic publication in 1904 by G. Stanley Hall entitled *Adolescence: Its Psychology and Its Relations to Physiology, Anthropology, Sociology, Sex, Crime, Religion, and Education* (Irwin, Burg, & Cart, 2002), which fit in well at the time with emerging theories of moral degeneracy, idiocy, and eugenics. In light of the pessimistic portrayal of youth in our society, it was relatively easy to perpetuate such negative views of adolescence, much as it had been with racism, sexism, and similar forms of ignorance and prejudice. As Stanley Hall clearly proposed, adolescence, for the most part, had long been viewed in association with danger, rebelliousness, crime, sex, and threats to the well-being of society.

But what has become of the well-being of adolescents? Although it is true that adolescence is a period of greater risk than any other in terms of academic failure, violence, and health-compromising behaviors, it is recognized more and more as a period of tremendous opportunity for establishing the skills and values needed for adult life. Needless to say, this period of development has always been challenging and fraught with ups and downs as teens seek their independence from their families and establish their own self-identities. Yet, the last two decades have seen considerable effort expended to understand adolescent development and begin to address some of the large gaps in education and services. Most important, studies examining adolescent behavior in its ecological context and in light of its special vulnerabilities and opportunities have dispelled many myths perpetuating the fearful view of adolescents as deviant. It is now realistic to believe that the next century will bring unparalleled attention to the significance of this period of development.

Major transformations have begun in how adolescent behaviors are understood and in appreciation of how healthy and adaptive behaviors can be promoted. These transformations began, in large part, with concerted efforts by government and nongovernmental agencies to target the high rates of health-compromising behaviors among adolescents. These efforts have been matched with increased funding for research on various aspects of adolescent development and ways to assist youth facing the difficult challenges of this period. What is emerging is a more youth-friendly and inclusive approach to the age-old problems of youth risk behavior along with innovative strategies to promote healthy, safe choices and lifestyles during this critical period of development.

One of the first major contemporary advances in understanding adolescence began with the recognition that many risk behaviors, such as substance use, sexual behavior, and antisocial behavior, are interconnected. Rather than studying youth risk behaviors in silos—as if they were separate and independent "diseases"—researchers and clinicians noted that the factors that increased the risk of one behavior, such as substance use, were highly similar to the factors that increased another behavior, such as unsafe sexual behavior. A good example of this convergence comes from the substance abuse literature, in which alcohol and drug abuse were seen as cousins, largely connected to (and sometimes responsible for) the youth's other problem behaviors. Similarly, researchers and clinicians involved with problems related to sexual behavior, violence, or crime likewise began to see the overlap in predictors of these behaviors, challenging past assumptions that each problem was independent of others.

Not only are risk behaviors related to one another, often occurring in the same individual, these behaviors are important in terms of the goals of adolescence. Jessor, who conducted much of the pioneering work in this area and formulated Problem Behavior Theory around the concept of co-occurrence and common causal factors, points out how some behaviors seen as problems are "functional, purposive, instrumental, and goal-directed, and that the goals involved are often those that are central in normal adolescent development" (Jessor, Donovan, & Costa, 1991, p. 378). Many of these goals are typical of ordinary adolescent development and not signs of disorder, which explains why risk behaviors that play an adaptive role during adolescence can be difficult to change, much less eliminate. Smoking, drinking, drug use, and early sexual activity, for example, can be instrumental in gaining peer acceptance and respect, establishing autonomy from parents, repudiating norms and values of conventional authority, coping with anxiety or failure, or affirming one's maturity. These activities can also be physically and psychologically dangerous and potentially compromise both short- and long-term health.

So where does this leave us? Because adolescence is a time when individuals prepare to manage adult roles and privileges, developmentalists generally accept that some amount of experimentation and transition is necessary. The issue becomes when, how, and with what adolescents will experiment as well as what role adults should play in ensuring they make safe and responsible choices. About 80 percent of high school students have tried alcohol, 60 percent have tried cigarette smoking, and 50 percent have tried marijuana (Johnston, O'Malley, & Bachman, 2003); it is equally telling that very few adolescents (about 6 percent) refrain entirely from such behaviors (Moffitt, Caspi, Dickson, Silva, & Stanton, 1996). The challenge faced by parents, teachers, and professionals is how to keep teens safe, given that the majority (but not all) will experiment with adult privileges such as smoking, sex, and alcohol use, as well as other illegal or unsafe activities.

There have also been major advances in accepting and supporting youth as valuable members of society, gradually rejecting the negative viewpoint based on fear and poor understanding. Catalano and Hawkins were innovators in exposing the illogic underlying services for youth. With the exception of education, they noted that services for youth largely exist to address or prevent youth *problems,* with little corresponding attention given to promoting youth *development.* Society's assumption that positive youth development occurs naturally in the absence of youth problems resulted in an assortment of youth services focused on "fixing" adolescents engaged in risky behaviors or preventing other youth from "getting into trouble." Burt and colleagues (2002) echo this concern about too little, too late and underscore how such interventions are restricted, almost unilaterally, to single issues such as substance use or early pregnancy. Insufficient attention is given to any of the other factors influencing youths' decisions and choices, such as their families, their environments, and the development context in which problem behaviors occur. Such single-focused, problem-driven approaches to the needs of youth have been very disappointing in terms of their ability to improve the lives of youth.

As described throughout this book, the most effective prevention programs empower young people to be involved in the work, which then becomes rewarding through the promotion of cooperation and mutual support. To foster healthy adolescent development, efforts to reduce or prevent risk behaviors are needed. These efforts need to be matched with an equal commitment to helping young people understand life's challenges and responsibilities and to developing the necessary skills to succeed as adults. Youths need developmentally appropriate knowledge and education delivered in a nonjudgmental and highly salient format, which emphasizes their choices, responsibilities, and consequences. In effect, they need to be prepared, not scared. Youth, especially youth at risk, need education and skills to promote healthy relationships, to develop peer support, and to establish social action aimed at ending violence in relationships. They need to feel connected not only to their peers (which is relatively easy) but also to their school, family, and community. Such connection requires a commitment to building capacity in each community to be inclusive of all youth—to see each adolescent as a person rather than a potential problem. The ul-

timate act of inclusion is to empower youth to identify the critical issues they face and the solutions that are most meaningful to the reality
of their lives and circumstances.

The most recent transformation, and one that forms a foundation for the themes and approaches described in this book, recognizes
the importance of *relationships* and how they protect against or increase risk behaviors. Youths' relationships and their peer culture play a
significant role in understanding many of the motives and beliefs underlying their healthy or harmful choices. Relationships include past
and present interactions with parents and family members, which
shape many of their current attitudes and provide the foundation for
making safe versus risky choices. These relationships also include their
peer group and peer culture, which set the context for new opportunities to experiment with adult privileges, challenge rules, or define their
own boundaries and choices. Rather than viewing youth behaviors primarily in terms of their degree of risk or harm, it is important to remember that risk behaviors almost always occur in the context of a relationship. As noted by Jessor et al. (1991), this relationship context
reflects developmental circumstances, such as resolving disputes with
parents or peers, seeking status or acceptance, or looking for new plea-
sures. Thus, the determination of an individual's degree of risk often
comes down to his or her skill at negotiating relationship issues, particularly with parents, peers, and romantic partners.

A relationship perspective is certainly not new to the fields of psychology, sociology, psychiatry, criminology, social work, and many
others. The distinction here is that the significance of relationships has
not been used to inform policies and programs for this age group. An
analogy to early child development is relevant here, for it shows some
parallels to adolescent development as well as some possible roads to
prevention of problem or risk behaviors.

Early parent-child attachment is tremendously important for
toddlers, because a positive (secure) attachment with one or more caregivers serves as an adaptive strategy for the infant to organize his or her
world and accomplish important developmental milestones. Accordingly, developmental researchers and many others have argued that the
early childhood years are critical in terms of family support and education concerning child-rearing strategies and healthy parent-child in-

teractions. Parents are often most willing to receive guidance during
these early years, because an infant's, toddler's, or preschooler's behavior can be challenging and, at times, upsetting. Children's early care-
giving experiences play an especially important role in designing the
parts of the brain involved in emotion, personality, and behavior
(Sameroff & Fiese, 2000). Children's attachment to their caregivers,
for instance, may increase their ability to learn and to cope with stress
(Waters, Merrick, Treboux, Crowell, & Albersheim, 2000), whereas
maltreatment or harsh parenting can prime the brain for a lifetime of
struggle with handling stress or forming healthy relationships.

Because of the significance of secure, positive parent-child relationships to healthy development, efforts have been made for many
years to foster them from an early age, with considerable success. According to attachment theory (Bowlby, 1980), infants are born with
many abilities to engage in relationship-enhancing behaviors, such as
smiling and crying. Nonetheless, researchers recognized that the process of parent-infant attachment (particularly among humans) was not
rigidly predetermined; rather, infant behavior has to become organized
into flexible, goal-oriented systems through learning and goal-cor-
rected feedback. Moreover, a child's internal working model of relationships—what he or she expects from others and how he or she relates to others—emerges from this first crucial relationship and is
carried forward into later relationships. This theory has now been
field-tested in many different cultures and has received wide support in
terms of its basic premise of the developmental processes involved in
forming attachment. Furthermore, this relationship-based theory has
led to important advancements in working with families at risk of maltreatment or facing other major stressors by fostering positive interactions and attachment (Olds et al., 1998).

Without stretching the analogy too far, there are many interesting parallels between the developmental milestones and behaviors of
young children and those of young adolescents, with one important
difference. Both age groups have higher levels of problem behaviors
than any other age period, especially in terms of noncompliant, disruptive, or difficult behaviors (Mash & Wolfe, 2005). Both age periods
are also marked by rapid physical and emotional development. Perhaps most telling is how both age groups have difficulty controlling or

regulating their emotions, usually under particular circumstances such as paying attention in class or sharing with peers or siblings. Once again, the child-caregiver relationship plays a critical role in this process by providing the basic setting for children to express emotions and have caring guidance and limits placed on them. Troubled child-caregiver relationships are highly stressed during these two stages; indeed, children are most likely to be assaulted by a caregiver during early childhood and adolescence.

An important difference between the developmental processes of young children and those of young adolescents is connected to the fundamental goals demanded of each of them by their environment and biology. Whereas the young child's "job" is to form a secure, close relationship to his or her caregivers, the young adolescent's role is the opposite: to begin the process of detaching from his or her parents and becoming an independent, autonomous individual (Erikson, 1968). Historically, this process has been regarded as one of Sturm und Drang; that is, adolescents are expected to be troublesome and aggravating as they plot a course from their childhood connections to their adolescent peer group and struggle with rapid hormonal and environmental changes. Although this view was an advance over the previous one of deviance and crime, it went a bit too far in attributing adolescent problems to their stage of development. Insufficient consideration was given to the true warning signs of problems in the assumption that adolescents would "grow out of" their difficulties or that there was little that could be done.

As a time of transition from childhood to adulthood, adolescence presents a period of instability and change (American Psychological Association, 1993). Transition periods are often more amenable to change, as a system is already in flux; it is more difficult to introduce change to a system that has achieved homeostasis and thus has considerable inertia. During adolescence, individuals often "try on" different characteristics and roles and are therefore more open to experimenting with new ways of relating to others. Adolescents start to make their own decisions about important issues affecting their lives. Self-reliance, self-control, and independent decision making all increase during the teen years, with a shift away from the family and onto the peer group. To the frustration of many parents, conformity to parental opinions gradually decreases while at the same time the tendency to be swayed by peers increases in early adolescence before it declines (Crockett & Petersen, 1993). Thus, by providing adolescents with growth opportunities that emphasize a more positive mode of relating to others, we can use this natural inclination to try new patterns to strengthen their interpersonal capacities. Conversely, if adolescents are not provided with strong messages about ways to develop healthy dating and peer relationships, they will be more vulnerable to the bombardment of other, less healthy messages conveyed by media and peers.

From Problem Focused to Youth Focused

We exist in a problem-focused society, whereby services and programs are established on the basis of a specific condition or problem. Many schools and communities have programs to deal with youth violence and crime, school failure and dropout, substance use, teen pregnancy, and so forth, and these are structured in much the same way as programs for adults. Understandably, these compartmentalized services follow from the structure of government agencies and requirements, whereby an individual has to have a rather narrow set of problems to receive help. Although many community services recognize that youths often have more than one presenting problem, these agencies may be limited to addressing one problem based on their funding source and mandate. Consequently, education and services have become less youth focused and more problem focused, despite the increasing recognition that youths' problems share very similar underlying factors and conditions. These conditions include economic disadvantage, family conflict, a family history of problem behavior, harsh or inadequate child-rearing methods, and poor neighborhood characteristics (Catalano & Hawkins, 1995).

Today, the idea of adolescent development necessarily being tumultuous has further evolved. Rather than seeing adolescence as a period of angst and rebelliousness, the importance of this transition from childhood into adulthood has gained more formal recognition. It is now recognized that many adolescents negotiate this life transition with few major disruptions or sustained high-risk behaviors. This contemporary view has important implications for investing in youth. On the one hand, most (but not all) adolescents maintain their relationships with their parents and siblings while they add new relationships and identities, and they require minimal assistance in managing new risks. On the other hand, some teens who do experience major problems or consistently engage in risk behaviors are in trouble now and have a significantly greater chance of being in trouble later in life (Burt et al., 2002).

From a developmental perspective, the processes of attachment (in the young child) and independence (in the teen) are both important to one's well-being, yet both often require some input and direction from the environment. Such efforts with young children and parents, as well as with preschools and community programs, have shown considerable promise in fostering a healthy interdependence between child and environment. Paradoxically, there have been many fewer corresponding efforts directed at the process of independence during adolescence, despite the recognized difficulties inherent in this challenging process for all involved.

The greatest categories of risk during adolescence include substance use, unsafe sexual behavior, school failure and dropout, and delinquency/crime/violence (Lerner, 2002). Not surprisingly, the leading causes of death among youth stem from accidents and violence resulting from high-risk behaviors (Irwin et al., 2002). Although significant, given proper understanding, resources, and priorities, these problem behaviors and consequences are largely preventable. The message is simple: successful, developmentally relevant interventions for youth have important payoffs in terms of both preventing harmful outcomes and promoting healthy lifestyles. Despite different origins and contributing factors, risk behaviors typically need to be addressed as a whole, rather than one at a time (Biglan, 2004). Ironically, youths from problem families or problem neighborhoods have ready access to problem activities and little access to positive ones. The solution is to address the known underlying conditions or causes of adolescent troubles while helping them achieve their fundamental developmental tasks (Burt et al., 2002).

For youth to make healthy and adaptive choices, their home, community, and societal structures must be supportive. Understanding which interventions are most appropriate requires understanding of the timing and nature of investments over the course of a lifetime and the factors and constraints that affect decisions to invest in children and youth by parents, family members, and young people themselves. Investing in youth preserves the benefits of prior investments in children, helps to recover some of the benefits for those who may not have had earlier assistance, and addresses new risks that arise during this period (Catalano, Hawkins, Berglund, Pollard, & Arthur, 2002). Only through more concerted efforts to assist youth will we be able to complete the chain of education and services beginning in infancy and childhood that will lead to lasting changes in health and productivity across the lifespan.

Having adults tell adolescents "Just say no" to sex, drugs, and violence is clearly ineffective without teens' active participation and discussion. One thing that has not changed significantly in 100 years is the axiom that adolescents do not welcome messages implying that they are the problem rather than a very dynamic part of the solution. The critical role of adults is to provide access to information and learning opportunities, facilitate relationships and enhance participation in organizations, and actively engage youth in decision making on issues pertinent to their lives.

An important part of understanding the adolescent landscape is grasping the extent of rapid change and new pressures that pose risks to their well-being. More than any other stage of development, adolescence seems like an endless series of crises. These crises, of course, are an extension of familiar adaptive processes that offer opportunities for growth, much like the first day of school or the first night away from one's parents. However, for the adolescent, these new challenges come in the form of overwhelming life events and catastrophes, with each one seemingly unconnected to the others. The resolution of these crises often depends on relationships, namely whom teens turn to and what kind of information they receive. Accordingly, adolescence is filled with milestones to celebrate as well as minefields to avoid, with a slim margin for error.

The essential challenge in raising adolescents is to acknowledge the rapid changes they are going through and be prepared to renegotiate the nature of their previously established relationships. In effect, the fundamental nature of the previous parent-child relationship changes as a function of normal adolescent development, and thus both parties need to be willing to adapt and allow their relationship to evolve. Popular books of advice for parents with teenagers widely acknowledge the nature of this changing relationship and its impact on family members. For purposes of illustration, we examined some of the themes in current books for parents and teens to see how they match up with our views. The basic problems and solutions focus on similar concepts. Again, the importance of maintaining a healthy relationship surfaces as being of core importance. These themes include:

- *The reality of generational differences.* Several authors emphasize the "double generation gap" that separates today's teens from their parents. Not only do today's teens represent a different generation, parenting styles learned in the previous generation may be obsolete or ineffective. The level of tolerance and diversity of ideas change dramatically over each generation, creating a new reality and sense of community. For example, a teen of divorced parents was more likely to feel isolated and different than his or her peers 30 years ago, whereas today divorce is seldom as stigmatizing. Today's debates, in contrast, are more often related to same-sex marriages, alternative lifestyles, and addressing homophobia in mainstream education.
- *The combined effects of pop culture and peers.* Taffel and Blau (2001) point to the reality that families of teens are competing with a "second family" comprised of peers and pop culture. Parents face a challenge to be both aware of and vigilant about the positive and negative effects of this powerful influence. The positive reality is that adolescents are adapting to a rapidly changing culture; the negative reality is that if parents lose their relationships with their teens, an amorphous peer culture may become dominant and inappropriately sway the socialization process. Research into gangs offers an extreme example—teens join gangs as a way of belonging to a "family" that replaces inadequate relationships with their parents.
- *Communicating with teens in the age of technology.* For

decades, experts on raising teenagers have emphasized the importance of establishing good communication between parents and their adolescents. This challenge is heightened by the fact that communication between parents and teens may be at an all-time low due to competition with technology and media (Grigsby & Julian, 2002). Not only are adolescents spending more time in front of computers and televisions, they are also acquiring knowledge at a rate faster than their parents can keep up with. Teens speak less to their parents than ever before, while the advice and information parents offer is sadly out of date. Parents who fail to understand technology are not only hampered in terms of monitoring their teen's activities; they may be falling further and further behind in terms of understanding and communicating with their son or daughter. Parents need to strike a balance between supporting their teen's important need for an independent identity and at the same time seeking ways to strengthen their relationship through nonjudgmental communication.

■ *Understanding adolescent brain development.* Current brain science research is now accessible to parents and teachers to help them understand the impact of brain development on teen behavior (Bradley & O'Connor, 2002). Because the most advanced parts of the brain are still developing throughout adolescence, teens may appear to be unpredictable and somewhat impaired in their judgment and decision making. Experimenting with drugs and alcohol may compound these developmental "limitations." From this perspective, parents need to develop appropriate expectations for adolescent behavior that encourages internal controls and safe choices.

Central to these themes is the vital role of relationships, both past and future. The traditional focus on teens as presenting a host of problems overlooks the importance of relationships as the necessary building blocks to positive communication and problem solving. Simply stated, adolescents who have had close relationships with parents, siblings, teachers, coaches, and friends in the past are more likely to have a strong base from which to develop future relationships and to resolve disagreements without resorting to violence or the abuse of power. Without this foundation, based on previous experiences and role models, a young person is more vulnerable to the powerful influences provided by the media and peers and more susceptible to their emotional impact. Exposure to positive models of conflict resolution is a core component of healthy relationships at home, school, and in the community at large. Throughout this book we present the argument that adolescent development flourishes in such a climate. This climate of healthy relationships has to happen by design and not be left to chance.

Summary

Our work has always focused on children and adolescents trying to adapt to different environments, be they violent homes, crisis shelters, youth institutions, or schools. In all of these environments we were faced with the challenge of promoting prevention at all levels, from treatment of identified children and early intervention with at-risk families to universal school-based programs for all students. Fortunately, this Herculean task has evolved into an important mission of many communities and organizations. Although the commitment to prevention is clear, the strategies, tools, and funding are still lacking. Funding is all too often directed to those who most qualify by their desperate circumstances in the mental health, educational, and correctional systems. Prevention and health promotion, in contrast, are easy to put off to sometime in the future when current crises have been brought under control—an unlikely scenario. We feel strongly that prevention must be built into the system from the ground up, rather than seen as an occasional visitor who drops by.

The gateway to adulthood is surrounded by a myriad of new opportunities, responsibilities, and hazards. Adolescents have to navigate through the murky waters of soon-to-be-theirs adult privileges, from smoking and drinking to sexual involvement and romantic relationships. To some these temptations prove too enticing to resist, launching them to become early starters. Early starters have the greatest risk for many of the health and injury consequences associated with such behaviors, especially those who lack guidance from home or other sources. For others, these new temptations come wrapped in perils that they wish to avoid altogether.

Some teens are less interested in exploring adult privileges and/or may possess the requisite skills and understanding to resist the pressure from peers. However, the majority of youth chooses to try out some or many of these newfound enticements, regardless of known or suspected risks, out of curiosity and the important need to fit in. Simply letting them learn for themselves is not a viable option, given the risk of injury or long-term health problems. Likewise, simply telling teens they can't do it ("Just say no") or putting up legal or family roadblocks to make it more difficult has not proven to be of much use, especially for the early starters and those at greatest risk of engaging in risk behaviors.

Adolescence represents a crucial link in the prevention of health-compromising behaviors as well as problem behaviors that pose a risk to others, such as violence, unsafe sex, and substance abuse. It is an important time for relationship formation, and it is also a period in which the scars of childhood or inadequate opportunities for adaptation can impair normal adjustment. The passive choice would be to continue addressing the needs of youth in an inconsistent, reactionary manner. The active choice involves a new paradigm committed to the needs and resources of youth. Helping all teens navigate this critical transition period is a valuable goal regardless of the extent of their current involvement with sex, drugs, or violence. Adolescence offers an ideal opportunity for education and skills that promote healthy relationships, and the vast majority of teens is interested in learning alternatives to violence and ways of counteracting strong negative messages from their peer culture.

Youth, especially youth at risk, need education and skills to promote healthy relationships, to develop peer support, and to establish social action aimed at ending violence in relationships. They need to feel connected not only to their peers but also to their schools, families, and communities. Such connection requires a commitment to building capacity in each community to be inclusive of all youth and to see each adolescent as a person rather than a potential problem. The ultimate act of inclusion is to empower youth to identify the critical issues they face and the solutions that are most meaningful to the reality of their lives and circumstances.

In this book we reclaim the importance of adolescence as a valuable window of opportunity for promoting positive adjustment. In so doing we emphasize that this age group requires universal, nonstigmatizing programs that fit adolescent interests and needs, can be delivered through existing and familiar community institutions (such as schools), and have at their very core the development of healthy relationships. An important starting point is a closer examination of this stage of development and the many reasons why adolescence offers so much potential for shaping positive relationships and reducing violence and risk behaviors.

2

Learning the Rules of Relating

From toddlers to teens, children's relationships are at the core of everyday life. Learning to relate to others is a process shaped over many years, influenced by numerous personal, family, and cultural factors that provide relationship rules and expectations. An understanding of how the rules of relationships develop forces us to examine how boys and girls learn to relate on the basis of gender roles, establishing implicit rules and expectations for acceptable male or female behavior. Throughout childhood, many of the rules learned at an earlier age become established and generalized to new situations. These gendered rules are then carried forward into future relationships with peers and romantic partners. Understanding the dynamics and rules behind relationships with same- and opposite-sex peers has important implications for understanding adolescent choices and behavior, because teens often base their decisions on carefully perceived gender-based peer norms and peer acceptance. In our view, the rules of relationships provide a crucial foundation for understanding the powerful forces at play during adolescence, for better or for worse. If we hope to engage youth in reducing harm stemming from experimenting with adult privileges, it is incumbent on us to take this gendered reality into account.

The rate at which emotional, social, physical, and intellectual changes occur between and within individuals creates an extremely diverse group of young people. Furthermore, all adolescents have to accommodate these rapid changes in a way that maintains important existing relationships in their lives and helps them form new ones. At the beginning of adolescence, youths are emerging from childhood relationships with parents, siblings, and other adults and are eager to find an independent identity. A short seven years later, on the verge of adult responsibilities, they are expected to be prepared for full independence.

These years may seem endlessly challenging for parents, who are constantly required to redefine their roles and relationships with a fast-moving target. Most teens think their parents change too slowly or not at all, whereas parents feel overwhelmed with the onslaught of new dilemmas, especially in the context of social norms that didn't exist a generation ago. Mark Twain captured this reality over a century ago with his now famous exhortation: "When I was a boy of fourteen, my father was so ignorant I could hardly stand to have the old man around. But when I got to be twenty-one, I was astonished at how much he had learned in seven years."

Researchers in adolescent development have long maintained that more meaningful distinctions within this broad developmental category are necessary for genuine insights into these rapid changes. These distinctions break down into three age ranges, although the exact boundaries are somewhat arbitrary: early (ages 11–13), mid (ages 14–16), and late adolescence (ages 17–20). Of course, there are no established rules for being an adolescent. Some preteens enter this stage well in advance of their biological age, while others have difficulty leaving childhood behind. At the other end of adolescence, we see a similar discrepancy in maturity and the rate at which individuals emerge into adult responsibility and personal autonomy. These age distinctions come as no surprise to parents and teachers, who for generations have been aware of the benefits of separating older and younger teens to facilitate their growth in social, academic, and athletic activities. This separation allows activities to be geared more specifically to the developmental demands faced during each stage of adolescence and also reduces the potential risk of exposing youths to older peers and premature demands that stretch them beyond normal limits.

What are these normal limits and expectations of adolescence, and how are they changing? These fundamental questions are at the root of most parents' struggles to keep up with their adolescent son or daughter in a climate of rapid social and technological change. Parents' roles, although still critically important, have been diluted by the sheer amount of resources and influences in the lives of their children. These resources and influences have multiplied the traditional impact of peers by adding new (and sometimes covert) ways to communicate using text messaging, cell phones, e-mail, and instant messaging. More than ever before, teens have a broad choice of methods to keep in touch and expand their peer relationships.

In addition to active communication, teens are also bombarded with passive yet significant messages from television, movies, video games, advertisements, and other entertainment and marketing innovations, all of which skillfully appeal to teens' desires to be independent and distinct from their parents. Although parents have always struggled with communicating and understanding their adolescent offspring, today more than ever these competing influences challenge their relationships with their sons and daughters. At best, parents learn ways to renegotiate their relationship in ways that respect these developmental transitions and accept a certain degree of reduced influence. At worse, they become a relic to their teen's world, seemingly irrelevant in the face of these outside forces.

Why Early Relationships Matter

How children come to see themselves in relation to others begins with the parent-child relationship, which is essential for early attachment and adaptation. Children can have multiple attachments to parents, grandparents, and other caregivers, all of which create the early foundation for learning to relate to others. Upon entering the school system, peer relationships become essential to children and act to further modify and shape their view of self and the manner in which they relate to others. In adolescence, relationships expand to include intimacy and romance but remain heavily influenced by the nature of previously observed and experienced relationships.

In effect, cognitive, behavioral, and emotional components shape children's views of relationships in a logical, organized manner. Expectations, behaviors, and beliefs about peers and romantic partners in adolescence are based on the experience of earlier relationships, especially those formed in early childhood with caregivers (Furman & Simon, 1998). This foundation shapes children's cognitive perspective of what to expect in future relationships, such as acceptance and intimacy or rejection and distance. This process is shaped by primary and interconnected views of relationships stemming from previous and ongoing experiences with caregivers, peers, and romantic partners. Although early attachment relationships are crucial, the process of relationship development itself is ongoing and dynamic. For example, successful peer relationships and closeness to friends in elementary school may portend healthy dating relationships. Thus, while early relationships are important, they are not deterministic; there is the opportunity for later corrective experiences to offset negative early experiences.

The early relationship process has been extensively studied by researchers in the field of parent-infant attachment. The field of attachment has identified the parent and child behaviors, some of which are innate, that provide the basis for a secure relationship. Infants are "preadapted" to engage in relationship-enhancing behaviors, such as orienting, smiling, crying, clinging, signaling, and, as they learn to move about, proximity seeking. Infant survival depends on becoming attached to a specific person who is available and responsive to their needs. Adults are similarly equipped with attachment-promoting behaviors to respond to infants' needs. These behaviors complement those of the infant—smiling, touching, holding, and rocking. Thus, what begin as instinctive behaviors follow an organized pattern through learning and feedback, primarily from caregivers (Sroufe, 1979, 2000).

The evolving infant-caregiver relationship helps infants regulate their behavior and emotions, especially under conditions of threat or stress. As such, attachment serves an important stress-reduction function. Infants attempt to maintain a balance between the desire to preserve the familiar and the desire to seek and explore new information. Self-reliance develops when the attachment figure provides a secure base for such exploration (Bretherton, 1995). Moreover, children's internal working model of relationships—what they expect from others and how they relate to others—emerges from this first crucial relationship and is carried forward into later relationships (Rutter & Sroufe, 2000).

In addition to the cognitive aspect, attachment also serves an important emotional-regulation function. Emotional reactivity and expression, such as distress or comfort, enable infants and young children to first communicate with the world around them. Their ability to regulate these emotions in an adaptive fashion is a critical aspect of their early relationships with caregivers (Emde & Spicer, 2000). Children experience emotions as powerful events, demanding that they find ways to reduce or regulate the emotions' force. The most adaptive way is to seek comfort from a caregiver, which gradually helps children learn how to self-regulate and adapt to new surroundings. To infants, who have very limited means of expressing and interpreting the many new things going on around them, emotions provide the initial filter for organizing massive amounts of new information and avoiding potential harm. Similarly, early relationships with one or more caregivers provide structure and regulation to these emotional responses.

Children have a natural tendency to attend to emotional cues from others, which helps them learn to interpret and regulate their own emotions. From a very young age, they learn to understand their own experience through the emotional expressions of others (Bretherton, 1995). Within their first year of life, children learn the importance of emotions for communication and regulation, and by their second year they have some ability to attribute cause to emotional expression. Children look to the emotional expression and cues of their caregivers to provide them with the information needed to formulate a basic understanding of what's going on. To young children, emotions are a primary form of communication that permit them to explore the world with increasing independence (LaFreniere, 1999). The child-caregiver relationship plays a critical role in this process, for it provides the basic context for children to express emotions and to have caring guidance and limits placed on them.

In maladaptive environments, this attachment process does not provide infants with the same self-regulatory capacity and understanding of emotions. Children who live in a world of emotional turmoil and extremes (such as abused children) have difficulty understanding and regulating their internal states. Because expressions of affect (such as crying or signals of distress) may trigger disapproval, avoidance, or abuse, maltreated youngsters learn to inhibit their emotional expression and regulation (Pollak, Cicchetti, Hornung, & Reed, 2000). When a new situation involving a stranger or peer triggers emotional reactions, they may not have the benefit of a caring smile or words from a familiar adult to assure them that things are okay. Thus, both the cognitive aspects of attachment (in terms of internal models of relationships) and the emotional-regulation function are impeded when an infant has to negotiate the attachment process with an abusive or neglectful adult.

As normal development proceeds, regulation of affect and behavior becomes less dependent on the caregiver and is more and more autonomous. Toddlers' developing self-regulation is now applied to new situations, and these successful experiences of mastery over the environment further strengthen their emerging view of themselves and others. It is during this period that children form complex mental representations of people, relationships, and the world. Their emerging view of themselves and their surroundings is fostered by healthy parental guidance and control that invoke concern for the welfare of others. Developmentalists refer to this process as forming *representational models* of oneself and others. Such models of how children relate to others are significant because they contain experience, knowledge, and expectations that are carried forward to new situations (Cicchetti, Toth, & Lynch, 1995). One key aspect of how people view themselves and their relationships to others that needs to be accommodated in these representational models is the notion of gender. While figuring out the people, relationships, and world around them, young children must also come to understand what it means to be male or female in that world.

Constructing Different Worlds for Boys and Girls

Gender identification is a universal process that children undertake in an effort to make more sense of their world. It results in the creation of a flexible or inflexible template for the formation of early peer relationships. Gender identification is fraught with cultural expectations and traditions that can lead to views of relationships based on rigid sex-role expectations and beliefs. We now examine some of these processes that occur as children come to an understanding of gender identity. An appreciation of these processes during childhood helps us understand how boys and girls come to hold different views of cross-sex relationships years later in adolescence.

From a very early age, children have a need to organize information about their social world and form an impression of how they fit into it. One of the most prominent ways that children approach this organization is by identifying male and female characteristics and roles, especially in terms of relationship expectations and views. Naturally, these early beliefs about the world around them are strongly influenced by what they see on a daily and routine basis. Such early views help young children make sense of the many confusing bits of information they come into contact with each day.

The gender identification process begins early in children's lives, as gender becomes part of who they are, how they interpret the world, and how they are expected to behave. It is remarkable how early gender-based discrimination develops and, in turn, influences the pace of further social and cognitive development. Infants can discriminate between male and female faces by 9–11 months of age, and over the following nine months toddlers start to recognize labels such as "man" and "woman" that go with certain faces. By the time they are 2 years old, children begin to label their own sex and categorize toys on the basis of whether they are meant for boys or girls. Girls begin to imitate what they perceive to be feminine activities around 24–26 months of age, with boys imitating masculine activities shortly thereafter (30–32 months).

As children come to view their world in terms of gendered relationships and activities, these views influence and are influenced by their relationships. Children are not passive recipients of gender role expectations; rather, they actively observe the world around them, notice that males and females do different things, figure out their own gender assignment, and then alter their behavior accordingly. Their behavior may at times be puzzling—for example, preschoolers may insist that men cannot be nurses or women cannot be doctors but have no rational explanation for this argument. Similarly, they may assume that their own gender is superior, simply because they identify with that gender (Blakemore, 2003).

These sometimes rigidly held beliefs are based on what developmentalists call "gender schemas." Cognitive structures, or schemas, are organized around the assumption that the sexes are different and thereby influence how children view their social world. Such schemas, or conceptual maps, develop readily during childhood because *gender is predictive.* That is, it is easy for children to recognize those tasks most commonly done by men or by women and, therefore, gender becomes a simple way of assigning expectations and roles (Serbin et al., 1993). If a child sees that most childcare workers, housekeepers, and grocery shoppers are women, for example, he or she easily comprehends that these are the tasks that women do. No matter how much parents wish to promote gender equality and flexibility in their young children, the realities that they encounter every day are much more powerful than what their parents may tell them.

As these schemas develop, beliefs and expectations about the world coalesce, thereby increasing children's convictions that males and females do different things. Naturally, children are motivated to figure out what is appropriate for their own sex while being careful to avoid behaviors associated with the opposite one. For some this gendered view of the world can take on more extreme and unyielding proportions, resulting in a dichotomous view of masculine and feminine roles that presupposes acceptable and unacceptable behaviors.

How this process leads to possible gender role stereotypes and rigidity merits attention. Such stereotypes can carry forward into adolescence to serve as a template for self-expectations as well as for the nature and quality of relationships with peers and romantic partners. Below we consider some of the family, peer, and cultural forces that influence gender construction in adaptive and maladaptive ways and examine how gender roles continue to play a part during early adolescence.

Children's social and cognitive development takes place in an ambient climate of peer and cultural influences. Children and youth shape and create their own culture and in the process form their understanding of gender as they themselves construct it (Corsaro, 1997).

Within their peer and family networks, boys and girls from a very young age actively learn to relate to each other in terms of their gender expectations. Cultural norms, influenced by established family patterns as well as current media portrayals of traditional gender roles, dictate the parameters for socialization agents such as parents, teachers, peers, and siblings. These agents, actively but often unwittingly, shape boys' and girls' definitions of their own gender and how it differs from the opposite sex (McHale, Crouter, & Whiteman, 2003).

As children actively construct these gender roles and expectations, they become very perceptive of where the borders are between male and female. This evolving construction helps them relate to others according to cultural expectations. Inherent throughout this process is the role of gender identity and expectations, which are constantly being created and adjusted. Children must carefully learn to "talk the talk" in a manner that strengthens their same-sex identification and distances them from the opposite sex. The processes of language and play reveal some of the cognitive foundations for significant differences in how boys and girls form and refine their view of same- and opposite-sex relationships.

Young children typically choose to play with others of the same sex, often actively avoiding cross-sex play with peers. About two-thirds of 3½- to 6½-year-old boys and girls show a strong preference for playing with same-sex peers, while only 10 percent prefer to play with opposite-sex children (Martin, 1994). In many Western cultures, segregation into same-sex groups is a prominent and visible phenomenon beginning in early childhood and lasting through much of elementary school. However, gender segregation is not universal, which suggests that this important developmental process varies considerably by cultural norms and expectations.

In early observational studies of the speech and play patterns of young children, researchers discovered that very different processes are at work for boys and girls (Lever, 1978). When boys are at play with other boys, their games and language reflect the importance of status and independence. Boys tend to play outside in hierarchically formed larger groups. They choose a leader and are likely to challenge one another in terms of "expertise" or leadership ability by giving orders or telling stories and jokes. Their play activity often centers on having winners and losers, with rules that are carefully monitored and argued. During such play, boys are more likely than girls to boast of their skills and make an issue over who is "best."

Girls' play activities are qualitatively and structurally different from those of boys. Girls are more likely to play in pairs or small groups with people they consider best friends. For girls, intimacy and closeness are primary, and therefore one's standing in the group is determined by her degree of relative closeness or connectedness to the others. Noticeably, their games are less likely to have winners or losers—they choose to play house or make crafts—and girls who excel at the chosen activity are expected not to brag. Rather than giving orders or forming hierarchies, they make suggestions to one another. Girls are less likely to challenge one another or jockey for status; rather, their activities reflect a clear preference for spending time together while sitting and talking.

As children choose to segregate themselves with members of their own sex, the play styles of girls and boys become more distinct (Serbin, Moller, Gulko, Powlishta, & Colburne, 1994). One of the important ways in which children explore and construct gender roles and norms, concerning everything from appearance to friendships, is through peer culture on the playground. Gender separation is most complete and evident on the school playground (Thorne, 1993), especially during preadolescence (ages 7–12). This segregation allows boys and girls to rehearse their understanding of gender roles and expectations. It is here they learn to make sense of and resolve ambiguities related to gender, and the playground is also the place where they may be forced to conform to boundaries and norms, sometimes with harsh penalties for nonconformance.

A recent study advanced these established observations by examining preadolescent children's same- and cross-sex play during recess periods and determining how themes evident on the playground relate to gender development and relationships (Boyle, Marshall, & Robeson, 2003). When girls were observed interacting only with other girls, most were seen to be confident and physically active. Most of the girls showed positive relationship skills, as demonstrated by negotiating with laughter and appropriate use of touch, eye contact, and sharing inner thoughts. Interactions of boys with boys, on the other hand, were marked by a "show of power," especially when another boy or girl attempted to gain entry to the group. There were more attempts to circumvent rules (for example, play out of sight of adults), challenge authority, and be aggressive with other boys.

There were many instances of "borderwork," that is, behaviors that reinforce the boundaries between girls and boys (Thorne, 1993), including contests, "rituals of pollution" (for example, "cooties"), and invasions of the opposite sex's territory. Not surprisingly, this borderwork was often asymmetrical, with boys having more power in the situation. The children at this age were also likely to use exclusion on the basis of gender, with boys applying a particularly overt style of exclusion with girls (such as telling them to leave or name calling). Interestingly, the observers also saw girls of this age successfully joining boys' teams, especially if the girl was confident and able to move back and forth between girls' and boys' activities.

It is not surprising that children's ability to manage this borderwork increases their popularity with other children; however, this borderwork competence is also reflected in adults' perceptions of children's overall social competence (Sroufe, Bennett, Englund, Urban, & Shulman, 1993). In a study using videotaped behavior codings of 10- and 11-year-old children at camp, researchers observed that children who violated gender boundaries had fewer friends. In addition, these children were particularly unpopular with their peers (based on individual interviews). While these results mirror previous findings about the importance of maintaining gender boundaries to achieve status with peers, this study also looked at counselors' ratings of the children. Camp counselors judged children who demonstrated low levels of gender boundary violation and high levels of boundary maintenance as more socially competent. These findings suggest that children learn to recognize and maintain these boundaries because they are expected to, and the regard of other children and adults alike may hinge on their ability to do so.

The way boys and girls play sheds considerable light on their relationship preferences, revealing what Tannen (1991) refers to as a paradox of independence and intimacy: boys tend to focus more on status (who's giving orders and who's taking them), are vigilant for signs of being told what to do, and find rough-and-tumble play more enjoyable. In contrast, girls find social negotiation and cooperative interactions more rewarding; they prefer monitoring their friendships for subtle shifts in alliance and feel some sense of status through being connected to a group of friends. A key issue is whether such gender construction is harmless and transitory or whether it establishes and perpetuates gender bias in our culture that creates inequality and justifies acts of abuse and violence toward women.

A basic consideration in determining the roots of gender segregation in children is the extent to which it may be biological, cultural, or both, and the extent to which it can or should be modified. Whereas there is evidence to support both nature and nurture influences (as is usually the case), our concern is the degree to which cultural norms and biases promote undue gender rigidity and discrimination and how these influences negatively affect adolescent relationships.

Basic physiological differences between girls and boys support the notion that some degree of gender segregation may be self-guided, especially at younger ages. For example, boys show more physiological arousal to distress-inducing stimuli, whereas girls find sympathy-inducing stimuli more evocative (Fabes, 1994). This finding could be due to biological differences in the nervous system response of girls and boys, such that playing with the opposite sex is less rewarding than playing with same-sex peers (Serbin et al., 1994). As a result, boys and girls may begin to avoid one another because playing together is less fun or stimulating. From this perspective, gender segregation is mainly an extension of peer preference for a companion with a similar style of play (Aydt & Corsaro, 2003).

Although gender segregation may have some degree of biological basis, there are significant family and cultural forces at work that make such differences pronounced and operative. A sociocultural perspective argues that boys and girls are rewarded differentially for certain behaviors, and these rewards heavily influence the development of gendered styles of interaction. For example, in one study in infant-caregiver interactions, no differences emerged in the frequency of assertive and communicative behaviors of infant boys and girls, but dramatic differences were found in how adult caretakers responded to these behaviors (Fagot, 1994). Boys were attended to more often than girls for their assertive behaviors (41 versus 10 percent, respectively), whereas girls received more attention than boys from the caregiver for positive forms of communication (65 versus 48 percent, respectively). Notably, caregivers responded to demands for attention by boys (such as screaming, crying, or pulling at the caregiver) almost three times more often than they did for girls (55 versus 18 percent of the time).

A follow-up of these same children one year later revealed clear sex differences in their behavior. Boys were more aggressive and assertive, and girls spent more time speaking and interacting with the adults. Researchers interpret these and similar findings as demonstrating that children are very adept at determining what makes them valued in their culture. In other words, girls learn to form and influence relationships through verbal negotiation, while boys learn to use more aggression and domination as means to relationships with peers. Although certainly not the only factor influencing behavior, these findings are consistent with the notion that boys are encouraged toward greater autonomy and given greater license to control the flow of interactions, whereas girls are encouraged toward greater compliance with authority and given less license to directly influence others (Biringen, Robinson, & Emde, 1994; Birns, Cascardi, & Meyer, 1994).

The above discussion brings us to our argument that the basis for understanding the imbalance of power between men and women and the implicit acceptance of various forms of men's violence toward women begins with gender construction and its associated pressures and barriers. It is well known that gender development is reinforced by traditional norms conveyed by parents and the broader culture through the many avenues of media, sports, and entertainment. Although such development is a critical process in forming healthy relationships, we must question the point at which the majority culture's norms impose restrictions that hamper this process.

Not surprisingly, the degree of gender segregation cross-culturally appears to vary according to the extent to which the adult culture considers men and boys to be aggressive and women and girls to be passive (Aydt & Corsaro, 2003). Traditional socialization practices, in which boys are raised to be strong, uncommunicative, competitive, and in control, and girls are raised to be compliant, other-oriented, and not to express anger directly, are associated with greater sex-role rigidity and inequality (Whiting & Edwards, 1988). Societies in which gender roles are more restricted tend to promote negative attitudes and power imbalances in male-female relationships (Dobash & Dobash, 1992).

Cross-cultural studies of children's gender concepts and behaviors lead to the conclusion that gender is culturally constructed. For example, African American boys and girls more often engage in playful, cross-sex arguments than do white children (Goodwin, 2001). Similarly, African American and Latina girls show more verbal conflict during games than white girls, such as arguing over the rules (Goodwin, 1998), behaviors ascribed mostly to males in studies involving mainly white participants. In China, girls are more assertive with one another than boys are, although this, too, varies by situation. For example, Chinese boys take the lead in work-related discussions, but girls dominate when relationships and courtship are at issue (Kyratzis & Guo, 2001).

In brief, some degree of gender segregation seems to be universal as children learn to play with one another. However, research is uncovering the manner in which traditional gender boundaries vary across peer cultures, largely on the basis of the larger adult cultural norms. Biological and cognitive development certainly play key roles throughout this process, but the cultural context in which children are raised makes a fundamental difference in how gender is constructed. Even within a particular culture, it is normal for boys' and girls' gender-related knowledge and behavior to wax and wane across development. In research conducted with North American children, gender stereotyping about the kinds of objects and activities associated with males and females has been shown to emerge between 2 and 4 years of age, reach a peak of rigidity between 5 and 7 years, and then show greater flexibility during middle childhood (Serbin et al., 1993; Signorella, Bigler, & Liben, 1993). Gender rigidity then reemerges during early adolescence, presumably as a function of increased pressure for gender typing (by parents and peers) in accordance with pubertal growth and change (Ruble & Martin, 1998). In the next section, we explore how young adolescents express this increased rigidity, and how it may be responsible for the eruption of homophobia and bullying during this period of development.

Shifting to the Peer Frontier

From early childhood, relationships with parents and family members typically provide the closest feelings of connection to others and serve as the base for resolving new developmental tasks and directions. Such close relationships are inherently constrained by kinships and norms. Pre- and early adolescence is a crucial time in relationship development, in that youth begin to shift the balance of influence from family to peers. Now, for the first time, individuals choose with whom they spend their time and develop close relationships. Because there is strong continuity in relationship style and adaptation over time, those who have established positive relationships with peers and adults are better prepared for navigating the critical roadway ahead, whereas those who have not face greater obstacles.

As youth begin to disengage from their families as the major socializing force in their lives, they rely more heavily on their peers and peer culture. The peer context is central to understanding many forms of youth behavior that represent their attempts to construct shared cultures through interactions with peers. Peer contexts are where adolescents explore, challenge, and transform adult expectations and governance. This developmental stage is when teens form more complex rules about social stratification and choose their friendships on the basis of particular values, attitudes, and activities.

Beginning with friendships in elementary school and continuing into dating relationships in high school, children and youth start to look to their best friends to meet their needs for intimacy, companionship, nurturance, and assistance formerly provided by the family (Lempers & Clark-Lempers, 1993). At the same time, those youth who lack adequate skills or self-regulation to be accepted by their prosocial peers, as well as those who do not conform to the gender expectations and boundaries, are more likely to gravitate toward others like them (Capaldi, DeGarmo, Patterson, & Forgatch, 2002). Peer hierarchies rapidly emerge, formulated by natural interests and compatibility (as they did in same-sex play in childhood) as well as by subtle and blatant forces that delineate an individual's standing in the peer group. These events are pivotal in terms of the manner in which adolescents feel connected to others and the extent to which they adhere to rigid gender role expectations with peers and dating partners. These experiences serve as the foundation for subsequent romantic relationships as adolescents begin to develop templates for how dating is both similar to and different from previous relationships with friends and family.

As is the case with respect to childhood development, gender differences in relationship styles and emphasis have different implications for adolescent boys and girls. Studies of mental health and stress-related disorders of girls and boys note the significance of these gender boundaries and pressures. Girls report feeling worse about themselves than do boys, in particular regarding their self-image. Over 40 percent of girls say they frequently feel ugly and unattractive, although they see themselves more positively with respect to interpersonal relations and social ability. In contrast, boys see themselves more positively with respect to achievement, academic aspirations, self-assertion, and body image. Adolescent boys also value control and perceive themselves as more willing to take on leadership roles and responsibilities. In contrast, girls tend to value social relationships, intimate personal relationships, and for others to initiate positive personal relationships with them (Bakken & Romig, 1992). Thus the differential gender roles put in motion in early childhood continue to exert an impact on the nature of relationships and the specific challenges faced by adolescent boys and girls.

Peer Culture and Hierarchies: The Pivotal Role of Gender

Social changes in Western culture over the past several decades have dramatically improved the political and social status of women, but there has not been an accommodating shift of the same magnitude for men. Because gender is constructed through relationships with others, it has been argued that these changes for women destabilize traditional views of masculinity (Pascoe, 2003). That is, while there have been massive changes in what it means to be a woman, there has not been a corresponding change in notions of masculinity or what it means to be a man.

In this section, we examine how teenage boys and girls face a heightened need for conformity to acceptable masculine and feminine ideals within their peer context (Basow & Rubin, 1999), which can create major upheavals in the way they relate to one another. We also consider how social positioning in the school's gender order affects the way in which boys construct themselves as masculine and girls as feminine and the social cost of this construction on their relationships.

High school is the staging ground for forming identity, where the culture and structure of the school shape students' lives. Conceptions of masculinity play a crucial role in this process of identity formation by creating adolescent subcultures and an informal class structure or hierarchy. While peer hierarchies have always been a prominent part of high school life, only recently have researchers discovered the extent to which the ranking and formation of these hierarchies is connected to gendered meanings. Being seen by others and by oneself as masculine is central to being a boy in high school (Pascoe, 2003). However, portraying oneself as masculine is not easy or simple, because it is highly related to one's social position in the school. Researchers refer to this process as "managing masculinity"(Martino, 1999).

As in the past, high schools today have highly delineated social groups, derived primarily from the status ascribed to different abilities and interests. Typically, Jocks, Preps, Cheerleaders, and/or student leaders lay claim to the top of the ladder, while students interested in drama and music share the lower end of the social spectrum with Freaks, Goths, and Tech students (Garbarino & deLara, 2002; Martino, 1999). Most students are usually located somewhere in the middle of this hierarchy, where they may escape a named distinction. Because the male Jock is the most recognizable masculine social group, boys tend to interpret their own masculine identity against this standard image. In her interviews with 20 teenaged boys at two high schools, Pascoe (2003) noted how each boy, in describing his own identity and position in the school hierarchy, referenced his position to that of the Jock. They referred to the image or symbol of the Jock and manipulated this image to permit them to be masculine. For example, if a boy was not particularly athletic, he drew on other masculine traits associated with the Jock, such as emphasized heterosexuality or dominance, to make up for what he might lack in sports ability.

By equating Jockhood and masculinity, boys who are good at sports can use this prowess as "Jock insurance" for being permitted to engage in traditionally less masculine activities such as music or drama

(Martino, 1999). Sports, in effect, help some boys manage the pressures to be seen as having a masculine identity, while permitting them more leeway in showing interests in less "masculine" pursuits. To completely reject the Jock identity boys have to create an alternative one. Boys who reject the symbol of the Jock must devalue the hierarchy and its incumbent forms of competition. Instead, they gravitate toward a "counterculture" identity and appearance to set them far apart from the hierarchy they despise. Interestingly, boys who reject the importance of athletics and sports tend to feminize Jocks.

These boundaries of what constitutes adequate masculinity contribute to what many argue are the two features of adolescent boys: a worsening record of academic achievement in comparison to girls and a propensity for violence (Ferguson, Eyre, & Ashbaker, 2000). The forms of masculinity that gain the most respect involve hierarchies based on toughness, threats of violence or actual violence, casualness about schoolwork, "compulsory heterosexuality," and the accompanying homophobia (Epstein, 1997; Martino, 1999). As a result, boys feel pressure to position themselves relative to these issues, whether they like it or not. As one can imagine, this pressure creates a need to be on the alert for threats from other boys and to guard against the failure to be properly masculine. Any vulnerable feelings must be hidden if they are to survive in the peer context—that is, boys have to follow the "boy code" to gain acceptance and status (Pollack, 1998). In this atmosphere, anyone who exhibits gender asymmetrical traits or characteristics risks being ridiculed or outcast from his peers.

In addition, because of the clear link between specific characteristics and traditional expressions of masculinity and femininity, attributes considered attractive or important for a boy (such as athletic abilities) are usually an impediment for girls. Likewise, attractive attributes for girls, such as intimacy and emotional expression, are to be avoided by boys if they wish to achieve status in the peer hierarchy. To manage these rigid pressures, teens must balance out any anomaly with clear expressions of gender-typed behavior.

Girls also experience a world of rigid gender expectations and pressures to conform during adolescence. A concerning finding is that the transition to adolescence is the time when female participation in sports and athletics notably and markedly declines, a pattern that has not been found for boys (U.S. Department of Health and Human Services, 1996). In addition, the peer culture becomes less tolerant of independent thinking and assertiveness in girls (L. M. Brown & Gilligan, 1993). These findings have been explained on the basis of peer pressure to conform to rigid feminine ideals (Kaplan, 1997).

Male-identified attributes are important to girls for overcoming hurdles before puberty, but this advantage reverses soon thereafter (Shakib, 2003). To acquire the all-important social status with peers, girls have to conform to gender ideals. Unlike boys, where sports raise their status, girls' participation in sports has the opposite effect. Girls who do pursue sports find they have to prove themselves to be accepted into the male peer group. This acceptance is accomplished through clothing, acting tough, not crying, and, of course, playing well. Not being viewed as feminine can lead to lower peer status but also to being seen as not heterosexually desirable. Equating participation in sports with a lack of sexual appeal in turn puts pressure on adolescent girls to do what needs to be done to be desirable to boys and avoid being labeled a lesbian. As a result, adolescent girls may contend with the apparent mutual exclusivity of athletic performance and heterosexual desirability by dropping out of sports. In effect, female sports attrition in the peer context is a function of homophobia and the rigid gender stereotypes evident during adolescence. Like boys, girls who decide to engage in "masculine" activities (such as sports) may have to emphasize the feminine gender ideals (such as dress and appearance) to counter their nonfeminine interests.

Of particular note is that Jocks, unlike the other social groups, is clearly a gendered category. Girls can also be Jocks, but female Jocks tend to be dispersed throughout the hierarchy instead of clustered near the top like male Jocks. Popularity for girls results from good looks, personality, and their boyfriends' social status (Martino, 1999). As well, being a Jock isn't always the same as being athletic—it is based on playing the right kind of sport (usually football or basketball). It also implies a dominant position in the hierarchy, with other boys as well as girls. As part of this masculine emphasis, girls function as status symbols or sexual objects, less so as girlfriends.

In summary, gender differences become more rigid during the

rapid transition of early adolescence, as gender role construction becomes more salient in shaping one's view of his or her social world. For boys, a strong masculine identity is rewarded overtly through peer status. The identification of masculine traits as valuable and feminine traits as undesirable reinforces the inequity of men and women in our culture. In comparison, adolescent girls are more apt to be punished by their male and female peers for engaging in activities designated as male endeavors. For both boys and girls, the decision to behave counter to these powerful peer norms about gender identity may be met with exclusion or overt hostility.

Dating and Romantic Relationships

The formation of intimate and romantic relationships is a core task of adolescence, although one that was historically overlooked in studies of normal and abnormal development. More recently, researchers have taken up the challenge of studying the dating process as adolescents move toward committed adult intimate relationships (Connolly, Furman, & Konarski, 2000; Florsheim, 2003; Furman & Shaffer, 1999; Furman, Simon, Shaffer, & Bouchey, 2002). This research sheds light on the ebb and flow of adolescent romantic relationships as they rework the familiar rules of relating, including the powerful conventions faced by sexual minority youth. Despite considerable gains in knowledge, many fundamental questions about romantic relationships remain unanswered that are potentially critical to engaging youth in harm reduction, which we return to in chapter 3.

Developmental theorists describe the course of forming and maintaining adolescent romantic relationships as progressing through four phases. The first stage of dating involvement derives from teasing and cross-sex chasing in early elementary school, which by grades 4 and 5, transforms into normative heterosexual interactions (Thorne & Luria, 1986). By early adolescence, small groups of mixed-sex friends are common and form the springboard for involvement in larger networks of mixed-sex peers. Romantic interest is first expressed in these groups with many group-based activities and little actual romantic interaction (Connolly, Craig, Goldberg, & Pepler, 2004). This early stage of dating is important for broadening self-concept and increasing the confidence of youth in their capacity to relate to others romantically (B. B. Brown, 1999).

In the second stage of dating a "romantic flavor" is added to group-based interaction, and romantic relationships take on importance for peer status (B. B. Brown, 1999). Although there is considerable variation in time of entry to this stage, by age 14 or 15 about half of all adolescents report some single- or group-dating experience (Connolly & Johnson, 1996; Feiring, 1996). Dating at this stage is a short-term, rapidly shifting affair, as adolescents learn methods of interpersonal and sexual relatedness and experiment with romantic identities. Due to the association of romance and status in this stage, adolescents are confronted with pressure to engage in romantic relationships that receive peer approval. Romantic relationships may be used to gain status with peers, and a "poor" romantic choice may result in diminished peer acceptance. At this point, many adolescents have begun to experiment with sexual intimacy. The U.S. Youth Risk Behavior survey found that 34 percent of grade 9 and 41 percent of grade 10 students reported having had sexual intercourse; 23 percent and 30 percent, respectively, indicated that they were currently sexually active—that is, had engaged in sexual intercourse during the past three months (Grunbaum et al., 2002).

After a period of experimentation in multiple casual relationships (stage 3), youth generally progress to more serious, exclusive dating relationships that become increasingly important sources of support relative to parents and peers (Furman & Buhrmester, 1992). By 18 years of age, most adolescents have had at least one steady relationship, and dyadic relationships are the norm (Connolly & Goldberg, 1999). In addition, adolescents' romantic relationships have become more intense, committed, and satisfying. At this point, adolescents work to balance in-depth romantic caring with practical considerations such as the possibility of lifelong commitment and similarity of adult goals and values. All adolescents have to navigate issues of identity, sexual scripts, and self-esteem as they integrate a new awareness of sexuality into their view of themselves (Maticka-Tyndale, 2001). For example, university students identify a range of behaviors that constitute sex, sexual partners, and unfaithful sexual behavior (Randall & Byers,

2003). Each adolescent must determine his or her own definition of sex and values related to engaging in various behaviors with different partners.

The difficult task of developing romantic and sexual relationships is further complicated for gay, lesbian, and bisexual youth by the issue of sexual orientation identity and navigating the coming-out process. Although a critical developmental task for gay youth, this process has received limited research attention. There are many societal barriers to the development of same-sex relationships, such as the lack of positive role models of same-sex couples, failure to acknowledge such couples in a formal sense, and the threat of hate crimes (Diamond, Savin-Williams, & Dube, 1999). Further, because of risk of rejection by peers and parents, disclosure of same-sex romantic relationships may be very limited. A four-stage model has been proposed as the ideal transition to an integrated same-sexual orientation identity (Troiden, 1989). The stages involve a progression from sensitization (that is, awareness of same-sex attraction) to confusion (marked by inner turmoil) to identity assumption (possibly following a same-sex sexual contact) to commitment.

A recent attempt to delineate trajectories of significant events associated with sexual identity orientation (for example, age of awareness, age of first disclosure, coming out) found five significant clusters of experience for these youth (Floyd & Stein, 2002). These clusters of youth differed from each other on dimensions of age of awareness, homosexual experience, age of first disclosure, disclosure to a parent, and gay/lesbian social immersion. The results suggested significant diversity in the experiences of gay, lesbian, and bisexual youth with respect to these developmental experiences. For example, although the mean age for awareness (with respect to same-sex attraction) was 10.4 years (SD = 3.4), the responses ranged from 3 to 18 years. Clearly, it is difficult to chart age ranges for these significant events, given this variability of experience.

In short, the developmental literature suggests that over the high school years there is a normative progression from multiple, casual dating relationships to more committed and intimate partnerships. At the same time, there is a good deal of variation around this normative path, and there is almost certainly no single "best" path of romantic development (Furman & Wehner, 1997). Social dating relationships that emerge during adolescence may represent a transition point between experiences of nurturance and care as a child and the establishment of healthy intimate relationships as a young adult.

Early dating relationships contain aspects of both childhood friendships and adult intimacy and function to help adolescents cope with conflicting desires for autonomy and connection. Furthermore, these relationships can facilitate or inhibit the achievement of a range of developmental tasks faced by adolescence—identity formation, school achievement, and individuation from family (Furman & Shaffer, 2003). Children and adolescents who have not developed many positive relationships prior to embarking on adolescent dating may have a higher likelihood of unhealthy dating relationships and becoming abusive or being abused as an adult (Bethke & Dejoy, 1993). For this reason, social dating may be a primary testing ground of one's acquired ability to express emotion and receive affection without resorting to abusive practices or submitting to attempts at coercion or intimidation by a dating partner.

Summary

The rules of relating are shaped throughout childhood and adolescence and form one of the most powerful forces for approaching the tasks and challenges of adolescence. In this chapter we identified relationships as the glue that supports adolescent development. We traced relationship development from infancy to adolescence and highlighted a pattern of continuity in terms of relationship quality over time. That is, children who develop strong relationships with their parents have a good foundation for peer relationships and subsequent dating relationships. Although important, this continuity in relationships is not inevitable: positive relationships can offset earlier experiences that were harsh or negative and vice versa. Nonetheless, healthy infant-caregiver attachments typically portend positive peer relationships in childhood and adolescence and set the stage for the development of healthy adolescent dating relationships.

During adolescence, youth shift from their family to their peers in terms of their emphasis on relationships. Although parents still have

an influence on their children, the role of peers is much more significant than in earlier childhood. Furthermore, youth of this age develop
their own peer culture, which is heavily influenced by the media. The
role of peers is essential in helping youth define their relationships.
This peer culture unfolds within the context of powerful media messages, as we discuss further in the next chapter.

We also identified the role of gender identity as being critical in
the formation of child and adolescent relationships. Gender identification is one of the earliest ways that children can make some sense of a
complex world. The categorization of people into male and female,
and the subsequent assignment of activities and characteristics to these
categories, appears to be universal. Gender segregation during childhood exists in one form or another cross-culturally; however, the extent of the segregation and the rigidity of these attitudes range broadly.
Throughout childhood, those who do not manage the boundaries between males and females face social repercussions from their peers and
possibly adults as well. In the next chapter, we discuss the intensifica-
tion of this process during adolescence and the accompanying forms of
relationship violence.

The emergence of dating relationships was identified as a key
characteristic of adolescence. The nature and flavor of romantic relationships change drastically during adolescence. In early adolescence,
relationships tend to be short-lived, affiliative in nature, and heavily
influenced by peer approval. Dating occurs in a group context, with
little intimacy. By the end of adolescence, dating relationships tend to
focus more on the dyad, are more intimate in nature, and more closely
resemble adult romantic relationships. The dating relationships experienced by adolescents will also affect other developmental tasks. In
parallel, exploring sexuality and sexual behavior presents challenges to
adolescents.

Establishing an integrated sexual identity and engaging in successful early dating relationships are further complicated for sexual minority youth, who have to navigate the coming-out process. Furthermore, the homophobic nature of adolescent peer culture and the
ensuing forms of relationship violence, as discussed in the next chapter, leave sexual minority youth particularly vulnerable to peer violence. The trajectories for gay, lesbian, and bisexual youth have not re-

ceived as much research attention, but recent attempts to describe the process of sexual identity formation suggest considerable variability for these youth with respect to timing of key events. Relationships are of central importance not only in the development of healthy relationships but also in the expression of various forms of violence, as we show in the next chapter.

3

The Dark Side of the Rules

The previous chapter traced normative relationship development from infancy to adolescence, with an emphasis on the crucial role of gender. The rules of relating also have a darker side, at times creating dissonance between one's personal values and those of the all-important peer group. The themes of relationships and gender rigidity evident in normative adolescent development are mirrored in the forms of violence and abuse that emerge at this age. In this chapter we examine some of the ways in which many forms of violence and abuse surface during the course of developing relationships with peers and romantic partners. In addition, we consider the contributions of media and technological advances in defining adolescents' behavior and attitudes, including the increased opportunities afforded by some of these advances for new forms of relationship violence.

Patrolling the Borders: Teasing, Bullying, and Harassment

Teasing, bullying, and harassment are not new phenomena, but their developmental significance has only recently come to light. Although many adults dismiss these behaviors in a "kids will be kids" manner, others recognize bullying as a serious behavior that can be extremely detrimental to those involved. In reality, these behaviors range from harmless, normative banter to more serious abuse that exerts a profound impact on victims. Teasing, in particular, serves a prominent function in the development of relationships, but it can be sometimes difficult to draw the line between playful teasing and more hurtful forms of verbal and emotional abuse. To understand the way in which these behaviors emerge, it is important to remember how peer and romantic relationships emerge in general. As the pattern of relationship development shifts from family to same-sex peers to mixed-sex groups to dating dyads, so, too, do abusive behaviors follow a similar pattern.

In pre- and early adolescence, cross-sex relationships exist mostly in a group context. Not surprisingly, relationship aggression at this age also tends to be group based and involves various forms of teasing and harassment. Teasing, a commonplace activity, typically involves making fun of the target individual, especially about some characteristic that deviates from the group norm, such as weight or appearance. Teasing can be playful and harmless, or it can escalate to the point of intimidation and hostile discrimination. Teasing may be particularly harmful when it is used by a more powerful (for example, older, larger, more popular) individual to dominate a less assertive or less powerful one. This power differential between perpetrator and victim is one of the fundamental characteristics of bullying in general and one of the dynamics that makes it difficult for victims to assert themselves or get help. Drawing on this parallel, some forms of teasing belong to the same class of behavior as coercive and openly hostile forms of abuse and thus may warrant consideration as an entry-level behavior for those inclined to control others in their relationships.

Paradoxically, teasing also plays an important role in the development of cross-sex relationships and, as such, may signal the transition into romantic relationships. For example, as children approach puberty, there is often a change from teasing about the *presence* of heterosexual interest to teasing about the *absence* of such interest (Shapiro, Baumeister, & Kessler, 1991). Teasing is also a viable strategy for the teaser to camouflage his or her intentions and express sentiments that could not otherwise be expressed. Because such teasing combines elements of sexual interest, aggression, and humor in an ambiguous manner, it permits the teaser to show romantic interest with little risk to self-esteem or social standing. If the romantic interest conveyed in a teasing manner is not reciprocated, the teaser can always retreat behind a façade of "just joking." The complex function of this behavior represents one of the important developmental challenges accompanying the early formation of dating relationships.

Although adolescent banter is normative for showing romantic interest, teasing can also be used to camouflage aggressive and hurtful sentiments. Such harassment initially emerges in the context of same-sex relationships and can include malicious whispering, name-calling, and note-passing. Same-sex harassment can also include, or be based on, the romantic interests and choices of an individual. Like teasing, harassment tends to be related to an adolescent's interest or lack of interest in romance and among boys often entails homophobic and misogynist insults (McMaster, Connolly, Pepler, & Craig, 2002).

Between grades 6 and 8, cross-sex harassment becomes increasingly common (McMaster et al., 2002). Although same-sex harassment sometimes has a sexual component, cross-sex harassment often entails behaviors that might be construed as sexual advances. Examples of these behaviors include making sexual comments, jokes, or gestures, rating sexual parts of someone's body, pulling at someone's clothes in a sexual way, or intentionally brushing up against someone in a sexual way. Although younger teens have some concept of the various forms of harassment and why they are wrong, verbally, physically, and sexually abusive behaviors among peers or friends are usually discounted as "just joking" (Berman & Jiwani, 2002). This minimizing view of harassment continues throughout midadolescence and can become a familiar excuse for dating violence and bullying. Because these teasing behaviors can also represent ways of expressing interest, it is difficult for teens and adults alike to differentiate the more harmful behaviors. As a consequence, adolescents may misinterpret abusive behaviors as signs of interest and commitment from a peer or dating partner.

Figure 3.1 shows the type of sexual harassment reported by adolescent girls and boys. Almost half of the girls and one-third of the boys reported that someone made sexual comments, jokes, gestures, or looks to them, and a significant number reported having been touched, grabbed, or pinched in a sexual way. Notwithstanding teens' views of

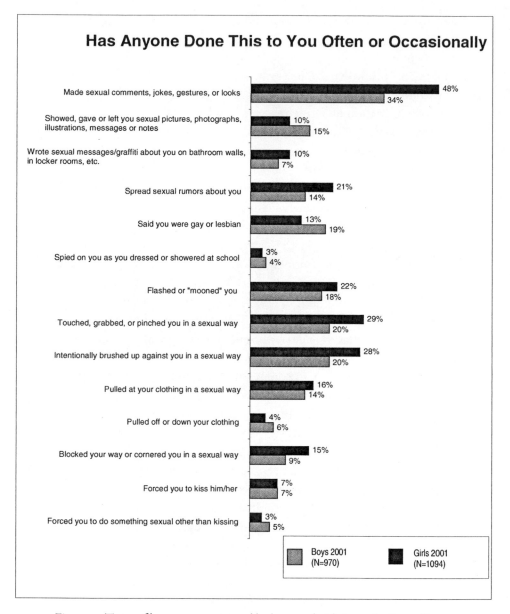

Figure 3.1. Types of harassment reported by boys and girls in grades 8–11. (American Association of University Women, 2001. Used with permission.)

harassment as harmless, cross-sex harassment can and does have negative consequences. Adolescent girls report that experiencing harassment results in them feeling afraid or embarrassed, being quiet in class, and achieving lower grades (American Association of University Women, 2001). Sexual and nonsexual forms of harassment take perhaps the greatest toll on girls, who report self-blame, reduced self-esteem, a sense of needing to change to be accepted, embarrassment, and shame much more often than boys (Berman & Jiwani, 2002). Furthermore, sexual harassment of others is often a warning sign of a developmental pattern of interpersonal aggression and a precursor for hostile interactions with dating partners (Connolly, Pepler, Craig, & Taradash, 2000; McMaster et al., 2002). In one of the few studies to track relationship aggression from childhood to adolescence, children who perpetrated the most same- and cross-sex harassment were substantially more likely to report perpetrating aggression in their dating relationships (Pepler, Craig, Connolly, & Henderson, 2002).

The cumulative nature of relationship quality is analogous to building a house—early relationships form the foundation for subsequent ones (Sroufe, 2000). Because there is continuity in one's manner of relating to others, children who develop coercive and hostile relationship patterns have a less tenable foundation for healthy relationships in the future. Although not inevitable, it is more likely that children who engage in bullying and harassment with their peers, for example, will carry forward these behavior patterns into adolescence and adulthood.

Researchers who follow youth throughout adolescence have identified teasing and harassment as potential entry-point behaviors for subsequent abusive and violent acts toward dating partners. Although these forms of relationship aggression typically begin with same-sex peers, by early adolescence harassment and other forms of abuse move into the realm of cross-sex relationships. In particular, teens who become prematurely engaged in serious romantic involvement and develop overly committed relationships at a younger age have increased risk of partner abuse and related risk behaviors. Not surprisingly, as men and women rely less on their peers and depend more on romantic relationships for support and intimacy in late adolescence and young adulthood, rates of relationship aggression continue to grow.

Dating Violence

Despite the importance of relationships during this time of transition, research on healthy and unhealthy adolescent dating relationships has been sparse. Initially, the lack of research attention may have stemmed from societal bias, in that adolescent romantic relationships were seen as trivial or somehow less genuine than adult intimate relationships. While there has been a shift in understanding the developmental importance of these relationships, research continues to be impeded by logistics. For example, adolescent dating relationships are short term (compared to adults) and their context and nature can change rapidly. As well, generational changes in adolescent subculture affect the dating lexicon and patterns, creating a moving target for researchers and parents alike. Terms such as "hooking up" or "seeing someone" have very different implications for the status of a relationship, and many teens prefer "going out" with someone as part of a group activity rather than as a couple. Finally, public health concerns about teenage pregnancy and sexually transmitted infections have pushed the study of adolescent sexual behavior to the forefront, eclipsing the context of romantic relationships in the process. These difficulties notwithstanding, there has been a more recent emphasis on understanding adolescent dating, in part because of an increased recognition of the levels and severity of abuse that can be part of these relationships. As such, a clearer picture of adolescent dating conflict and violence is emerging.

As with their other relationships, adolescents must learn to resolve conflicts in their romantic relationships. Although most conflicts are not severe, teens have an average of seven disagreements per day (Laursen & Collins, 1994). Mothers top the list of people with whom they have the most conflict, followed by siblings, friends, and romantic partners. Fathers, along with other peers and adults, are identified less often. The preference for how conflicts are settled has echoes of childhood preferences for relationship styles, where girls focus on connectivity to others and boys focus on status and hierarchies. Thus, during conflicts with dating partners girls are generally more likely to emphasize compromise between the partners rather than submission; boys, on the other hand, rely almost exclusively on submission of one or both parties to resolve such disputes.

The potential for violence in adolescent relationships increases significantly from middle to late adolescence for both girls and boys, partly as a function of increased jealousy and conflict. Girls as well as boys engage in abusive behavior with dating partners during adolescence, although for different reasons and with different consequences (Wolfe, Scott, & Crooks, 2005). By virtue of size and strength, most boys have more options available to escape a potentially dangerous or harmful situation; in contrast, adolescent girls are more likely to see self-defense as an acceptable reason for aggression (Cauffman, Feldman, Jensen, & Arnett, 2000). Beyond self-defense, abuse toward dating partners in mid- to late adolescence is often attributed to the relationship's dynamics, the partner's behavior, or an attempt to gain control over one's partner. Few teens identify their own abusive behavior as wrong or take personal responsibility for their actions, possibly reflecting the powerful messages received from family, entertainment media, and peers that imply coercive tactics are acceptable under certain circumstances (Wolfe, Wekerle, & Scott, 1997).

Motivation for dating violence is also tied to feelings of anger, jealousy, and emotional hurt. Male and female adolescents both report jealousy as a common motivator for relationship aggression (O'Keefe & Treister, 1998). Girls are more likely to perpetrate relationship aggression as a means to demonstrate anger or to retaliate for emotional hurt, whereas boys use aggression in retaliation for being hit first and, according to their victims, as a means to gain control over their partners (Follingstad, Wright, Lloyd, & Sebastian, 1991; Gagné & Lavoie, 1993). Girls also report using abusive or violent tactics against their dating partners in an attempt to tease or engage (Jackson, Cram, & Seymour, 2000) as well as to fight back in response to partner aggression (Watson, Cascardi, Avery-Leaf, & O' Leary, 2001). In contrast, physical and emotional abuse by boys is more likely to be attributed (by others) to behavior problems or alcohol and drug consumption (Hammock & O'Hearn, 2002; Odgers & Moretti, 2002).

In addition to differences in motivation, there are differences in consequences of dating violence for boys and girls. As we noted previously, childhood and adolescence are formative periods in which gender socialization is prominent and profound lessons are imparted about gender inequality and sexism. The valuing of masculine characteristics and activities and the devaluing of anything seen as feminine translates to the way in which dating violence is experienced by individuals. Female victims of dating violence are more likely than males to experience fear, anxiety, or hurt and express a desire to leave the situation for self-protection. Male victims, in contrast, report being amused or angered by female aggression (Jackson et al., 2000). One study of high school youths found that girls reported their use of aggression as most typically expressive (that is, feeling angry, frustrated), whereas boys reported their use of aggression as often playful (Scott, Wekerle, & Wolfe, 1997). In a similar vein, in responding to their worst incident of violence, adolescent males typically reported they laughed it off, while females reported they cried (40 percent), fought back (36 percent), obeyed their partner (12 percent), or ran away (11 percent) (Cascardi, Avery-Leaf, O'Leary, & Slep, 1999).

Related to this notion of differential impact is the possibility that boys and girls have different interpretations of violence in dating relationships. Young women are more likely to overlook a physically abusive experience, whereas young men draw attention to their victimization, possibly to justify their own behavior (Currie, 1998). The possibility also remains that males may deny or minimize their violent behavior and females may be too ready to assume blame due to sex-role stereotypes that are part of Western culture (Sharpe & Taylor, 1999).

Regardless of differences in motivation, mutual violence remains the most common pattern of violence seen in adolescent dating relationships right through to late adolescence. Youths involved in mutually violent relationships tend to report sustaining and initiating more total violence, engaging in more severe violence, and experiencing more injuries than those who reported victimization or perpetration alone. Mutual violence may emerge when two individuals who have experienced or witnessed violence in previous relationships select similar partners (H. M. Gray & Foshee, 1997). Based on their previous experiences, each partner may bring distorted expectations of control and intimacy to the relationship as well as increased acceptance and normalization of abusive behavior. This supposition underscores the need to study dating violence within the context of the dating relationship and the reciprocal effects of aggressive male and female partners, as opposed to studying individual behaviors.

Gay Baiting and Homophobia

Gender socialization again emerges as a dominant theme in the origin of abusive behaviors directed toward peers. Boys come to believe that their identity and the perception of their peers depend on being different from girls and, to a lesser extent, the opposite holds true for girls as well. Boys' views of what male characteristics are acceptable, for example, give license for them to behave in a gender-consistent manner. By the same reasoning, any boy who exhibits characteristics that are gender inconsistent (that is, feminine) are justifiable targets of coercive methods to "bring them in line." In other words, teasing, bullying, and harassment may be used to force individuals to conform to acceptable gender roles and behaviors. Those who do not conform risk exclusion and further abuse from members of the group.

At the core of these abusive behaviors is the construction of power and status (important goals boys have learned to value) and the acceptability of using abusive means to maintain the status quo. Likewise, girls may use a gender lens to evaluate the appropriate behavior of other girls and exclude those who fail to meet their expectations. They, too, may assert their power in abusive ways, albeit the predominant methods for doing so are linked to relationship preferences; that is, they are more likely to reject another girl from their peer group than engage in physical violence. In essence, boys and girls engage in the dark side of relationship formation for similar reasons—maintaining their gender construction. Their choice of methods is dictated by their gendered preferences for physical versus relational aggression (Crick & Grotpeter, 1995).

Homophobic insults and abusive language explode during early to midadolescence, and this pattern shows signs of worsening. In fact, the biggest change in the type of harassment experienced by teens between 1993 and 2001 is the incidence of being called gay or lesbian: a jump from 17 percent to 36 percent (American Association of University Women, 2001). By early adolescence teasing takes on a clearly homophobic intent, whereby insults can be handed out freely to pressure conformity. Boys, in particular, find it necessary to police their own and others' behaviors to defend themselves against humiliation and being considered not adequately masculine. Policing relationships with other boys and vilifying others as gay serve the function of asserting masculinity and avoiding being bullied. The term *gay* becomes an insult rather than a matter-of-fact description of sexual orientation, used when boys want to discredit another boy who falls outside of their own gender beliefs and expectations. The ubiquity of homophobia affects not only the target of ridicule but also the identities and experiences of all boys in general, regardless of social class or ethnicity (Epstein & Johnson, 1998). Boys' homophobic actions can be seen as readily available defensive ways of shoring up their masculinity by constructing feminine traits as threatening and distancing themselves from any boys they see as not properly masculine. Homophobia is intertwined with misogyny in its focus on avoiding and devaluing characteristics associated with girls (Phoenix, Frosh, & Pattman, 2003). Not surprisingly, boys see homophobic insults as insignificant ("just a joke"), much as they do negative comments about girls and women (Capaldi, Dishion, Stoolmiller, & Yoerger, 2001).

The manner in which gender construction carries over into boys' views of other ethnic groups was illustrated in a qualitative study of 11–14-year-old boys (Phoenix et al., 2003). Asian boys were constructed as not powerful or sexually attractive and were more likely to be subjected to homophobic insults. Black boys, in contrast, were less likely to be called gay and, in fact, could spend a lot of time with girls and not lose their status because they were seen as strongly heterosexual. Young African American men are viewed in some ways as supermasculine, possessing the most attractive masculine traits—toughness and authentic male style of talk and dress. While being "heroes of a street fashion culture that dominates most of our inner cities" (Sewell, 1997, p. ix), the price they pay is increased discrimination in schools due to perceptions of them being poor students and threatening to others (Phoenix et al., 2003).

Homophobic taunting has been implicated in some of the most extreme cases of school-based violence seen over the past 20 years. A review of the school shootings that occurred in the United States between 1982 and 2001 highlighted the role of chronic bullying and harassment in the perpetration of lethal violence (Kimmel & Mahler, 2003). The boys who committed the school shootings were all bullied extensively and culturally marginalized in their schools. Furthermore, the homophobic nature of the harassment was underscored. The researchers quote several of the shooters' classmates, who, when interviewed after the lethal violence, still identified the presence of these "queers" in their school as the only problem. The classmates completely overlooked the pervasive and relentless victimization of these marginalized youth as a contributing factor in the violence. The role of gender has been largely overlooked in other analyses of lethal school-based violence as well. Many experts identify the roles of violent media, family backgrounds, and bullying in leading to these instances of fatal violence, yet they ignore the fact that all of the perpetrators were male. Ironically, if the killers in the schools had all been girls, gender would have been the only story (Kimmel & Mahler, 2003).

The significance of homophobic name-calling has not been given proper recognition and is often overlooked as a form of bullying. Its role is to buttress versions of masculinity by putting others down. This threat-driven homophobia is likely responsible for the explosion of antigay and antiwomen aggression during this developmental stage (Parrott, Adams, & Zeichner, 2002). Given the homophobic nature of bullying in general, youth who are developing gay, lesbian, or bisexual sexual identities are especially susceptible to being bullied, harassed, and physically victimized. Indeed, the majority of lesbian, gay, bisexual, and transgendered (LGBT) youth experience harassment in school. In a New England study that questioned 136 LGBT adolescents between the ages of 13 and 18 about their school experiences, 60 percent said they experienced some form of victimization in their school, most commonly verbal insults or threats of violence (Elze, 2003). Disturbingly, 32 percent reported experiencing more serious forms of victimization, including various types of physical violence. Approximately half of those interviewed had seen antigay/heterosexist graffiti in their school, and about the same percentage of these students believed that LGBT youth were harassed in the locker rooms. Peers are not the only perpetrators of this harassment; 41 percent of the youth reported having heard homophobic jokes from their teachers.

A similar study, conducted in the Chicago metropolitan area, questioned 34 gay, lesbian, or bisexual youth between the ages of 15 and 19 (Jordan, Vaughn, & Woodworth, 1997). Nearly half (47 percent) of the youth who reported experiencing some type of harassment at school said it often ended in physical aggression. The majority of the students surveyed reported sometimes feeling threatened or afraid, different or separate, alienated, alone, and rejected. The impact of this ongoing harassment and intimidation can be profound. Research in the United States and in Canada has identified higher rates of suicide and substance use among LGBT youth, which may reflect "attempts to escape from a present and future that appear untenable" (Maticka-Tyndale, 2001, p. 13).

The National School Climate Survey attempted to document the extent to which sexual minority youth in the United States feel comfortable in their school environment (Kosciw, 2004). Information was obtained from 887 middle and high school students from 48 states and the District of Columbia. The findings of the report identified these youths as a vulnerable group with respect to peer-perpetrated abuse. More than four out of five LGBT youths reported being verbally, sexually, or physically harassed in the school environment because of their sexual orientation. A vast majority (91.5 percent) reported hearing homophobic remarks, such as "faggot," "dyke," or "That's so gay," frequently or often. Another important finding of this report was that LGBT youth who experienced significant harassment were twice as likely to report not having the intention of going to college, and their GPAs while in school were significantly lower. In addition, a majority (82.9 percent) of the students interviewed reported that faculty rarely or never intervened when they witnessed harassment against sexual minority youth. Approximately two-thirds of LGBT students admitted to feeling unsafe at school because of their sexual orientation, and one-third reported they felt uncomfortable discussing these issues with their teachers. This survey underscores the need for teachers and administrators to be aware of harassment targeting lesbian, gay, bisexual, and transgendered youth and to take action against these injustices that render the school environment hostile for sexual minority youth. The report itself stresses the urgent need for support systems, policy adjustment, and creation of harassment policies and gay-straight alliance groups in the school systems.

In our own discussions with teachers, many have identified feeling helpless and overwhelmed by the pervasiveness of homophobic insults. During a recent presentation to teachers, one noted that she would have to stop her class 50–100 times a day if she tried to intervene every time she heard the words "fag" or "homo." Those who do try to intervene often feel ineffectual—adolescents say they are "just joking," and teachers feel their attempts to curtail these behaviors make no difference. As we discuss in the later chapters of this book, there is no simple answer for teachers attempting to curtail these homophobic insults. The entire school setting needs to be mobilized to create new norms for acceptable behavior and awareness among all members of the school community with respect to the inappropriateness of these insults.

Gang Violence

As discussed throughout this chapter, all youth seek affiliations and relationships with peers. When relationships with prosocial youth and adults are unavailable or rejecting, adolescents turn to other alienated youth to fill this void (Dodge, Coie, & Brakke, 1982). Identifying with a particular gang is one way that these rejected youth can develop a sense of belonging and relatedness, albeit with the potential for significant harm. The issue of youth gang involvement is an important one. More than 16,000 active gangs with at least half a million members proliferate in all areas of the United States (Harper & Robinson, 1999; Huff, 1997). A survey of nearly 6,000 eighth graders conducted in 11 American cities discovered that 11 percent of these students were currently gang members, while 17 percent admitted to belonging to a gang at some point (Esbensen & Deschenes, 1998). While the predominant stereotype depicts gang members as young boys of an ethnic minority, the reality is much more diverse, ranging from young, white, affluent females to 9-year-old Latino boys.

Why is such a significant percentage of today's youth involved in gangs? What is missing in their other relationships that they attempt to remedy with gang membership? Pride and honor are two of the commonly stated adolescent motivations for joining gangs (Parker, 2001; A. Y. Wang, 1994). While these may be the explicit reasons provided by teens involved in gang activity, the complete picture is much more complex. Often adolescents who are not receiving sufficient fulfillment of their relationship needs through family, school, peers, and the community look to gang membership to fill these needs. Gangs offer individuals a sense of protection and belonging perhaps previously unknown to them in their family or community environment (M. L. Walker, Schmidt, & Lunghofer, 1993).

Research investigating motivation to join gangs has identified a range of factors. Alienation from and defiance toward parents may be an initial cause of adolescents' turning to delinquency and gang membership. Socioeconomic factors appear to contribute to gang affiliation: a dysfunctional family system, low self-esteem, poor academic performance, and poor vocational training are common traits (Kodluboy, 1997). Furthermore, parents' educational levels have been shown to be low, and many gang members lack positive male role models. The families of gang-involved adolescents are frequently chaotic and detached, and there may be a history of child neglect, alcoholism, and violence (Clark, 1992). In many ways the gang is a surrogate family for youth who face family problems such as poverty, alcoholism, drug addiction, poor housing, and family criminal activity (Morales, 1992). Young gang members are often seeking feelings of security that were absent in their own homes and feel they will be understood by the other gang members. It is clear that these youth experience a multitude of risk factors that converge to make them likely candidates for gang membership. For many adolescents involved in gangs, there appears to have been a breakdown of the fundamental relationships that form the basis for healthy relationship development.

The dynamics of gender-based harassment and violence that emerge in adolescents are magnified in gang culture. Gangs serve as a crucible that intensifies many of the negative processes discussed in this chapter. The book *Guys, Gangs, and Girlfriend Abuse* (Totten, 2000) draws the link between the experiences of these marginalized male youths and how their subculture encourages them to perpetrate physical, sexual, and emotional violence toward their girlfriends, whom they claim to love. Although gender rigidity is evident in any high school, there is a big difference in the degree to which gang members endorse a rigid code of male conduct. They may have witnessed this code of conduct in their own homes, where male authority was absolute. Within the context of this exaggerated masculinity, the abuse of females and gay and ethnic minority youths goes unchallenged.

Peer Culture: A Closer Look at the Media

Relationship development and the central role of gender identity all unfold within the larger context of peer culture and mass media. Adolescent peer culture is characterized by insidious forces—teens are bombarded by masses of information. Numerous forms of media play a notable role in providing information and entertainment for adolescents and comprise a force to be reckoned with during the teenage years. Television, radio, movies, video games, music and music videos, magazines, and the Internet are all so pervasive in young people's lives that youth are hardly aware of their presence. These media have become an invisible force that defines the reality of many teenagers.

Of course, it is not only teenagers who are affected by the pervasiveness of media, but they are the biggest consumers. According to a survey conducted by the Kaiser Family Foundation, American children between 2 and 18 years of age spend an average of 6 hours and 32 minutes each day using media, including television, commercial or self-recorded video, movies, video games, print, radio, recorded music, computer, and the Internet (Roberts, Foehr, Rideout, & Brodia, 1999). A survey conducted by the Environics Research Group on behalf of Media Awareness Network (2000) found that virtually all high school students use the Internet; 48 percent are on it for at least half an hour every day, and nearly 60 percent regularly engage in chat room discussions and instant messaging.

Young women are relentlessly targeted through the bombardment of images of fashion and beauty, particularly in teen magazines such as *Cosmo Girl* and *Seventeen* as well as via music videos and advertisements. The persistent media image of emaciated models wearing expensive clothing has in many cases come to define beauty for these young women, often damaging their self-esteem and affecting their own body image. These images may be particularly salient for adolescent girls in light of the gender role rigidity characteristic of the age. Young women are also media targets at a younger age through increasingly sexualized fashion trends.

Television advertisements are another familiar avenue by which the media use women in a sexist manner. In a study that examined beer commercials, researchers found that women were often portrayed as sexual objects and were used to sell the product. Most of the images focused on desirable lifestyles, and many were sexual in nature (for example, females in these ads served the function of sexual imagery or attractive background decorations). In addition, nearly all of these ads with beer and sports images, and most of the beer ads without sports content, featured traditional gender role/sexist female presentations (Rouner, Slater, & Domenech-Rodriguez, 2003).

The degree to which media have become a pervasive force is unprecedented. Reality TV shows, allowing viewers to follow people's lives around the clock, are becoming increasingly popular. E-mail and text messaging allow people to remain in touch 24 hours a day, 7 days a week. This omnipresent media culture is having a significant impact on adolescent lifestyles. Youth are becoming less active and more isolated as a result of having so much information and stimulation within arm's reach. With this ubiquitous media culture it is becoming increasingly difficult for parents to monitor their children's viewing and listening habits, especially when it comes to the Internet. Due to the amount of media being consumed by adolescents, parents and society need to be aware of the potentially negative effects of these forms of entertainment, particularly with respect to violent and negatively gendered content (Kaiser Family Foundation, 2003).

The mass media today, including movies, television, music videos, and video games, contain an unprecedented amount of violence. Furthermore, there is evidence of "ratings creep" in that the level of violence has increased in each category of movie ratings (Kids Risk Project, www.kidsrisk.harvard.edu). Although there is some disagreement in the research community as to whether or not this type of subtle or overt violence viewing pushes young people to act in aggressive ways, there is consensus that the media have the potential to desensitize children to violence and to normalize aggressive behavior (Huesmann, Moise-Titus, Podolski, & Eron, 2003).

A recent study attempted to measure the extent of desensitization that occurs after a child has been exposed to violent media. While desensitization is obviously difficult to measure, the researchers monitored the levels of pro-violence attitudes and empathy following the subjects' involvement with violent media. They found that of the media forms investigated, video games had the most significant impact on the children, and pro-violence attitudes increased significantly after playing violent video games. These authors attribute this phenomenon to the intense involvement in video game play (more intense than watching a movie), which makes it difficult for the child to distinguish between play and reality (Funk, Baldacci, Pasold, & Baumgardner, 2004). The mechanical, interactive quality of "first-person shooter" games makes them potentially more dangerous than movie or television violence (Grossman & DeGaetano, 1999). In an attempt to assess the level of violence in video games, a group of researchers conducted an evaluation of teen-rated (T-rated) video games. Out of a random selection of 81 T-rated video games, 79 games involved intentional violence for an average of 36 percent of game playtime, and 34 games contained blood. More than half of the games depicted five or more types of weapons, with players able to select weapons in 48 games. Thirty-seven of the games rewarded or required the player to destroy objects, 73 games rewarded or required the player to injure characters, and 56 games rewarded or required the player to kill. The rate of human deaths occurred at an average of 61 per hour of game play (range 0 to 1,291; Haninger, Thompson, & Ryan, 2004).

In addition to an unacceptable amount of general violence, video games have also been shown to perpetuate sexist gender roles and often depict violent behavior specifically toward women. In a study of video games, 41 percent of the 33 popular Nintendo and Sega Genesis games had no female characters present whatsoever; in 28 percent of them women were portrayed as sex objects, and 21 percent displayed violence against women (Dietz, 1998). Video games, therefore, can serve to reinforce traditional and degrading gender stereotypes and situations and propagate aggressive behavior toward women.

Finally, some researchers distinguish between violent content per se and the framework in which it is presented. From this viewpoint it is not the violence itself but the context in which it is portrayed that can make the difference between learning about violence and learning to be violent (Bar-on et al., 2001). In explorations of dramatic forms of violence, such as *Macbeth* and *Saving Private Ryan,* which depict violence as a human behavior that causes suffering, loss, and sadness to victims and perpetrators, viewers learn the danger and harm of violence by vicariously experiencing its outcomes. However, most entertainment violence is not presented in this larger context but rather is used to trigger immediate visceral thrills in its audience without portraying any human cost. In a similar vein, the fact that the violence shown most often on television and in movies and experienced in video games is generally considered acceptable and is often even depicted as "funny," in large part explains youth desensitization to violence (Grossman & DeGaetano, 1999).

Innovative technological advances have created an array of new opportunities for learning and discovery. Unfortunately, the inventions of instant messaging, websites, and chat rooms have also created new methods for perpetrating relationship violence. Internet harassment, defined as an intentional and overt act of aggression toward another person online, is just one of the many risks associated with cyberspace (Ybarra & Mitchell, 2004). Internet bullying is becoming a significant problem, initially involving rude comments or intentional embarrassment of another user and often leading to more serious infringements of another person's rights. A 2002 British survey found that one in four youth ages 11 to 19 has been threatened via computers or cell phones, including death threats (National Children's Home, 2002). Bullying and harassment among youth are facilitated by the anonymity associated with the Internet, which allows a bully to project aggression without having to face the reaction of the victim (Janovsky, 2004). Making a website in order to embarrass another person is all too easily done: simply by posting a few embarrassing photographs on the web and adding some nasty comments for all eyes to see. The young victim may feel the effects of this type of teasing for a long time to come.

Cell phones are another example of a technological device that has been misused for the purposes of bullying and harassment. According to the British survey executed by the National Children's Home (2002), 16 percent of young people report having been bullied or threatened via text messages. Many cell phones are equipped with Internet access and can also be used to send e-mails and engage in chat room discussions and are thus unfortunately another potential means of harassment among youth. The added ability of these phones to take pictures has led to numerous incidents of embarrassing photos being posted on the Internet, with a devastating impact on victims. Not only is the Internet a means by which youth can harass and bully each other, it also introduces adolescents and children to potential exploitation by adults. Virtual chat rooms make it impossible to discern the age of the person with whom you are chatting, and youth can easily be tricked into thinking they are forming a relationship with someone their age when in fact they may be conversing with an Internet pedophile.

Although still a somewhat new area of research, information about chat room use patterns and correlates is growing. A relationship between chat room use and sexual solicitations has clearly emerged; chat room users are four times more likely than nonusers to be exposed to unwanted sexual solicitations online (Mitchell, Finkelhor, & Wolak, 2001). Which adolescents tend to form the closest online relationships and be targets of sexual material via the Internet is not a mystery: depression, victimization by peers, and alienation from parents are commonly associated with exploitation. For example, a study of chat room users found disproportionate numbers of sexual abuse victims, adolescents who had run away from home, adolescents who were intrigued by risk, and adolescents who used alcohol and other drugs (Beebe, Asche, Harrison, & Quinlan, 2004). The vulnerability of these adolescents may leave them ill equipped to recognize and fend off attempts at exploitation.

While various forms of media have the potential to inform and entertain youth in a positive manner, the preceding analysis highlights the potential for profound negative effects, such as a hostile depiction of women, sexualization of young girls, and exposure to violence. To counter some of these influences it is essential that parents and teachers supervise and guide children and youth in their choices of movies, music videos, video games, and similar forms of entertainment that involve abusive and violent behavior.

Summary

In early to midadolescence we see the issue of gender role expectations reemerge with considerable force, defining how teens are expected to behave among their same- and opposite-sex peers. As their peer networks rapidly expand teens are caught in the middle between their family and peer values. They often face considerable pressure to conform to peer expectations at school or in the community while maintaining allegiance to family values at home. Although this divergence from the family is a normal and healthy part of development, it can be fraught with tension and dispute as teens try to adapt to the ever-changing yet all-important expectations of their peers.

Learning to relate is an ongoing process, and one that takes a particularly difficult new direction in early adolescence. As youths become more engaged with their peers they rely once again on familiar gender role expectations to improve their chances of fitting in and being accepted. Much as it did in early childhood, this reliance on familiar roles and expectations helps them through this process by providing some structure to this demanding situation. However, this time around the process of learning to relate is more challenging than ever and accompanied by its darker side: bullying, harassment, dating violence, gay baiting, lethal violence, and gang involvement. We described how these behaviors share very similar dynamics and are often connected to one another by virtue of their role in maintaining one's style of relating and gender role boundaries. For children who have structured their previous relationships on the basis of victims and victimizers, sticking to this template becomes the easiest solution to relating to peers. Teasing can become bullying and bullying can transform into harassment and dating violence, such that abuse can become the critical dynamic by which relationships are defined and maintained.

In each of the preceding areas of violence and abuse, perception of gender expectations plays a central role in guiding behavior. It is no coincidence that the theme of gender rigidity is common to all of these types of behavior. To be accepted by peers and avoid the pitfalls of the darker side, many youths stick to the safest route and adhere carefully to gender role expectations. By disparaging those who fail to meet such expectations, teens protect themselves from falling outside the perimeter and remain safely within the acceptable boundaries defined by the comments and behavior of their peers and culture. Homophobic taunting is ubiquitous in adolescence and plays a particularly significant role in the different forms of relationship violence that emerge. Disturbingly, the antigay nature of this peer culture can create an extremely antagonistic environment for sexual minority youth.

All of these behaviors emerge within the context of larger forces such as media and peer culture. The potential for media to affect perceptions of gender roles negatively and to glorify violence, particularly toward women, deserves careful consideration. In addition, the interactive nature of some forms of media, especially first-person shooter video games, may have the potential to shape the behavior of vulnerable adolescents in a way that places them on a pathway toward becoming more violent and abusive to others. Although these extreme outcomes are rare, they demonstrate the pressures all adolescents face. In the next chapter, we focus more closely on these challenges and pressures and explore the different trends and patterns with respect to violence, substance use, and sexual behavior.

4

Choices and Pressures
of Today's Youth

Adolescents have always had to navigate the murky waters of adult privileges, from smoking and drinking to sexual involvement and romantic relationships. These temptations may prove too enticing to resist, causing some teens to become early starters. Although most teens will eventually try at least some of these behaviors, premature experimenters run the greatest risk for many health and injury consequences associated with such behaviors. Part of adolescent development is learning how to establish one's own principles and boundaries. Nonetheless, simply letting teens learn for themselves is not an appealing option given the known risks of injury or long-term health problems. Likewise, simply telling teens to "just say no" or putting up legal or familial roadblocks to make their involvement more difficult will not remove the risks, especially for early starters and those at greater risk of engaging in health-compromising behaviors. To understand how teens learn to navigate this important transition period, it is essential to examine the physical, emotional, and social changes they face and how the experience and timing of these adjustments ultimately affect adolescent health (Halpern-Felsher, Millstein, & Irwin, 2002).

Adolescence represents a crucial period in preventing health-compromising and problem behaviors. Many of these critical health-damaging behaviors—such as substance use and abuse, unsafe sexual practices, and dating violence—begin largely during adolescence and can form the basis of lasting behavioral patterns. In thinking about how best to prevent these lifestyle behaviors that can cause negative long-term consequences for both adolescents and those around them, we are faced with a choice of being passive and reactionary or taking an active stance. The passive choice would be to continue addressing the needs of youth in an inconsistent, reactionary manner. The active choice involves shifting to a new paradigm committed to the needs and resources of youth. A starting point is to understand the pressures and choices faced by teens as they undergo rapid physical, cognitive, and emotional maturation. Choices that may seem straightforward to adults take on many shades of gray to teens due to their evolving internal and external worlds.

Adolescence is a time of tremendous transformations of the body, mind, and personal responsibilities. One of the main changes that occur during adolescence is puberty, a purely biological transformation that we address in greater detail below. More advanced thinking abilities also develop during the teen years, and along with these come social change and the transition into new roles in society. The rate at which these changes take place is uneven, leaving a gap between physiological changes on the one hand and cognitive and emotional maturity on the other. This gap may account for some of the observed risk-taking behavior characteristic of adolescents. The pubertal changes increase novelty and sensation seeking, but the self-regulatory competence that offsets sensation seeking does not fully mature until adulthood. As a result we should begin with the premise that adolescents are inherently more likely than adults to take risks, and we should focus on reducing the harm associated with risk-taking behavior (Steinberg, 2004). An understanding of all the different changes taking place during adolescence provides the foundation for understanding the observed rise in a range of risk behaviors.

Navigating puberty is one of the major challenges faced by adolescents (Silbereisen & Kracke, 1997). Adolescents undergo significant psychological and emotional changes in conjunction with physical changes. For example, they face transformations in physical appearance such as breast development in females and growth of facial hair for males and a dramatic increase in height. During this period, most youth will physically mature from children into adults, although males continue to grow into their early 20s. Self-image may be temporarily threatened as teens come to terms with all the physical changes, including bodily maturations and facial changes, each influencing the way they feel about themselves. The impact of puberty differs across the board: some youth feel attractive, grown-up, and confident, while others feel self-conscious, ugly, and afraid. These physical changes are intertwined with psychological and emotional transitions. Physical changes affect self-image and behavior while also prompting changes and reactions in others. Changes in a child's physical appearance may, for instance, elicit different types of behavior from parents, peers, and others. In addition to these types of challenges, adolescent moods tend to fluctuate throughout the day.

The extent to which early or late onset of puberty may affect involvement in risk behaviors is worthy of consideration. Early onset of puberty in girls is associated with a number of risk behaviors, including cigarette smoking and consumption of alcohol (Stattin & Magnusson, 1990). Furthermore, girls who mature younger tend to start dating earlier and often choose older partners (Silbereisen & Kracke, 1997). Involvement with older partners has been identified as a link in the observed relationship between premature physical maturation and earlier onset of sexual activity for girls (Stattin & Magnusson, 1990). In addition, early pubertal development relates to a younger age of sexual debut for both males and females (Capaldi, Crosby, & Stoolmiller, 1996). Earlier age at menarche also correlates with riskier sexual practices, most likely by increasing the likelihood of affiliating with older boyfriends, which in turn increases the chances of engaging in sexual risk behavior (Mezzich et al., 1997).

In addition to outward pubertal changes taking place during adolescence, hormonal and synaptic changes in the brain affect teens' behavior. One significant hormonal change is the increased activity of the hypothalamic-pituitary-adrenal (HPA) axis, which plays a central role in the biological response to stress (E. Walker, 2002; E. Walker & Bollini, 2002). Heightened stress levels during adolescence have been attributed in large part to this more active HPA axis. The prefrontal cortex—the part of the brain where emotional control, impulse restraint, and rational decision making take place—also grows quickly during adolescence. However, because this part of the brain is still developing, most teens have not yet fully achieved the abilities of self-control and affect regulation. To a certain extent, this lag in neurodevelopment explains why many teenagers engage in high-risk and impulsive behavior: their passions are ignited, yet they lack the cognitive and self-regulatory skills to consistently make positive, well-considered decisions.

As a result of these neurological processes and experience in general, adolescents' intellectual abilities become more sophisticated, their expectations about relationships become more realistic, and their ability to regulate emotions becomes more finely tuned. In addition, more advanced cognitive skills such as reasoning and problem solving emerge and are consolidated. More advanced thinking abilities also imply an increased propensity to consider hypothetical situations and abstract concepts—skills that affect how one thinks about the self, relationships, and the world. Along with cognitive maturation comes the ability to think from more than one perspective or angle—to consider what is being observed versus what is possible. As adolescents mature, they also gain the ability to plan ahead, anticipate the response of others, and become better debaters and arguers, all of which contribute to and are affected by increased problem solving skills and the ability to reflect on moral dilemmas.

This increased ability to think about possibilities may also lead to becoming lost in thoughts and worries. Adolescents become capable of metacognition, or "thinking about thinking," and as a result, they experience an increased propensity to monitor thoughts, more intense self-absorption, and often a belief that their own behavior is the focus of everyone else's concern and attention. Social cognition—thinking about people, relationships, human behavior, and social conventions such as social norms, guidelines for social interaction, and justice—is also an important part of adolescent growth.

Adolescents develop an increased comprehension of their own emotions and the ability to understand or analyze why they feel a certain way, which facilitates more intimate relationships. Emotional self-regulation continues to develop, increasing the capacity of youths to form more long-lasting, mutual, and healthy relationships. As feelings toward others mature during these years, teens generally begin to place less value on appearance and more on personality, thus finding themselves in more meaningful and intense relationships.

The importance of peers and the development of romantic relationships are two distinguishing features of adolescence. Most teens shift their focus of interest from parents to peer relations and develop greatly increased capacity for intimacy with other youth. Along with this shift to peer relations is a desire for more privacy from family members, often resulting in changes in their family relationships. Although this move toward independence leads to less exclusive and intense relationships between parents and children, this shift does not necessarily mean a decrease in the importance of the parent-child relationship. While youth turn to their peers for help with more superficial decisions about things like clothes and curfews, parents are more influential than peers in more serious matters of religious beliefs, moral values, and political ideas (Savin-Williams & Berndt, 1990; Steinberg & Morris, 2001).

Relationships are of central importance in adolescence to the extent that some researchers have coined them the organizing principle of adolescents and their peer networks (Collins & Sroufe, 1999). The development of romantic relationships in particular encourages independence, assists with identity formation, and fosters skills for intimacy. These fledgling romances also provide a training ground for the development and refinement of interpersonal skills such as negotiation, reciprocity, emotional closeness, and disclosure. As noted in chapter 2, romantic relationships also serve a function within the peer group and may be a way to gain status and acceptance.

While all of these adjustments to family and peer relations are taking place, social status and social roles also transform. Newfound rights, privileges, and responsibilities are acquired during the latter phases of adolescence, such as the permission to drive, marry, vote, drink, and smoke. These changes in social status allow teens to try new activities and roles. Social positioning also changes as adolescents begin training for adult roles, such as work, starting their own families, and responsibilities in their community. This is also the time in life when individuals generally attain adult status and training, with the completion of formal schooling and/or job training.

While simultaneously attempting to cope with all of these physical, cognitive, and emotional changes, adolescents must also deal with the challenge of developing a psychological identity. As mentioned earlier, teens establish an identity beyond their family role by developing relationships with others and becoming more emotionally detached from their parents. Healthy same-sex relationships play a key role in the growth of an individual and a sense of self in relation to others. Questions arise during adolescence as to who they are and where they are heading in life. It is also a period of role experimentation—trying on different roles until the "true self" is found. Adolescents may even change their identity from context to context, particularly around the ages of 14 to 16 (Steinberg & Morris, 2001). For example, an individual might be typically shy at school but behave in an outgoing manner at summer camp. At the same time, the need to be seen as a unique person while also fitting in with others poses an inner struggle for most teens. These challenges are all part of the changes in identity, self-esteem, and self-conceptions that occur during the teenage years, as new activities and roles trigger a new evaluation of self. Cultural identity is another critical part of this process, especially for adolescents who are not part of the white Anglo majority (Phinney, 1990).

Along with these changes comes the need to establish a sense of autonomy, independence, and achievement. Teens strive to assert their own independence and to be seen as self-sufficient by others. In order to do so they must become less emotionally dependent on parents; therefore, the ability to make independent decisions and establish a personal core set of values and morals are vital adjustments during these years. Attempts to achieve a balance between autonomy and connectedness lead to the push–pull behavior some parents observe in their adolescents: youth may be affectionate one moment and aloof the next. Intimacy takes on an important role as well, as adolescence is a time of forming close and caring relationships with others. Most teenagers experience a change in their capacity for intimacy with others, especially as far as their peers are concerned. They move from sharing activities and interests to relationships that involve openness, honesty, loyalty, and keeping confidences. Adolescence is also a time for forming trusting and loving relationships, and expressing sexual feelings and enjoying physical contact with others represents one expression of such intimacy.

The Adolescent Landscape: Choices, Pressures, and Consequences

On top of these dramatic physical and psychological changes adolescents face an onslaught of choices and pressures unmatched in any other developmental period. Unfortunately, there is undue prejudice against youth in our culture, stemming in large part from lack of knowledge of youth development and overexposure in the media of tragedies and fear-inducing events. Headline stories about a murder committed by an adolescent, for example, result in demands for more youths being sentenced as adults, getting tougher with teens through boot camps, and capital punishment (Steinberg & Scott, 2003). Broadly speaking, there is an overall movement toward "zero tolerance" of adolescent misconduct, in the hopes of eliminating problems through punishment and exclusion. These attitudes have developed in spite of overwhelming data suggesting a drop in violent crime committed by teens (Federal Interagency Forum on Child and Family Statistics, 2004) and the ineffectiveness of zero tolerance and abstinence-based programs, as discussed in chapter 6.

We hear less about reductions in adolescent health-compromising behaviors and about improvements in educational achievements than we do about the risks. For example, the public at large often perceives that the education system fails to produce literate students, when in fact the past two generations have witnessed dramatic increases in student retention in secondary school and continuation into further education (National Center for Education Statistics, 2000). Despite the common belief that teens are engaging in more promiscuous behavior, resulting in a higher number of unwanted pregnancies, the evidence from national surveys in the United States and Canada indicates that the teen birth rate has hit a record low (Dryburgh, 2000; Federal Interagency Forum on Child and Family Statistics, 2004; Maticka-Tyndale, 2001).

Educational achievements and lowered rates of teen pregnancy notwithstanding, important areas of concern remain. Of particular note is that common risk-taking behaviors, such as drug and alcohol abuse, unsafe sexual activity, violence, injury-related behavior, tobacco use, inadequate physical activity, and poor dietary habits, account for

70 percent of adolescent mortality (Irwin et al., 2002). Enhanced surveillance of the well-being of children and youth by federal governments and researchers has provided greater specificity about the extent and breadth of problem areas and identified some worrisome concerns that confirm the need for ongoing efforts at health promotion targeted at adolescents.

Between the ages of 11 and 16, teens start to experiment with alcohol, drugs, smoking, and sex in their peer and dating relationships. Whether or not they get involved with these potential risks directly, they will undoubtedly find themselves in situations where they have to make choices. For some, their role may become one of crisis counselor or bystander, and they may even encourage their peers to make safer choices. For others, the escalating experimentation of their peers may influence them to make harmful choices. More likely, most adolescents will find themselves in both roles during their teen years. Regardless of their role, youths are desperate for information and guidance to help them handle the choices, pressures, and consequences associated with this tumultuous stage. For example, 93 percent of young teens are in favor of sexual health education at school; they particularly seek accurate information and practical skills (Byers et al., 2003).

Addressing the topic of adolescent choices and risks is fraught with controversy. The dilemma for parents and adults in authority is to understand the reality of these behavior trends and strike a comfortable balance between the two extreme approaches that are sometimes chosen. At one extreme, some parents assume their teen can be constantly monitored, and any foray into risk behaviors can be forbidden and strongly sanctioned to eliminate potential problems. At the other extreme, parents may relinquish control of their adolescent, adopting a laissez-faire attitude in the hopes their teen will learn through natural consequences. Neither of these extremes fits well with the realities of today's society. Without sensitivity and concern for the pressures their son or daughter faces, parents may become irrelevant or even contribute to rebelliousness through their unreasonable and rigid demands. Likewise, parents who leave the process too much to chance or try to approach their adolescent as a friend may not provide the guidance adolescents require to minimize the likelihood of serious negative consequences.

In our view, adolescents benefit from open discussion about the pressures and choices they face. Most teens appreciate adult guidance that evolves from a trusting relationship and welcome advice that is based on up-to-date information and respects their circumstances. Like younger children, adolescents need a parenting strategy that balances sensitivity to their stage of development with a greater emphasis on self-regulation and safe choices. Further, child-rearing approaches that may have been effective with young children may backfire if attempted with adolescents, who are seeking independence and autonomy. In fairness, few parents have the natural expertise and ability to guide their adolescent without the support of other caring adults and positive peers. Schools in particular provide an ideal forum to address the complexity and challenges of adolescence and offer unique opportunities for adults and teens to discuss healthy, adaptive choices together (Tutty et al., 2002).

To approach the challenging hurdle of educating youths about risk behaviors, it is vital to understand current information about normative conduct and experimentation among adolescents. Below we describe the typical choices and pressures teens face with respect to sexual behavior, substance use, and conflict resolution with peers and dating partners. We consider how some of these patterns differ for boys and girls as well as for youths from different ethnic and socioeconomic backgrounds. We also address the consequences of negative choices pertaining to each risk behavior. This developmentally informed perspective underscores adolescents' normal or typical experimentation and attraction to risk behaviors to highlight the context in which prevention efforts must be designed.

Sex

Issues of sexuality are of primary concern during adolescence. Over the last couple of generations sexuality transformed from the most private of topics to a prominent and public theme throughout North American culture. From television and magazines to computer games and Internet sites, children and youth are bombarded with sexual situations and graphic images unlike anything faced by previous generations. It has become more and more difficult for parents to even pretend they are the primary source of information about healthy sexuality. Perhaps more than any other topic, the domains of sexuality and sexual behavior are rife with misinformation and misperceptions about appropriate expressions of intimacy.

For adolescents and young adults alike, the pressure to have sex is exceeded only by the pressure to drink (Kaiser Family Foundation, 2003). About one-third of adolescents acknowledge they feel pressure to have sex well before they are ready, and as a result many start at younger ages: about 12 percent of young adult males and 3 percent of females report having had sexual intercourse by age 12 (Meschke, Bartholomae, & Zentall, 2002). Even though most teens avoid sexual activity at such an early age, in the 10 years between puberty and adulthood the vast majority of teens (about 80 percent) chooses to become sexually active. As part of their choice to either abstain, postpone, or engage in different sexual behaviors, teenagers must navigate such decisions as the age of first intercourse, number of sex partners, and contraceptive use and confront such issues as sexually transmitted infections (STIs) and unintended pregnancy (Meschke et al., 2002).

How many adolescents are choosing to become sexually active? Approximately 46 percent of American high school students reported having had sexual intercourse at least once (Grunbaum et al., 2002); similarly, half (52.6 percent) of grade 12 students and one-third (31.7 percent) of grade 10 students in a Canadian study reported having had sexual intercourse (Hampton, Jeffery, Smith, & McWatters, 2001). Studies have also shown that African American students are more likely than Hispanic or white high school students to have had intercourse. Nonetheless, these rates of sexual intercourse are lower than in previous generations, as are the rates of contraction of STIs and unwanted pregnancies, while the use of contraceptives is more common (Irwin et al., 2002). Likewise, HIV infection rates continue to fall for adolescents (Centers for Disease Control and Prevention [CDC], 2001 online, #29). At the same time, there is growing awareness that simply measuring rates of sexual intercourse does not capture the whole picture. For example, recent media and research awareness of the significant number of young adolescents engaging in oral sex gives cause for concern about this behavior and the associated risks (Prinstein, Meade, & Cohen, 2003; Schuster, Bell, & Kanouse, 1996).

The age at which an adolescent begins sexual activity is strongly correlated with his or her future sexual experiences. Youth who have sex at an early age are more likely to have more sexual partners, have sex more frequently, and be less likely to use contraception at first intercourse (Stedman, 2003). Similarly, females who are sexually active for the first time before age 15 are less likely to practice safer sex with subsequent partners (Langille & Curtis, 2002).

Although rates of contraceptive use and STI preventative measures by both male and female adolescents increased during the 1990s, they are still lower than that of adults (CDC, 1997), a particular concern given that adolescents are more likely to have multiple partners. Recent studies suggest that three out of four teens use contraception at first intercourse but are less consistent thereafter (Abma, Chandra, Mosher, Peterson, & Piccinino, 1997; Grunbaum et al., 2002). Although more youths recognize the importance of contraception than before, they are still not committing to using it consistently and on a long-term basis (W. A. Fisher & Boroditsky, 2000). There are also many harmful myths about sex and contraception prevalent among teens. For example, many young people see oral sex as a safe substitute for intercourse, without realizing that many STIs are transferable this way. Similarly, over 70 percent of young people regard sex with forms of birth control other than condoms as "safer" sex, although most of these other contraceptives do not protect against STIs (Kaiser Family Foundation, 2003). Along other lines, the myth that HIV is a "gay disease" has not been dispelled; recent statistics indicate heterosexual HIV transmission is more common among adolescents, with females being almost as likely to become infected as males.

Although the teen birth rate has been declining in the United States over the last decade, pregnancy and abortion remain of concern: 8 percent of adolescents (ages 15–17) report that they or a partner have been pregnant, with highest rates among African American and Hispanic youth (CDC, 2002). American youth have higher pregnancy rates and birth rates than other developed countries despite similar levels of sexual activity, suggesting they may be particularly poor users of contraceptives (Darroch, Singh, & Frost, 2001). This rate of contraceptive use is of acute concern because even though the age at which people are getting married and the average number of years of schooling have increased, at the same time the average age of first intercourse has decreased. These changes are creating an extended period of time when youth are unmarried, financially dependent, and sexually active (Stedman, 2003). Moreover, about one in three adolescent pregnancies end in abortion (Singh & Darroch, 2000).

Drugs

The initiation into substance use is another benchmark of adolescence. In fact, most people who experiment at some point with drugs or alcohol do so for the first time in their adolescent years. Substance use generally begins in the early teens: alcohol at around age 13 and cannabis slightly later at around age 14 (Adlaf, Paglia, & Ivis, 2003). Substance consumption increases linearly from early to late adolescence, peaking in young adulthood. Adolescents are not specialized users and tend to experiment with various substances in rapid succession (Young et al., 2002). Typically, rates of substance use peak around late adolescence and then begin to decline during young adulthood in conjunction with the adoption of adult roles such as work, marriage, and parenthood (S. A. Brown & Abrantes, in press). For some youth a pronounced pattern of early-onset risk taking signals a more troublesome course that can threaten both their short- and long-term well-being. Concern is particularly warranted when high-risk behaviors begin before adolescence, are ongoing rather than occasional, and occur among a group of peers who engage in the same activities (Lerner & Galambos, 1998).

Alcohol remains the most prevalent substance used, and abused, by adolescents (Substance Abuse and Mental Health Services Administration [SAMHSA], 2003; Young et al., 2002). About four in five high school seniors, two in three 10th graders, and half of those in grade 8 report having used alcohol in their lifetime (Johnston et al., 2003). About one-third of these users reveal a history of binge drinking. Cigarettes are the second most commonly used substance among adolescents, with about 60 percent of high school seniors reporting use of nicotine in their lifetime and one-third smoking cigarettes in the last month (Grunbaum et al., 2002). Disturbingly, over half of youth in grade 7 have tried smoking at least once (Ellickson, Tucker, & Klein,

2001). On a more encouraging front, cigarette use among adolescents is currently declining (SAMHSA, 2003) following a sharp increase in rates of smoking throughout the 1990s. For the first time since the mid-1990s, adolescents have a lower smoking rate than the overall population (Health Canada, 2004).

Illicit drug use is also relatively common among North American adolescents. Over half of U.S. students surveyed reported having tried one or more illicit substances—typically marijuana—by the time they finished high school (Johnston & O'Malley, 2003), and 10–25 percent are current illicit drug users (Grunbaum et al., 2002; SAMHSA, 2003). There have been wide fluctuations in the rates of illicit drug use in North America over the past several decades. In the United States, marijuana use decreased steadily through the 1980s, increased in the early 1990s, and has since leveled off with some modest declines (Johnston & O'Malley, 2003). Illicit drug use other than marijuana, such as MDMA (Ecstasy), opiates, cocaine, and crack, has increased over the last decade, with hallucinogen and inhalant use decreasing marginally (Adlaf et al., 2003; Johnston et al., 2003). Reasons for such fluctuations range from availability to cost, with no single factor accounting for the variance.

Although alcohol, marijuana, and other substance use is prevalent among adolescents, only a minority engages in repeated and excessive use (Young et al., 2002). For example, while two-thirds of high school students reported drinking alcohol in the past year, only 18 percent reported drinking once a week and less than 1 percent drank daily (Adlaf et al., 2003). Alcohol consumption among adolescents occurs fairly infrequently: fewer than 30 percent of those aged 12 to 20 reported consuming alcohol in the past month (SAMHSA, 2003).

Other promising news is the large minority of adolescents that virtually abstains from substance use altogether. Two out of three high school students have not used any illicit drug, including cannabis, in the past year, and 30 percent have not used any substance including alcohol and tobacco (Adlaf et al., 2003). Similarly, Zapert and colleagues (2002) found that over one-third of adolescents between grade 6 and grade 11 had engaged in virtually no substance use. Another 25 percent were described as "alcohol experimenters" who engaged in almost exclusive use of alcohol (as opposed to drug use), and this usage increased only minimally over time. Therefore, the notion that substance use is a grave problem for a large proportion of our youth might be reframed as being a serious problem for a select group of adolescents, with the majority engaging in some experimentation without heavy or continued use.

Although past surveys have found that girls typically use fewer types of drugs and use them less often than boys, sex differences in the lifetime prevalence rates of substance use are converging, mostly due to increased substance use among girls (Wallace, Brown, Bachman, & Laveist, 2003). There are still some areas in which gender-specific differences are consistently noted. Although substance use has not recently increased for males, there does continue to be a greater overall use among adolescent males than among females (Adlaf et al., 2003; Hussong, 2000; Young et al., 2002). Also, teenage boys are more likely to binge drink, while adolescent girls tend to smoke and use stimulants (Young et al., 2002).

Evidence for gender-specific trends with respect to tobacco use has been inconsistent. Some studies report that adolescent girls are more likely than boys to use tobacco (SAMHSA, 2003). However, other studies report similar rates of tobacco use in boys and girls (Adlaf et al., 2003; Johnston & O'Malley, 2003) or greater use in males than females (Grunbaum et al., 2002). There are also some associations between race, ethnicity, and education patterns and tobacco use. For instance, white youth are more likely than Hispanic or African American youth to report daily cigarette use (Grunbaum et al., 2002; Johnston et al., 2003), and the prevalence of cigarette smoking has been found to be inversely related to education (SAMHSA, 2003).

One group of particular concern is Native youth in both the United States and Canada. In the United States, the National Household Survey on Drug Abuse found that among adolescents aged 12 to 16, American Indian and Alaskan natives were more likely than other racial/ethnic groups to have used cigarettes and illicit drugs and to have engaged in binge drinking in the past month (Office of Applied Statistics, 2002). Based on a large U.S. sample of adolescents, substance use (as indicated by alcohol, marijuana, and smoking) was highest among Native American youth, a bit lower among white, Hispanic/Latino and African Americans, and lowest among Asian American teens (Wallace et al., 2003). Moreover, adolescents from single-parent and remarried families tend to report higher substance use than those from married families (Zapert et al., 2002).

As with sexual activity, early starters have an increased risk for the onset of substance use problems and subsequent disorders (S. A. Brown & Abrantes, in press; Lewinsohn, Rohde, & Seeley, 1996). Across 15 studies, 60 percent of youths with a substance abuse or dependence problem had a comorbid diagnosis such as conduct disorder, oppositional-defiant disorder, or depression (Armstrong & Costello, 2002). The National Longitudinal Survey of Youth (NLSY) found that the odds of developing alcohol dependence decreased by 9 percent for each year that the onset of drinking was delayed (Grant, Stinson, & Harford, 2001). In general, researchers find that alcohol use before age 14 is a strong predictor of subsequent alcohol abuse or dependence (Grant & Dawson, 1997), especially when early drinking is followed by rapid escalation of alcohol consumption (Chassin, Pitts, & Prost, 2002).

Similarly, early smoking has been linked to a wide range of problem behaviors. A longitudinal examination of smoking behavior in youth found that compared with nonsmokers, early smokers (grade 7) were at least three times as likely to frequently use tobacco and marijuana, engage in the use of hard drugs, be involved with drug dealing, have multiple drug problems, drop out of school, and experience early pregnancy and parenthood by the time they are in grade 12. They were also more likely to be involved in delinquent behavior and use relational violence (Ellickson et al., 2001). Adolescents who smoke by age 11 are more likely to engage in a variety of health risk behaviors such as not using seatbelts, carrying weapons, and engaging in violence and substance use (DuRant, Smith, Kreiter, & Krowchuk, 1999).

In terms of health risks, substance use becomes a serious problem for a significant minority of adolescents. The National Survey on Drug Use and Health found that nearly 9 percent of all youth aged 12–17 in 2002 had a substance abuse or dependence problem (SAMHSA, 2003). One in four adolescents over age 16 meets the criteria for substance abuse, and one in five could be considered as substance dependent; although alcohol is the most commonly abused substance (10 percent), rates of marijuana dependence are higher than for that of alcohol (Young et al., 2002).

Emerging research also suggests that heavy drinking may be physically more dangerous at 15 years of age than it is even a few years later at age 20, because it may disrupt or disturb ongoing neurodevelopmental processes. When compared to teens with lower substance use levels, teens with long histories of heavy drinking performed poorly on tests of memory and attention in addition to showing other signs of abnormal neurological development (Tapert, Granholm, Leedy, & Brown, 2002). Because neurological development continues throughout the adolescent years, heavy alcohol use during this period may inhibit development, damage memory, and affect learning abilities.

Impaired driving is another well-known health risk associated with drug and alcohol use. One in seven youths reported driving a car within an hour of consuming two or more alcoholic beverages, and one in five admitted to driving after using cannabis (Adlaf et al., 2003). Nearly 3 million underage youths (ages 16 to 20) report having driven under the influence of alcohol at least once in the past year (SAMHSA, 2003). Not surprisingly, alcohol use is associated with the most prevalent causes of death and disability among adolescents (Perry et al., 2000). In 2002, 29 percent of 15- to 20-year-old drivers killed in motor vehicle crashes had been drinking, while 24 percent were intoxicated (National Highway Traffic Safety Administration, 2003). Among young drivers (ages 15–20), alcohol involvement is higher for males than for females; in 2002, 27 percent of males involved in fatal accidents had been drinking, as compared to 11 percent of young women.

Violence

Recent statistics suggest that dating violence is more common than previously believed. Rates of physical and sexual assault in dating relationships, including being beaten up and forced to have unwanted sex, range from 10 percent to 25 percent of high school students (Wolfe, Wekerle, Reitzel-Jaffe, & Lefebvre, 1998). When less severe aggressive behaviors are considered, such as verbal insults, threats, and intimidation, even higher estimates result: between 25 percent and 35 percent of youth report engaging in these behaviors (Cascardi et al., 1999; Halpern, Oslak, Young, Martin, & Kupper, 2001). Sexual violence is another significant problem that falls under the category of dating violence; a disproportionate number of rape victims are teenaged girls. Approximately 8 percent of teens experience a nonvoluntary first episode of sexual intercourse, but this number nearly triples among those whose first intercourse was before age 14 (Abma et al., 1997).

Similar to other areas where early initiation can be a risk factor, failure to delay dating activities and the early establishment of committed relationships is a predictor of unhealthy relationship patterns and associated problems in social and emotional development. Early starters of intense romantic relationships experience interference with healthy exploration and commitment to the process of identity formation and attainment of education and employment goals (Samet & Kelly, 1987). Moreover, early dating initiation has been associated with a number of adolescent problem behaviors, such as teen pregnancy, decline in academic grades, smoking, drinking, and delinquency (Neemann, Hubbard, & Masten, 1995). Adolescents' limited skill and experience in negotiating self-other boundaries in intimate relationships may help explain why dating during this period is also associated with high rates of abuse. Although similar rates of physical and psychological aggression are experienced by male and female adolescents in their dating relationships, females are more likely than males to experience sexual aggression from their partners and are much more likely than boys to experience severe injury (Wolfe et al., 2005).

The health consequences of dating violence are wide ranging, especially for girls. Adolescent girls who experience dating violence have higher rates of associated problems with substance use and sexual activity as well as unhealthy weight control and risk of suicide (Silverman, Raj, Mucci, & Hathaway, 2001). Sexual violence is associated with many short- and long-term problems, including physical injury and psychological symptoms similar to victims of war and natural disaster (National Research Council, 1996). Rape victims often experience feelings of anxiety, guilt, nervousness, and alienation, which can lead to phobias, substance abuse, sleep disturbances, depression, sexual dysfunction, and aggression (DeLahunta & Baram, 1997).

Another serious area of concern is youth violence that takes place on the streets and in schools. Even in schools that adults consider safe, an alarming number of teens report they do not feel safe (Garbarino & deLara, 2002). Although prevalence rates of violence among children and adolescents have steadily declined since the mid-1990s, they continue to be disconcerting. Adolescents and young adults are more likely to be involved in interpersonal violence, either as a perpetrator or a victim, than individuals in any other age group (Snyder & Sickmund, 1999). In the United States, more adolescents die from firearms than from all diseases combined (American Psychological Association, 1993). Although incidents of serious physical violence receive the most attention, ongoing harassment and emotional violence may affect youth just as adversely as outright physical assault.

A nationally representative survey of U.S. high school students found that 36 percent reported being in a physical fight during the past year, 18 percent admitted to carrying a weapon in the last month, and 8 percent had carried a weapon on school property (Brener, Simon, Krug, & Lowry, 1999). In another nationwide investigation, 20 percent of adolescents reported they had experienced at least one of the following forms of victimization during the previous year: being jumped, having a knife or gun pulled on them, or being shot and/or cut or stabbed (Guterman, Hahm, & Cameron, 2002). Similarly, one in five high school seniors and dropouts reported doing at least one of the following actions in the preceding year: attacking someone with intention to hurt or kill, carrying a hidden weapon, using strong-arm methods for extortion or robbery, or participating in gang fights; adding "hitting or threatening" to the above list raises the percentage to 54 (Ellickson, Saner, & McGuigan, 1997). Disturbingly, from 1999 to 2000, approximately 1.5 million violent incidents (including rape, sexual battery other than rape, physical attack or fight with or without a weapon, threat of physical attack with or without a weapon, and robbery with or without a weapon) occurred in public elementary and secondary schools in the United States. More than half of school-associated violent deaths occurred during transition times, such as the beginning or end of the day or during lunchtime.

Boys' rates of interpersonal violence are clearly higher than girls, but changes in the way such behavior is defined has complicated the picture about true sex differences (Odgers & Moretti, 2002). That is, girls' aggression appears to be on the rise, largely due to how such behaviors are counted today. Official statistics suggest that girls' violence rose 15 percent to 20 percent, although this 33 percent increase is likely due to an expanded definition of aggression that includes less serious violence such as pushing, shoving, and weapon carrying as well as indirect or relational forms of aggression (Cote, Vaillancourt, Farhat, & Tremblay, 2002). Both Canada and the United States are experiencing increasing levels of moderately violent crime among female youth. Over the last decade in Canada, there has been a 66 percent increase in violent crime charges among girls (in comparison to relatively low base rates) and a 7 percent increase among boys (Odgers & Moretti, 2002).

The consequences of interpersonal violence are well known. Homicide is the second leading cause of death among Americans aged 15–24 and the leading cause of death for African Americans in this age group (CDC, 2001). In 1999, almost 5,000 youths in this age group were murdered, an average of 14 per day; 81 percent of these homicide victims were killed with firearms. In North America, mortality rates for males have been consistently higher than for females over the years (S. Murphy, 2000); this pattern is usually linked to boys being more likely to engage in high-risk behaviors such as impaired or dangerous driving and violence (Grunbaum et al., 2002).

Sex, Drugs, and Violence: What Accounts for the Links?

As we noted in chapter 1, the adolescent risk behaviors described above are not independent of one another. These risk behaviors are linked most consistently by the formation of peer and romantic relationships that rapidly emerge in early adolescence. In this section we examine some of the data that describe the overlap among these risk behaviors. In the chapter to follow we investigate several factors that account for the connections among these adolescent risk behaviors, including common etiologies in relation to abuse or violence in the family of origin, fewer family resources, less parental supervision, peer problems, and lower school performance.

The relationship between substance use and other risk behaviors has received the lion's share of attention from the research and clinical communities and has produced convincing conclusions. For example, teens who use alcohol and drugs are more likely to have sexual intercourse, to initiate sexual intercourse at an earlier age, to have multiple sex partners, and to be at greater risk for sexually transmitted diseases and pregnancy (National Center on Addiction and Substance Abuse at Columbia University, 1999). Early onset of drug use is associated with increased numbers of sex partners, and teens with more partners are likely to be heavier drug users (Shrier, Emans, Woods, & DuRant, 1996). Furthermore, almost one in five teens who have had sexual intercourse reported regretting sex that occurred while under the influence of drugs or alcohol (Kaiser Family Foundation, 1996). High-risk alcohol users are also more likely to report having dating problems, fighting, having trouble with friends, and experiencing school trouble, compared to low-risk youth (Maney, Higham-Gardhill, & Mahoney, 2002).

The association between substance use and violence is also clearly recognized, confirming that the majority of violent adolescents report abusing alcohol, tobacco, and illicit drugs (O'Keefe, 1997). In a large-scale study of 11 to 16 year olds, only 3.7 percent of nondrinkers had been in a fight in the previous year, compared to 45 percent of teens who drank more than weekly (Sutherland & Shephard, 2002). A similar pattern of results was found for cigarette use: 44 percent of teens who smoked had been in a fight in the previous year, compared to 10 percent of nonsmokers. This same study found illicit drug use was also related to violence.

A number of other studies demonstrate this overlap among risk behaviors. For example, youth who become sexually active at a younger age and also use alcohol and drugs have a higher-risk profile for AIDS/HIV (O'Hara, Parris, Fichtner, & Oster, 1998) and other sexually transmitted infections (Irwin et al., 2002). In addition, these youth are more likely to engage in numerous aspects of risky sexual behavior, such as being less likely to use condoms at first intercourse (St. Lawrence & Scott, 1996) and in subsequent sexual encounters, as well as have higher rates of pregnancy. Others have found that the number of sexual partners is inversely related to condom use (DiClemente, 1992), and that the number of years an adolescent has been sexually active is positively correlated to a variety of sexual risk behaviors (Gillmore, Butler, Lohr, & Gilchrist, 1992). Finally, girls who report dating aggression are five times more likely to use alcohol than girls in nonviolent relationships, whereas boys are two and one-half times as likely (Pepler et al., 2002). According to one American study, youths who self-reported past-year delinquent behavior were more likely to have used illicit drugs in that year than were other youths (SAMHSA, 2003).

The overall picture that emerges from such findings is cloudy. On the one hand it is clear that there is considerable overlap among these behaviors. On the other hand, it can be confusing to piece all these results together. While these behaviors are clearly linked, does that mean that teens who engage in one engage in all? Are there different outcomes for teens who have different patterns of these behaviors? One way to begin to answer these types of questions is to look at profiles of behavior rather than single variables.

Different levels of risk can be defined according to the pattern or profile of multiple problem behaviors that a youth exhibits, such as substance use, violence, and early sexual activity. A large school-based survey of youth in Minnesota took this approach, identifying the different combinations of behaviors (Resnick, Harris, & Blum, 1993). Most youth (about 80 percent) participated in at least one problem behavior, yet relatively few (about 10 percent) participated in many. They examined nine problem behaviors to determine which, if any, clustered together in a meaningful way. The first cluster of behaviors—or profile—included polydrug use, school absenteeism, unintended injury risk (drinking and driving, not wearing seatbelts, unsafe sex, and so on), and delinquent behaviors. The researchers labeled this profile "acting out behaviors." The second profile, labeled "quietly disturbed behaviors," included poor body image, disordered eating, emotional stress, and suicidal ideation or attempts. The utility of identifying such profiles is the ability to investigate risk and protective factors that are specific to each profile. In this analysis, for example, school connectedness and family connectedness emerged differentially as the most important protective factor, depending on the profile and gender of the individual.

In our own research examining high-risk behaviors with students entering grade 9, we have identified four behavioral risk profiles (McIntyre-Smith, 2004): (1) adolescents who are not engaging in any risk behaviors (27 percent); (2) adolescents who are drinking alcohol but are not engaging in any other "risky" behaviors (24 percent); (3) adolescents who are using alcohol and engaging in violent behaviors (13 percent); and (4) adolescents who are using alcohol, drugs, and engaging in violent behaviors (10 percent). Because of the small number of teens in our sample who were sexually active (8 percent), a behavioral profile of risky sexual behavior did not emerge. That is, teens who were sexually active at the start of grade 9 did not cluster neatly into one of the four profiles, suggesting that sexual behavior was more independent than the other risk behaviors, particularly at this young age.

In general, our findings using a profile approach reveal that the riskier the behavioral profile among teens, the greater likelihood of mental health and general well-being concerns. For example, teens not engaging in any type of risk behaviors, such as drugs, alcohol, and violence, report feeling most connected to their school, peers, and teachers. In contrast, teens engaging in all three risk behaviors report feeling least connected to their school, peers, and teachers. A similar pattern emerges when we examine suicide and self-harming behaviors: teens using alcohol and drugs and engaging in violent behaviors report the highest frequency of suicidal and self-harming behaviors. Riskier behavior profiles are also associated with more childhood trauma experiences, such as physical neglect, physical abuse, and sexual abuse. Again, teens who self-identified with this triad of risky behaviors—drugs, alcohol, and violence—report more childhood neglect experiences and more total traumatic experiences overall. Thus, it is the pattern of risk that is important rather than the experience of any one of these factors alone.

One of the most interesting findings from our profiles is that there is a significant difference in the various clusters in the proportion of students who have started dating. Teens with the lowest risk profile, that is, not engaging in any risk behaviors, had the lowest frequency of dating experiences (44 percent), whereas the proportion of students who were dating was significantly higher in the riskiest profile (alcohol, drugs, and violence), where almost all students reported dating (97 percent). Early onset of dating may be an important contextual piece for multiproblem risk profiles, as we discuss below.

There are likely many different trajectories along which youth can travel to find themselves involved in multiple high-risk behaviors. For some, early onset of substance use may lead to engaging in other high-risk behaviors, such as unprotected sex and fighting, when under the influence of drugs or alcohol. For others, being in an abusive relationship may lead them to engage in substance use in an attempt to cope with the abuse. Given the importance of the relationship context, it is not surprising that premature dating emerges as a possible thread connecting these behaviors. In particular, both early substance use and premature involvement in serious dating relationships may be important precursors to a range of other negative outcomes.

Early substance use has been implicated as part of a developmental sequence leading to difficulties with adopting adult roles, education attainment, and physical and mental health (White, Bates, & Labouvie, 1998). Longitudinal studies have been able to trace the timing of these difficulties and note that substance abuse is often the earliest overt sign that an individual is heading toward engaging in a range of risk behaviors. Given the cognitive, emotional, and social implications of substance abuse, it is not surprising that early involvement can derail some of the developmental tasks. In fact, research efforts have identified different trajectories of binge drinking and the different antecedents and consequences of these trajectories (Hill, White, Chung, Hawkins, & Catalano, 2000). This focus on trajectories shifts the emphasis away from a single behavior (that is, binge drinking) to a pattern or type. Identification of particular risk patterns or types, in turn, helps us to understand the factors that signal the most problematic trajectories. Different trajectories of early substance use that led to risky sexual practices in young adults were identified in a prospective study of youths from age 10 to age 21 (Guo et al., 2002). The order of onset for these behaviors—that is, specific substance use patterns that preceded unprotected sex and sex with multiple partners—was clearly identified. These studies that identify trajectories and types of individuals—and follow them longitudinally—have helped researchers and clinicians to better understand these overlaps in risk behavior problems.

In addition to the trajectories associated with early substance use, there is evidence that early serious adolescent dating is not merely a correlate of other problematic behaviors. Rather, it is part of a causal sequence that promotes a precocious transition into adult sexual and social activities and neglect of adolescent developmental tasks such as scholastic achievement. For most youth early romantic relationships are short-lived and affiliative in nature, qualitatively different from the committed relationships of older teens and adults, but not all youths follow this sequence for emergence of dating. Some youths bypass this early stage of group dating and affiliative relationships and progress prematurely to serious relationships—marked by exclusivity, intensity, and sexual involvement—that they are not emotionally and socially equipped to handle. This type of intense early romantic involvement predicted increased conduct problems and decreased academic achievement by middle adolescence, even after accounting for continuity in problem behavior and romantic involvement (Neemann et al., 1995). Similarly, developmental pathways characterized by increasing dating involvement over the high school period were associated with increased problem behaviors (Davies & Windle, 2000).

Youths differ in their vulnerability to problematic dating outcomes. Because relationships are an organizing principle of development, individuals with a history of problematic relationships in their families and with their peers are more likely to have difficulties in their romantic relationships (Collins & Sroufe, 1999). Moreover, there is mounting evidence that the pattern and nature of the development of adolescent romance, in and of itself, may exacerbate and/or escalate problems of early adolescence (Davies & Windle, 2000). For example, overinvolvement in dating in middle adolescence predicted declines in functioning between ages 12 and 16, especially for girls (Zimmer-Gembeck, Siebenbruner, & Collins, 2001).

Although much research remains to be conducted, especially in terms of following profiles of youth over time, early serious involvement in dating may be an important marker for a range of negative trajectories. Given the developmental importance of establishing healthy dating behaviors, youths who engage too early in this behavior may face a number of problems. First, they may be trying to redress unhealthy early relationships with family and peers yet fall into the same patterns of relating. Second, they lack the skills and maturity to develop healthy intimate relationships. Finally, premature commitment to a serious dating relationship may interfere with some of the other developmental tasks, such as identity formation.

Summary

In this chapter we identified some of the physical, social, and cognitive changes that adolescents undergo and the manner in which these changes influence risk behaviors such as sex, drug use, and violence. Important patterns emerged in examining these risk behaviors that support our contention that relationships are the crucial link underlying the expression of many experimental and problem behaviors. Moreover, although there are some positive signs of improved health in the areas of teen pregnancy and smoking, there are still numerous areas where effective prevention is required. Trends in sexual behavior and outcomes suggest a good news/bad news picture. On the bright side, rates of teen pregnancy are unquestionably lower than in the past. However, there is still plenty of evidence that youth do not perceive the risks of different forms of sexual behavior. Many continue to engage in behavior that places them at risk for significant negative physical and psychological outcomes.

Data from many large epidemiological surveys suggest that most teens will engage in some experimental substance use during adolescence, although a sizeable minority abstains altogether. After a period of rising rates of drug use in the 1990s, substance use appears to be stabilizing or in some cases declining. Although some experimentation with substance use may be considered normative and likely does not have long-term consequences, there is a group of adolescents for whom initiating substance use is the beginning of a long and serious pattern of abuse and dependence. Furthermore, the overlap between alcohol use and other types of problems raises the likelihood of serious negative outcomes, even among teens who may drink only occasionally. Thus, heavy alcohol use, even on a limited number of occasions, has implications for safety during adolescence due to its overlap with sexual assault and motor vehicle accidents as well as being a risk factor for long-standing problems with alcohol.

As adolescent dating relationships develop, a large number of youth use abusive or violent acts to control or threaten their partners. These behaviors range in severity and may lead to significant physical and psychological injury to victims. There is not much information on historical trends of dating violence among adolescents because the phenomenon has only recently come under study. Nonetheless, researchers and service providers now realize that addressing adolescent dating violence is a critical point to intervene in the cycle of violence. As well, youth violence in schools and communities continues to be a serious concern. Although there is more media focus on the most se-vere physical assaults, the levels of emotional violence and harassment experienced by the majority of youth also require attention. Incidents of violence perpetrated by girls have increased recently, although the relatively low rate of serious violence committed by girls compared to boys results in statistics that may overstate the rise in female violence. Forms of violence predominately exhibited by girls, including social exclusion and rumor spreading, have only recently come into view. They are now recognized as prevalent forms of violence that may be equally devastating to victims.

Although individual youth may follow a range of pathways, two behaviors that appear to be candidates for signaling early difficulties with the transition to adolescence are early substance use and prema-ture involvement in serious dating relationships. Both of these risk be-haviors are precursors to other, more substantial problems. We stress that it is the timing of these behaviors—rather than the behaviors themselves—that is often most problematic. Regardless of the order in which these emerge, the overall picture is one that emphasizes the links among these risk behaviors. As we discuss in the following chapter, the main components of the links are the shared risk and protective factors for each domain that emerge in the context of peer and romantic rela-tionships.

5

Making Sense of
Making Choices

Adolescence is a stage marked by experimentation with new behaviors, roles, and relationships. In this chapter we consider the reasons why some teens manage the risks associated with such experimentation while others seem less able to stay out of harm's way. In particular, we focus on many of the identified factors important for understanding adolescents' choices and actions in the context of this critical stage of development. Considerable knowledge exists of the factors that influence their choices, including risk factors that can make dangerous outcomes more likely and protective factors that lower the risk of making unsafe choices. Our discussion is informed by a variety of theories that explain the processes leading to risk behaviors and define the major constructs that form pieces of the puzzle. While no one factor can begin to explain adolescent risk behaviors, together they form an increasingly clear picture.

As a result of concerted efforts to curtail adolescent substance use, in particular, there has been a tremendous increase in understanding the causes of risk behaviors, ranging from broad cultural factors to an individual's biological makeup. Research has identified many potential variables influencing teen behavior and has moved away from single-focused explanations to a greater appreciation of the interplay of multiple risk factors and how they shape development over time (Romer, 2003). Because many risk factors share common roots, it is necessary to organize these influences in a theoretically meaningful manner to make sense of the complex patterns that emerge. Similarly, protective factors may accumulate in fertile soil and offer multiple layers of protection that may insulate teens from many of the negative influences they face in early to midadolescence. Because children enter adolescence with a wide range of advantages or disadvantages, these influences also interact with each teen's strengths and vulnerabilities to become to a greater or lesser degree salient in affecting the course of his or her development.

Explanations for Experimental Risk Behaviors in Adolescence

Getting a grasp on the myriad explanations for youth risk behavior is daunting, since such behavior is clearly multidetermined. Although numerous theories attempt to explain why some youth engage in particular risk behaviors, especially substance use and delinquency, few consider multiple risk behaviors and their underlying connections. A narrow, single-problem focus made sense when researchers were attempting to identify the vast number of variables needed to explain a single problem behavior. Today, it is necessary to consider how similar factors, such as poor parenting or role models, can lead to diverse outcomes, such as substance abuse or unsafe sex. Identifying the common theoretical constructs and processes provides a more complete picture of an adolescent's experience and best informs universal efforts at education and prevention.

The field of adolescent risk behavior has shifted dramatically with the increasing recognition that many of the same risk and protective factors predict diverse outcomes, including substance abuse, delinquency, violence, teenage pregnancy, and school dropout (Catalano et al., 2002). Researchers also determined that risk and problem behaviors are correlated, implying that the same individuals often show a number of risk behaviors beyond the one or two that may have initially been of concern (Dryfoos, 1990; Jessor et al., 1991). Such discoveries had an important bearing on theoretical explanations for risk and problem behaviors and have spawned a growing movement toward a more comprehensive, integrated study of adolescent risk and problem behaviors.

Researchers have proposed many theories for why adolescents engage in risk behaviors. Some of these theories focus more narrowly on specific cognitive or behavioral processes that precede such behavior, while others involve processes rooted in childhood, early family interactions, and wide-ranging cultural factors. While no one particular theory or conceptual model can fully accommodate all of the likely processes contributing to adolescent risk behaviors, each has added pieces to the puzzle that permit a more complete picture. Fortunately, theories stemming from the fields of sociology, psychology, criminology, and many others have become less isolated from one another, allowing their important contributions to be integrated and more readily applied.

Trying to explain why an adolescent makes unsafe choices, such as binge drinking, is no easy task. There are numerous familiar explanations made popular through media reports, which attempt to simplify the causes into something manageable, such as "He wanted peer acceptance" or "She comes from a broken home." Yet, the number of factors that potentially influence a teen's binge drinking and similar unsafe actions defies a simple explanation. This recognition forces us to look beyond the immediate precursors to the teen's family background, peer group, and community norms that increase or decrease his or her susceptibility. Understanding the risk and protective factors that contribute to adolescent behavior requires consideration of the multiple social systems that make up an adolescent's world.

Our task herein is to make sense of the multitude of factors explaining youths' safe and unsafe choices in a practical manner that leads to harm reduction. We begin by examining several of the more influential theories, for each one contributes to a greater understanding of the processes that increase risk. We focus particularly on theories that have empirical support and that consider the interplay between different levels of risk factors such as individual, peer, family, and so forth. These theories involve cognitive and social learning processes, issues of attachment and formation of conventional values and norms, and individual characteristics such as beliefs, attitudes, and emotional adjustment. What these perspectives share is an approach to organizing knowledge about adolescent risk behavior into a framework that considers the breadth and complexity of the adolescent experience and a commitment to applying this framework to developing the most comprehensive intervention and prevention efforts.

The following discussion of theoretical perspectives is intended to serve as an overview of the major causes of experimental risk behaviors. We highlight the themes and constructs identified by prominent theorists to provide a road map for understanding the levels of influence affecting such behavior. The discussion draws heavily from theory and findings pertaining to adolescent experimental substance use, since much of the research on risk behaviors stems from this problem area. Drawing from a substantive and influential review by Petraitis, Flay, and Miller (1995), we use illustrations and concepts from major theories about the causes of risk behaviors. From these theories a practical framework emerges for examining the critical influences on adolescent risk behaviors and, by implication, the most promising avenues for prevention initiatives.

Beliefs and Attitudes

How adolescents perceive the risks and benefits of engaging in certain behaviors is a central feature of social learning and cognitive perspectives. A teen's decision to experiment with alcohol, for example, stems from his or her alcohol-specific expectations and perceptions, which are in turn shaped and influenced by peers and other factors. This perspective places primary emphasis on the cognitive processes that immediately precede a teen's decision to try something that carries uncertain risks or to behave aggressively toward a peer or dating partner.

In practical terms, adolescents experiment with new behaviors by first taking an interest in the activity, such as drinking, through normal processes of awareness and intrigue. Their decision to do so is then largely determined on the basis of familiar cognitive processes: attitudes about the risks and benefits, normative beliefs about what others may be doing, and self-efficacy, or the extent to which they feel they have control over the successful completion of the behavior. For example, teens will hold positive attitudes about drinking if they weigh the risks and benefits and decide that the expected benefits outweigh the possible costs. This cognitive process is highly influenced by their perceptions of the degree to which others consider this behavior as normal or expected and their desire to please or comply with the wishes of important others (Ajzen & Fishbein, 1980). Accordingly, youth may feel strong pressure to use alcohol if they believe that important others are doing so, such as friends and family members. They may also feel undue pressure if they overestimate how common such behavior is among their peers and other important influences (Chassin & Ritter, 2001).

In addition to attitudes and normative beliefs, self-efficacy is believed to play an important role in shaping behavioral intentions. Using a different example, adolescents will avoid practicing safe sex if they feel it is beyond their ability or control, even if they hold positive attitudes about safe sex and expect others will approve. Two types of self-efficacy have been identified: use self-efficacy refers to one's ability to obtain and use substances, and refusal self-efficacy reflects one's belief in his or her ability to resist social pressure to begin using substances (Petraitis et al., 1995). The same concepts apply to the ability to obtain and use condoms, to resist social pressure to become sexually active, or to manage conflict in relationships. Although a teen may have no intention of binge drinking, for example, he or she may lack the skills needed to refuse peer pressure. Similarly, theories explaining abuse in peer and romantic relationships highlight beliefs that aggression is normative, justifiable, and expected and that abusive behavior may increase the likelihood of desired outcomes (Dodge, Pettit, & Bates, 1994a; Riggs & O'Leary, 1989).

Social learning theorists have looked beyond the immediate causes of risk behaviors to consider what factors shape adolescents' current beliefs and attitudes. At the top of the list are influential role models, both past and present, who shape an adolescent's current beliefs, intentions, and self-efficacy (Bandura, 1986). Central to this view is the idea that adolescents' relationships, based on experiences with family members and peers, have a critical role in shaping their risk behaviors coupled with other cultural factors. Involvement with substance-using role models, for example, takes them through a process in which they have the opportunity to observe and imitate these behaviors, receive encouragement and support, and expect positive social and physiological consequences from participation. In the process adolescents learn to expect more personal benefits than costs from engaging in the behavior, which increases their risk of experimentation and harm.

Exposure to others who take part in certain risk behaviors directly shapes adolescents' outcome expectations, that is, their beliefs about the most immediate and most likely consequences of the behavior. For example, observing his father abuse his mother may shape a boy's belief that violence against intimate partners is justified or necessary, especially if the abuser escapes punishment and appears to achieve his objective. Furthermore, these attitudes and beliefs are not necessarily learned through direct observation alone but may be shaped as well by favorable statements or attitudes expressed by such role models, like "Sometimes you have to keep women in line."

Social learning and cognitive explanations for experimental risk behaviors have received considerable empirical support and inform several important intervention and prevention efforts. Early interventions based on elements of this theory focus on ways to influence behavior-specific beliefs, thus affecting the chain of decision making from the start. One method is to use persuasive messages to target the negative consequences of risk behaviors, such as health dangers, and to decrease teens' expectations regarding potential benefits. Such messages have also attempted to alter teens' perceptions of the relative costs and benefits by presenting the health risks as more costly and potentially long lasting. Messages challenge the perception that "everyone else does it," and adolescents are provided with information and skills to bolster their refusal self-efficacy and strengthen healthy choices. In addition, prevention initiatives attempt to make role models who engage in risk behaviors less salient, while making more salient those who do not.

Relationships and Connection

A fundamental issue that has been around since early studies of delinquency and crime is why some youths develop stronger bonds to deviant peers and adhere to unconventional values instead of developing conventional attachments to family, school, and societal standards of behavior. These theories propose that most children and youth develop strong attachments to conventional standards and values due to important contextual influences, especially their ties to family, teachers, and their communities. Such ties place needed limits on their behavior and provide invisible but effective boundaries for guiding them in their choices. In the case of youths who engage in high-risk or deviant behaviors, such ties and limits are often absent or weak, and as a result their emotional attachments to others more like themselves become more prominent.

Weak conventional bonds mean a lack of commitment to conventional society, its values, and its institutions and socializing forces, such as schools and religion. Teens who feel uninvolved with or uncommitted to such important institutions are less likely to adopt the values and standards of conventional behavior. Furthermore, this lack of connection makes them more inclined to connect with others who engage in unconventional risk behaviors and, in turn, experiment with such behaviors themselves. Weak conventional bonds also mean weak attachment to conventional role models, including teachers, family members, and especially parents. Similar to attachment to social institutions, if they feel unattached or estranged from these conventional influences they are more likely to gravitate toward unconventional and nonconforming peers. These social learning processes assert that once adolescents have weak attachments to conventional norms they perceive they have little to lose by becoming more like their high-risk peers, which in turn is strengthened through modeling, social pressures, and social learning (Petraitis et al., 1995).

Addressing the reasons why some adolescents develop a weak commitment to normal conventions brings us to the role of their social and cultural environment and how it affects their expectations. The underlying reasons behind this developmental process and how it shifts over time form the key concepts for theories of social control (Elliott, Huizinga, & Menard, 1989) and social development (Hawkins & Weis, 1985). Essentially, these theories propose that youths form stronger attachments to high-risk peers, and thus engage in high-risk behaviors, as a function of several key influences. One major influence concerns their social surroundings, including their families, schools, and neighborhoods. If these critical socialization agents are disorga-

nized and ineffective youths have fewer opportunities to develop conventional goals and establish positive attachments. Similarly, they may
become frustrated in their academic and occupational expectations if
they perceive they have few choices or options, and thus feel uncommitted to conventional standards and goals. Seeing few options, they
choose instead to associate with peers who reject such norms and engage in high-risk behaviors.

In addition to the influence of cultural forces, the social development model further takes into account ways in which risk behaviors
may result from the interaction between an individual and his or her
environment. Drawing on adolescents' developmental shifts, noted
previously, which gradually transform their sphere of influence from
parents in the early years to peers during adolescence, this model emphasizes the key elements that build attachment to either prosocial or
deviant peers and role models. For example, teens are especially likely
to engage in risk behaviors if, during phases of earlier development,
they had few opportunities for or little reinforcement of positive interactions with parents and teachers and/or they lacked the necessary academic and interpersonal skills to bring these about. Such lack of skills
in turn reduces their opportunities for reinforcement and attachment
to positive role models and conventional goals. Failure at school or rejection by peers obstructs their ability to develop strong social attachments and increases their chances of becoming alienated from conventional sources of reward. Simply stated, regardless of an adolescent's
personal strengths and abilities, he or she requires the attention and
guidance of important role models. Consequently, it comes as no surprise that many teens who are attracted to high-risk peers share common family backgrounds of impoverished stimulation, harsh discipline, or inadequate monitoring and guidance.

As in the other theories, the importance of relationships is para-
mount in this explanation, since feelings of frustration and resignation
derive from poor relationships with parents, teachers, and other adults.
Even if their neighborhoods and families are not chaotic and they are
not frustrated by their surroundings, teens require proper socialization
and child-rearing that matches their developmental needs. Moreover,
these and related theories note the importance of individual characteristics and traits that may motivate some teens to be early starters or en-

gage in risk behaviors to mark their transition to adulthood. These characteristics include, for example, biological predispositions that might promote their interest in experimentation or make them more susceptible to the effects of substances. Such dispositions may include an individual's temperament, genetic susceptibility, or tendency for sensation seeking, among others, which increase their interest in risk behaviors and motivation to engage in them (Jessor, Costa, Jessor, & Donovan, 1983).

The social attachment and social development explanations for youth risk behavior have clear implications for prevention that involve fundamental skill building from an early age. Rather than directly targeting risk behaviors or high-risk peers, the direction implied by these models is to address the critical building blocks of early relationships. Successful efforts have been made in prevention initiatives that nurture children's interpersonal and academic skills well before they form unconventional beliefs and connect to high-risk peers. These efforts range from family-focused approaches aimed at positive, healthy parent-child or parent-teen relationships to school-based programs that improve success and connection to school to community-based efforts to improve neighborhood safety and foster commitment to conventional standards.

The above models add important pieces to the puzzle of experimental risk behaviors and contribute to the growing integration of important themes and concepts (Elliott, Hamburg, & Williams, 1998; Weissberg, 2003). Contemporary explanations are also sensitive to developmental processes that account for the progressive influences, beginning with family experiences and followed by school, peer, and community experiences. The central themes include:

- Cognitive factors, such as beliefs about norms and pressures, costs and benefits, and beliefs about their ability to engage in or avoid such risk behaviors
- Behavioral factors, such as refusal skills and interpersonal and academic competence
- Social factors, such as attachment to high-risk peers and alienation from or limited exposure to healthy role models and positive socialization agents

Constructs emerging from the above theories cover all major domains of influence, including cultural and community; family; school; and individual and peer influences. Together, these domains provide a comprehensive account of the reasons adolescents experiment with or engage in certain risk behaviors. Notably, the same influences in one form or another emerge from studies of substance use, safe sex, dating and peer violence, and related problem areas and thus appear to be fairly universal in their importance for various risk outcomes. For over a decade, prevention programs for substance use, unsafe sex, and similar issues have sprung from these empirical findings of common risk and protective factors associated with related risk behaviors. However, few programs have attempted to integrate knowledge of these common risk behaviors into a comprehensive prevention strategy that addresses the common underlying factors and solutions. As an overview to the discussion below, table 5.1 organizes risk and protective factors associated with experimental risk and problem behaviors into logical domains of cultural and community; family; school; and individual and peer influences. This organization highlights their association both within and between each domain and facilitates their value as potential targets for the intervention and prevention efforts discussed in the remaining chapters.

Cultural and Community Influences

We begin with community influences simply because they establish the overall backdrop to many of the other well-known risk factors. Community standards and norms, which may vary from one neighborhood to another, provide teens with an overall template of what options are available to them and what to expect from their efforts. Many theories of adolescent experimental risk behaviors describe community risk factors in terms of boundaries and impediments that add to the strain of day-to-day problem solving and coping for families and individuals. Communities that, for one reason or another, have declined in their overall economic and social development put teens at risk of forming positive attitudes toward engaging in risk behaviors. Researchers have identified several community protective factors that contribute to more healthy attitudes and behaviors (Arthur, Hawkins,

Table 5.1 Risk and protective factors influencing experimental and problem behaviors

Cultural/community	Family	School	Individual and peer
Low neighborhood attachment	Poor family management practices	Inadequate schools	Rebelliousness
Community disorganization	Abuse and violence	Academic failure	Favorable attitudes toward antisocial behavior, drug use, violence
Crime and unemployment rates	Family history of substance use or violence	Low school commitment	
Transitions and mobility	Parental attitudes favorable to substance use, violence, and antisocial behavior	Few opportunities for rewards/success	Perceived risk of drug use violence
Community norms favorable to risk behaviors (e.g., drugs, violence)		*School connectedness*	Interaction with antisocial peers
		School opportunities for prosocial involvement	
Weak public policies	*Family attachment, connection, communication*	*School recognition for prosocial involvement*	Friends' drug use, violent behavior
Media depictions of risk behaviors			Sensation-seeking
Perceived availability of desired substances (e.g., drugs)	*Family opportunities for prosocial involvement*		Peer recognition for involvement with substances or violent behavior
Community opportunities for prosocial involvement	*Family recognition for prosocial involvement*		
Community recognition for prosocial involvement			Gang involvement
			Antisocial behavior
			Religiosity
			Social skills
			Belief in the moral order

Note: Protective factors are in italics.

Pollard, Catalano, & Baglioni, 2002). These come as no surprise and include opportunities for becoming involved in positive community activities such as sports and school functions and receiving proper encouragement and recognition for such involvement.

Resources are a limiting factor in a community's ability to influence adolescent development and risk behaviors. Consequently, poverty often defines the parameters of opportunity and risk experienced by teens each day. Poverty is highly associated with youth violence, delinquency, and related problem behaviors, largely because of its close association with community disorganization and inadequate opportunities for positive development (Beyers, Loeber, Wikstrèom, & Stouthamer-Loeber, 2001). Community disorganization is characterized by familiar concerns: presence of crime, drug selling, gangs, poor housing, economic and social flux, high resident turnover, and high rates of single-parent or otherwise disrupted families, all of which increase the likelihood of youth violence and risk behavior (Hawkins et al., 2000). Youth living in such community disorganization at age 14, for example, have more than twice the odds of being violent at age 18 than those from healthier communities (Herrenkohl et al., 2000). Similarly, the greater availability of drugs and firearms in such communities increases the likelihood of a young person committing a violent act by young adulthood.

One of the noted reasons why North American youth have among the highest rates of drug and alcohol use relates to access and community tolerance, which are also a function of community norms and resources (Johnston & O'Malley, 2003). The relative affluence of North American youth has created a market for illicit drugs, providing many youth with easy access to substances and awareness of their psychoactive properties. For example, almost all grade 12 students (95 percent) report they could get alcohol if they wanted to (Johnston et al., 2003). Youths also report it is fairly easy to obtain drugs, especially marijuana, as well as harder drugs such as cocaine and heroin (SAMHSA, 2003).

Alcohol use is presented in a positive light throughout many community and cultural events. It appears in over 90 percent of movies (Roberts, Henriksen, & Christenson, 1999), usually with few or no negative consequences. Similarly, alcohol advertisements are common and often depict scenes that appeal to adolescents. The commonness of alcohol, coupled with a tolerance of underage drinking, instills in youth a feeling that alcohol consumption is a normal, if not safe, behavior. For example, despite the fact that the percentage of youth who view binge drinking as dangerous has increased (thought to be due to public service campaigns), fewer than half (42 percent) of grade 12 students see great risk in this behavior (Johnston et al., 2003).

Access alone is not responsible for the level of youth involvement with substances and related risk behaviors. Community influences such as family mobility, increasing sizes of secondary schools, increasing urban population, and shifts in the labor force are all implicated as background factors that shape the role and influence of a given community and neighborhood. These changes, in effect, all contribute to less adult supervision in the family and community and less positive role modeling and transmission of values from adults to young people. Characteristics of neighborhoods and communities, such as economic conditions, residential stability, level of social disorganization, and availability of adequate services, have also been linked to high-risk sexual behavior among youth (U.S. Public Health Service [USPHS], 2000).

Although community influences seem beyond the reach of most prevention programs, their importance in the overall planning of health-promotion and risk-prevention initiatives cannot be ignored. As we argue in chapter 9, many well-developed programs have failed to have a lasting impact on behavior because they fail to mobilize existing community resources and build on community strengths. Programs that make inroads in this respect tend to engage youth and their families in seeking positive, cooperative solutions to community problems. Rather than targeting or isolating youth as the central problem, successful programs empower youth to be part of the solution. Similarly, existing community agencies and resources are seen as core elements of policies and programs aimed at stemming the tide of tolerance and frustration associated with youth risk behaviors. Media campaigns can help improve the sense of community connection and common goals and provide greater commitment to community norms, such as enforcing underage laws. The importance of economic and social changes remains fundamental and may be required in the poorest communities prior to any further investment in programs targeting youth and families. Despite these formidable hurdles, awareness of the significance of community influences underscores the importance of aligning prevention efforts with the unique resources and needs of each community. Today, universal and targeted prevention initiatives must go beyond the needs of individuals and groups to include the community and cultural contexts from which much problem behavior develops.

Family Influences

Relationships with family members play a powerful role in shaping adolescents' values, expectations, and beliefs about many aspects of life, including risk behaviors. The degree of parental warmth and supervision, reinforcement and assistance, and family stress and disorganization are all significant predictors of adolescent involvement in risk behaviors. The early parent-child relationship forms the basis for relating to peers and other adults and influences children's attachment to role models and their motivation to comply with the pressures from others. We examine several of the key family influences, beginning with events that, although well beyond an adolescent's personal control, often set the stage for problems in relationships.

Poor family management practices include the overall pattern and quality of interactions among family members and incorporate the day-to-day expectations and monitoring of a child's or teen's activities. The style a parent adopts with his or her child carries into adolescence and plays a critical role in the transition to healthy or unhealthy romantic relationships (M. R. Gray & Steinberg, 1999). Parents who achieve a balance between the amount of warmth they express and the degree of firmness they need to maintain (known as authoritative parenting) are generally more successful at maintaining a meaningful and close relationship with their adolescent. Parents must be sensitive to and knowledgeable about their teen's developmental needs, while at the same time ensuring they monitor the teen's activities and set clear rules and boundaries. Accordingly, factors such as inconsistent and inappropriate discipline, inadequate supervision and monitoring of youths' activities, and failure to set clear behavioral expectations are often associated with risk behaviors in adolescence, including delinquency and violence (Lavoie et al., 2002; Patterson & Yoerger, 1997).

The evolving relationship between adolescents and their parents is of continued importance in the progression of adolescent risk behaviors, despite the growing independence that accompanies this stage. Parental support serves to protect youth against high-risk experimentation, while decreased parental involvement and poor management practices are associated with the intensified influence of peers (Litrownik et al., 2000; Spoth, Goldberg, & Redmond, 1999; Spoth, Redmond, & Lepper, 1999). Poor parenting, lack of parental support, high levels of family conflict, and lack of closeness between adolescent and parent are all associated with early initiation into substance use and increased use over time (Farrell & White, 1998; Hawkins, Catalano, & Miller, 1992; Kilpatrick et al., 2000). Similarly, inconsistent, unclear family management practices, poor monitoring, few or inconsistent rewards, and excessive or inconsistent punishment are associated with greater risk for drug abuse (Hawkins et al., 1992; Kim, Crutchfield, Williams, & Helper, 1998). Other family characteristics linked to adolescent substance use include a parental history of substance abuse, poor parent-teen communication, and family conflict (Fergusson & Horwood, 1999). Very similar family factors increase the risk of precocious sexual behaviors, such as earlier onset of intercourse, less contraceptive use, and a higher risk of adolescent pregnancy (B. C. Miller, 2000) as well as the risk of adolescent dating violence (Wolfe et al., 2004).

To illustrate, a study of drinking initiation among sixth graders found that low parental expectations for abstaining predicted earlier onset of drinking and also interacted with adolescents' own alcohol expectancies. That is, if teens held positive expectations about alcohol use and believed their parents did not hold strong expectations for them not to drink, they were much more likely to initiate alcohol use during grade 6. If they held these same beliefs but thought their parents had clear expectations for them not to use alcohol, they were not as likely to initiate (Simons-Morton, 2004). This finding was present for girls and boys and for both white and African American youth and demonstrates that even at a time when adolescents are turning toward their peers for cues about acceptable behavior, parental attitudes still play an important role. Interestingly, it seems to be the teens' *perception* of parental monitoring that is important, although presumably there is a correlation between adolescent perceptions of parental monitoring and actual parental practices. For example, research with six cross-sectional data sets found a significant protective effect of perceived parental monitoring in predicting lower levels of substance use in each of the six cohorts (Rai et al., 2003).

There is some evidence that family influences show different patterns for boys and girls. For example, a study of 700 grade 9 and 10 students found higher levels of parental monitoring were associated with less alcohol use in boys but had no effect on girls' behavior (Borawski, Ievers-Landis, Lovegreen, & Trapl, 2003). In this same study, trust between adolescent girls (but not boys) and their parents was a strong deterrent for risk behaviors. Although these results are tentative, they underscore the importance of investigating gender differences in the establishment of risk behaviors. In light of the significant differences in adolescent development for boys and girls discussed in chapter 2, it is not surprising that different risk or protective factors may be operating.

In general, three family protective factors emerge in studies of high-risk adolescent behaviors: (1) parental monitoring; (2) the quality of the parent-adolescent relationship; and (3) parent-adolescent communication about risks and responsibilities that accompany new relationships and peer activities. For example, frequent and positive parent-adolescent communication is beneficial and, contrary to parental fears, does not increase teens' involvement in high-risk or precocious sexual behavior (Meschke et al., 2002). Positive communication is associated with fewer sexual partners, later and less frequent sexual behavior, and use of birth control methods. Communication of parental values may also play a role.

Richer discussions about dating and sexuality are one mechanism by which a better-quality parent-teen relationship influences adolescent choices to delay sexual activity. These discussions could include messages about the parent's attitudes and values about sexuality, advice giving, and warnings about potential negative consequences of teenage sexual activity. Parents who set high standards and have high expectations for their adolescents, and enforce these standards with consistent discipline, tend to have fewer problems. Even their teen's susceptibility to peer pressure is reduced to the extent that teens feel a close connection to their parents. In essence, parents are encouraged to provide an atmosphere of acceptance and psychological autonomy where the teen's views and individuality can develop freely, balanced with clear messages of personal safety and responsibility (M. R. Gray & Steinberg, 1999; Resnick et al., 1997).

Social learning and social attachment theories note the importance of parental attitudes and behaviors in shaping adolescents' decisions to experiment with risk behaviors. Some of these effects stem directly from parental problem behaviors: parental substance use or addiction influences both the onset and frequency of adolescent substance use (Hawkins et al., 1992; Younoszai, Lohrmann, Seefeldt, & Greene, 1999). More typically, adolescents are influenced by indirect or subtle family attitudes and modeling of risk behaviors, which is the case with smoking, alcohol, and drug use (Resnick et al., 1997; Sieving, Maruyama, Williams, & Perry, 2000). Similarly, parental attitudes and beliefs favorable to violence and antisocial behavior are powerful influences on alcohol use by adolescents and are one of the strongest predictors of youth aggression (Orpinas, Murray, & Kelder, 1999). Indeed, young children whose parents endorse attitudes favorable to abusive or violent behavior have twice the likelihood of being violent by age 18 (Herrenkohl et al., 2000).

Experiencing abuse and violence in the home, whether involving direct actions toward the child or indirect exposure to violent adult role models, has a profound effect on child development and on future relationships. Accordingly, child abuse and domestic violence have achieved prominence as predictors of many long-term adjustment problems in adolescence and adulthood, including high-risk sexual behavior, substance use, and interpersonal violence (Wolfe, 1999). Child maltreatment, in particular, is related to the inhibition of healthy relationship skills development and lower perceived competence and self-efficacy in social situations. Maltreatment leads to emotional and cognitive deficits associated with difficulty in accurately inferring emotional reactions in others; these deficits, in turn, result in problematic interpersonal interactions with both peers and dating partners (Rogosch, Cicchetti, & Aber, 1995). Not surprisingly, relationship difficulties carry over into adolescence, whereby those with a history of maltreatment have a limited ability to demonstrate basic relationship skills such as empathy and positive, nonthreatening communication

(Birns et al., 1994). As children form new partnerships in adolescence, this pattern may translate into an increased vigilance for signs of aggression, such as an expectation to encounter hostility from others and the belief that aggression is a viable and acceptable interpersonal conflict resolution strategy (Bugental, 1993; Dodge et al., 1994a).

Because self-efficacy is acquired through direct and indirect experiences, children who are abused or who witness violence may form highly situation-specific expectations regarding conflict resolution with intimate partners. Maltreated adolescents, especially girls, hold a low concept of their efficacy to resolve conflict in a nonviolent and non-threatening manner and are not confident that they can avoid being treated in a violent or threatening manner during a conflict (Wekerle et al., 2001). Whether direct or indirect exposure to parental aggression occurs, children may learn that aggression is a viable, and perhaps preferred, behavioral option. For example, female college students' interpersonal problems with dominance, intrusiveness, and vindictiveness fully mediated the association between childhood exposure to family violence and aggressive dating relationships (C. M. Murphy & Blumenthal, 2000). Instead of acquiring a tendency to repeat specific forms of aggression that one experienced in childhood, such individuals may acquire a generalized tendency toward domineering and controlling behavior.

Another developmental process affected by violence in the home is the ability to regulate strong emotions such as fear and anger, which in turns affects children's ability to relate to others. A main relational theme in these children's lives is a power imbalance in which there is a helpless (victim) versus hostile/controlling (victimizer) dichotomy associated with relationships. Such experiences pair anger and fear as being a major part of close relationships and may establish one's views of others in terms of being threatening, abandoning, and not trustworthy (Wolfe et al., 1997). Consequently, adolescents who grew up in a family atmosphere of abuse and violence are more likely to alternate between victim and victimizer roles during the course of an argument or conflict with peers or dating partners and to have difficulty regulating their emotions (Dodge et al., 1994a).

As a result of their early childhood experiences, youths with histories of maltreatment are especially at risk for relationship-based difficulties (Bank & Burraston, 2001) and have more than three times the risk of being involved in adult domestic violence (Coid et al., 2001). Studies of the development of maltreated children draw connections between maltreatment and difficulties inferring emotions and intent of others, which in turn results in coercive interactions with peers and dating partners (Rogosch et al., 1995; Wolfe et al., 1998). As well, some teens with maltreatment histories acquire a generalized tendency toward domineering and controlling behavior, which reemerges in the context of intimate relationships. Due to these challenges, peer and social dating relationships among maltreated youth are more likely to be accompanied by poor interpersonal adjustment, typified by fear, mistrust, and hostility toward others, and limited personal resources such as poor problem solving, lower self-efficacy, and distorted beliefs about relationships. These factors further tax their ability to form healthy, nonviolent relationships (Wolfe et al., 2001).

We and our colleagues have been investigating the connection between child maltreatment and the emergence of dating violence in adolescence. We studied over 1,400 high school students with self-reported maltreated and nonmaltreated backgrounds. Compared to their nonmaltreated counterparts, youths who grew up in maltreating families reported more hostility and interpersonal sensitivity, such as self-deprecation and feelings of uneasiness, and lower self-efficacy in solving interpersonal problems. They were also assigned higher self- and teacher ratings of peer aggression. Past maltreatment was significantly related to boys becoming perpetrators (as well as victims) of physical violence and threats and to girls being recipients of such violence in adolescence. We followed up with these adolescents a year later and found that boys and girls who experienced maltreatment in their families continued to have higher levels of dating aggression and trauma-related emotional problems, such as anxiety and anger. These symptoms, in turn, significantly predicted their abusive behavior toward dating partners over time (Wolfe et al., 2004). As the adage states, what goes around comes around.

Although most of the research on risk behaviors has focused on families that are affected by different types of disadvantage, a new stream of research has identified some of the challenges for youth coming from affluent families. This research has attempted to make sense of the higher rates of some emotional and behavioral problems among youth from affluent families compared to their peers (for reviews see Jaffe, Crooks, & Goodall, 2004; Kindlon, 2001; Luthar, 2003). The range of character development and emotional concerns identified in the literature include depression, narcissism and selfishness, low motivation, poor work ethic, and problems with delayed gratification and frustration tolerance. Detrimental behavioral outcomes include delinquency, substance abuse, and other high-risk behaviors.

Luthar (2003) and Kindlon (2001) both identify a combination of two dynamics that appear to create these observed difficulties—a combination of high pressure to achieve and isolation from parents. Kindlon in particular talks about this paradox—parents who are overinvolved in children's activities in terms of pressure to succeed but underinvolved in terms of finding time to really know their children as individuals. Thus, while affluent adolescents may experience privilege of material things, a lack of happiness, feelings of emptiness, and depression are some of the most consistently observed phenomena among affluent adolescents (Alderman & Shine, 1998).

Although at first glance these problems of affluence may seem very different from the types of difficulties emphasized in this book, the underlying themes of relationships and connections make them more similar than not. As with all adolescents, youths from advantaged homes and neighborhoods need opportunities for challenge and to learn responsibility; perhaps most of all they fare better when they enter this time of transition with strong connections to parents and family. Yet, affluent teens sometimes have less parental supervision during this critical time due to parental career or other demands, and less parent-adolescent contact in general due to extensive after-school activities and scheduling (Luthar & D'Avanzo, 1999; Rosenfeld & Wise, 2000).

There are many potential avenues for prevention efforts involving family influences, many of which focus on establishing a healthy parent-child relationship from the beginning. Such early intervention efforts have shown considerable promise in altering the course of children's development by strengthening the parent-child relationship and building important child-rearing skills and knowledge. Intervention and prevention efforts to address contemporaneous family influences on adolescent risk behaviors have also evolved from the above studies showing the connection between high-risk teen behaviors and poor parenting practices. Most of these efforts have been delivered to parents and teens who have been identified as engaging in problem behavior in an attempt to reshape the parent-child relationship, increase communication, and offer a less authoritarian and more developmentally sensitive approach to managing adolescent risk. Other than these identified families, however, there has been less effort at addressing the important role of the family from a preventative stance.

As we will see in chapters 7 and 8, there are broader applications for prevention and education efforts to strengthen family influences and reduce risk. For example, parents can benefit from current knowledge of adolescent development and norms, with the intention of making them more aware of current pressures and choices their teens may face. In addition, parents often welcome clear, informed guidelines regarding expectations for their adolescents' behavior, their own role in setting boundaries and monitoring behavior, and the significance of their own attitudes and modeling of risk behaviors on their teens' choices (Stanton et al., 2003).

School Influences

In general, factors such as poor attitude toward or performance in school have a small but important effect on risk behaviors in adolescence (Hawkins et al., 1992). For instance, poor academic achievement has been consistently linked to later delinquency, and low educational aspirations in midadolescence predict increased risk for involvement in violence in later adolescence (Herrenkohl et al., 2000). Low bonding and commitment to school is a predictor of later violence in adolescence (Herrenkohl et al., 2000) and, conversely, bonding to school is a protective factor against crime and similar problem behaviors (Jessor, van den Bos, Vanderryn, Costa, & Turbin, 1995). School attendance is also related to youth violence, in that adolescents with poor attendance records at ages 12 to 14 are more likely to be violent in later adolescence and adulthood (Farrington, 1989).

Certain characteristics make some schools far more conducive to violence and substance use, many of which relate to their general community surroundings. For example, schools located in disorganized neighborhoods have higher rates of violence than schools in other neighborhoods. In general, levels of school crime and violence are greater in schools with poor academic quality than schools with strong academic quality. In addition, the chances of being the victim of a violent crime are more than two and one-half times as great in schools where gangs are present (Snyder & Sickmund, 1999). Several characteristics make up ineffective school climates, including a widespread sense of futility among students and staff, low student attendance rates, high rates of teacher and staff absenteeism, low levels of staff commitment, and high rates of teacher and student mobility (McEvoy & Welker, 2000).

In contrast, effective school climates are characterized by student expectations for high achievement, effective administration leadership, strong commitment among teachers and staff, students' sense of learning efficacy, and student perceptions of a safe environment. The way adolescents feel about school—in particular, how connected they feel to their school community—predicts lower risk for use of substances (Williams, Holmbeck, & Greenley, 2002). This concept of school connectedness is a nonspecific risk factor; that is, adolescents who feel engaged with and supported by their school tend to get involved in less substance use, violence, sexual behavior, suicidality, and other problems compared to youths who feel more alienated from school.

Awareness of the importance of the school climate, including safety, connectedness, academic standards, and clear behavioral expectations, has straightforward implications for prevention. For example, comprehensive, restrictive policies such as developing and maintaining smoke-free school policies and ensuring their enforcement are associated with decreased substance use (Flay, 2000). The National Commission on Drug-Free Schools recommends that school policies include support for alcohol and other drug prevention, descriptions of violations and consequences, definitions of key terms, areas of jurisdiction, procedures for implementing policy, no-use rules for all, and procedures for communicating the policy to parents, students, and staff (Modzeleski, Small, & Kann, 1999). Some educators have also suggested involving students in school policy development, school changes, academic services, and so forth to increase the protective factor of school bonding and connectedness (Skroban, Gottfredson & Gottfredson, 1999). Furthermore, school-based programs that address youth risk and health-promoting behaviors more comprehensively are replacing problem-based strategies that address one or two risk behaviors. As a result, the important role of teachers and other school personnel is increasing among programs for adolescents, as are ways to incorporate healthy messages and positive skills into the regular curriculum.

Individual and Peer Influences

Personality characteristics that predispose a teen to high-risk experimentation may stem from basic temperament characteristics, such as increased sensation seeking or impulsivity (Wills & Dishion, 2004). Sensation seeking has been described as a preference for novel, complex, and ambiguous stimuli and has been linked to a range of high-risk behaviors. For example, higher levels of sexual risk-taking behavior are reported among youth who also score higher on measures of sensation seeking and who perceive themselves as having little behavioral control (Mezzich et al., 1997; Neumark-Sztainer, Story, French, & Resnick, 1997). Sensation-seeking and risk-taking traits have also been linked to adolescent violence—risk taking assessed in early adolescence more than tripled the odds for violence in later adolescence (Herrenkohl et al., 2000). A recent longitudinal study looking at two samples of adolescents between grades 8 and 10 found sensation seeking to have strong predictive value for both current and future marijuana and alcohol use (Crawford, Pentz, Chou, Li, & Dwyer, 2003). The relationship between sensation seeking and substance use was strongest for predicting marijuana, followed by alcohol and, to a lesser extent, cigarette use. Furthermore, there were both sex and ethnicity differences in levels of sensation seeking—males tended to score higher than females, and white adolescents tended to score higher than those with other ethnic backgrounds. One of the most important findings from this study was that sensation seeking is not stable over time, again suggesting there may be a window of opportunity to intervene.

Related forms of psychosocial vulnerability, including poor self-control and decision-making skills, coupled with social influences favorable to substance use, also predict some portion of alcohol use across white, black, and Hispanic populations. These factors have different predictive influence for male and female adolescents and for adolescents with different ethnic backgrounds (Griffin, Botvin, Epstein, Doyle, & Diaz, 2000). Similarly, high grades, negative alcohol expectancies, and negative norms or low social acceptability of alcohol consequences account for lower alcohol use overall, especially for white, black, and Hispanic use. In contrast, low self-esteem, traditionally thought of as a contributing factor to teens' involvement in risk behaviors, accounts for only a small percentage of the variance in substance use and similar risk behaviors. Consequently, activities aimed at improving self-esteem have little impact on experimental risk behaviors (Stoil, Hill, Jansen, Sambrano, & Winn, 2000).

Other personality and behavioral characteristics, such as hyperactivity, impulsivity, and attention problems have also been regularly linked to antisocial and violent behavior (Herrenkohl et al., 2000). For example, boys with restlessness and concentration difficulties were five times more likely to be arrested for violent acts than boys without these difficulties (Klinteberg, Andersson, Magnusson, & Stattin, 1993). While the exact pathways between hyperactivity, inattention, impulsivity, and violence still need to be properly investigated, these difficulties may be linked to concurrent problems in executive brain functions associated with these disorders, such as impaired cognitive processes that reduce one's ability to evaluate consequences and actions. Children with behavioral and attentional problems also have greater difficulty regulating negative emotions, which increases their likelihood of physical aggression and abusive behavior (Melnick & Hinshaw, 2000).

In brief, psychological well-being encompasses a number of related individual factors that influence one's level of stress and coping and, in turn, one's involvement in risk and problem behaviors. Adolescents with higher levels of stressors such as a history of physical or sexual assault, witnessing violence, or family members with substance use problems generally have an earlier age of onset and show greater risk for current substance abuse/dependence. Those who suffer concurrent disorders such as PTSD have an even greater risk of soft and hard drug abuse/dependence (Kilpatrick et al., 2000).

Given the important role that peers play in adolescents' lives in general, it is not surprising that peer influences play a large role in determining experimental risk behavior. The influence of peers seems to operate in more than one way. For example, associating with deviant and substance using peers makes a teen more likely to adopt beliefs supporting drug use, since they tend to have similar beliefs to their friends. At the same time, affiliation with these peers also increases access to substances and other risk factors. In addition, the idea of a false consensus, or the belief that everyone is doing it, exerts pressure on youth to engage in substance use: the extent to which individual teens think their peer group is using substances is strongly related to their decision whether or not to use substances (Musher-Eizenman, Holub, & Arnett, 2003). Peers are also influential within the context of dating violence. Friend involvement in dating violence is correlated with dating violence among both males and females and is a particularly strong predictor of dating violence by females (Foshee, Linder, MacDougall, & Bangdiwala, 2001). By following their sample of teens over time the Foshee et al. study determined that girls are influenced by their friends' dating violence, as opposed to simply selecting similar friends after they have become involved in dating violence. Similarly, association with peers who use drugs or have favorable attitudes toward drug use is a clear risk factor for adolescent substance use (Sieving, Perry, & Williams, 2000).

A study investigating the role of parent-teen communication in determining youth sexual behavior also found that a lack of communication with parents may cause adolescents to turn to peers, and that peers may then influence their behavior (Whitaker & Miller, 2000). On the other hand, parents discussing initiating sex or use of condoms was associated with adolescents' greater belief that parents rather than peers were the best source of information about sex. Parent discussions were also associated with less risky sexual behavior and less conformity to peer norms. A similar study clarified that perception of condom use among teens' friends was a strong influence on their own choice to practice safer sex (Shrier, Goodman, Chiou, Lyden, & Emans, 1999).

Given these findings, we can conclude that the most immediate influence on an adolescent's decision to engage in some form of risk behavior, be it smoking, drinking, or unsafe sex, is his or her perceptions and beliefs about what others do, especially those the teen admires or wants to please. Social normative beliefs are based on adolescents' perceptions that others want them to engage in the behavior and on the adolescents' motivation to comply with the behavior-specific wishes of those people. Consequently, teens will feel strong pressure to engage in a behavior if they believe that important friends and family members endorse the behavior. They might also feel strong pressure to engage in a behavior if they overestimate the prevalence of the behavior among peers and adults in general (Griffin, Scheier, Botvin, & Diaz, 2000). Ironically, adolescents overestimate prevalence of their peers' substance use as well as their peers' acceptance of substance use (Donaldson, Thomas, Graham, Au, & Hansen, 2000).

A similar process plays a role in youth involvement in relationship violence against peers and dating partners. For example, attitudes and beliefs justifying relationship violence under certain conditions reflect peer norms and pressures to behave in a sex-stereotypical manner. Such attitudes are linked to aggression in dating relationships among high school students, especially in accounting for male-to-female aggression (Avery-Leaf, Cascardi, O'Leary, & Cano, 1997; Foshee et al., 2001). For example, violence in men's family of origin predicted the development of negative beliefs about gender and interpersonal violence among university students, which in turn predicted their own use of violence or coercion in relationships and their association with deviant peers (Reitzel-Jaffe & Wolfe, 2001). Similarly, attitudes accepting aggression, coupled with antisocial behavior toward partners and others, accounted for two-thirds of the variance in dating violence among college-aged men but only one-third of the variance in women's relationship aggression (Riggs & O' Leary, 1996).

The contributions of individual and peer level influences to risk behaviors make both of these domains critical targets for prevention. At the individual level programs can target a variety of areas, including attitudes, skills, and knowledge. Because of the importance of peer groups in adolescence, prevention programs need to target them both in terms of decreasing negative peer influences and increasing positive peer influences through establishing "positive" peer groups, peer leaders, and mentors and increasing "alcohol-free" events in both the school and the community (Perry et al., 2000). Indeed, peers may be the most salient protective factor in adolescent substance use (Youno-szai et al., 1999).

Summary

We have examined the myriad of factors that influence adolescents' choices and the extent to which normal experimentation may result in undesirable health outcomes and behavior patterns. Trying to make sense of why some teens choose to engage in risky behaviors, even in the face of overwhelming evidence of harm or danger, requires a good understanding of typical and atypical adolescent development. The field has moved well beyond single-factor explanations of why teens engage in high-risk behaviors, embracing the importance of multiple layers of influence affecting adolescent decision making. The purpose of adolescence is to prepare for the challenges of early adulthood, but unfortunately some adolescents make life-altering choices that may impose significant limits on their future.

Contemporary explanations as to why many youth make poor decisions that pose harm to themselves and others consider the importance of family, school, peer, and community experiences. These explanations converge on several central factors: (1) cognitive factors, such as beliefs about norms and pressures, costs and benefits, and adolescents' beliefs about their ability to engage in or avoid such risk behaviors; (2) behavioral factors, such as refusal skills and interpersonal and academic competence; and (3) social factors, such as attachment to high-risk peers and alienation from or limited exposure to healthy role models and positive socialization agents. For example, adolescents may choose to drink alcohol after weighing the risks and benefits, derived from their perception of how others handle such choices. Their behavior is further determined by their feelings of self-efficacy, which reflect the extent to which they believe they can obtain alcohol or resist social pressure to do so. Importantly, these decisions are shaped by relationships with influential role models, past and present, who influence their current beliefs, intentions, and self-efficacy.

The importance of protective factors is also underscored in studies of high-risk adolescent behaviors. The role of parental monitoring, the quality of the parent-adolescent relationship, and the extent of parent-adolescent communication about risks and responsibilities were all shown to be significant factors in promoting safe choices and reducing harm. Similarly, school climate, including safety, connectedness, academic standards, and clear behavioral expectations, emerged as a critical determinant of positive, responsible choices.

These explanations for youth risk behavior have clear implications for prevention that involve fundamental skill building from an early age. For example, our knowledge of the importance of attitudes and beliefs on adolescent decision making supports the role of persuasive messages to highlight negative consequences of risk behaviors, such as health dangers, and to decrease teens' expectations regarding potential benefits. Information that alters teens' perceptions of the relative costs and benefits by presenting the health risks as more costly and potentially long lasting are also supported, as well as messages that challenge the perception that "everyone else does it." In addition, prevention initiatives attempt to make role models who engage in risk behaviors less salient while increasing the salience of those who do not. Of course, shaping beliefs and attitudes is easier said than done, and in the latter half of this book we present ways to use relationships and social influence to this end.

Rather than directly targeting risk behaviors or high-risk peers, these contemporary explanations suggest that a more universal strategy can be applied that bolsters the building blocks of relationships for everyone. These efforts range from family-focused approaches aimed at positive, healthy parent-child or parent-teen relationships to school-based programs that improve success and connection to school to community-based efforts to improve neighborhood safety and foster commitment to conventional standards. School-based programs that address youth risk and health-promoting behaviors more comprehensively are replacing problem-based strategies that address one or two risk behaviors. As a result, the important role of teachers and other school personnel is increasing among programs for adolescents, as well as ways to incorporate healthy messages and positive skills into the regular curriculum. In the next chapter we investigate the characteristics of successful and unsuccessful prevention programs in each of the three areas of sex, drugs, and violence to identify the principles of best practice.

6

What Works in Prevention
Promises and Pitfalls

Efforts to curb sex, drugs, and violence among youth are certainly not new. Programs designed to prevent or redress these problems have been in place for upward of 30 years. In all three of these areas, there are well-designed programs that have been empirically evaluated and found to be effective. At the same time, there are also fad programs that are not based on research or theory and are ineffective or even harmful. A discussion of both—the promising programs and the pitfalls—provides a solid foundation for moving toward an integrated intervention that addresses all three areas simultaneously yet is built on the best practices in each individual area. In addition to summarizing the research with respect to characteristics of effective programs, we describe a sample model program in each of the areas to illustrate the components deemed effective.

Preventing Violence

Violence is one of the most difficult behaviors to change, yet perhaps one of the most urgent concerns of our communities. Aggression in youth requires complex, intensive, multipronged interventions, and even then some individuals continue to be violent well into adulthood.

Among adults, entrenched patterns of relationship-based violence are extremely difficult to alter. For example, interventions for men who abuse their intimate partners have but modest success, and only when they are integrated into a responsive legal system (Gondolf, 2002). Due to the intransigence of violence, prevention has long been recognized as the only viable long-term solution. Although there are some excellent violence-prevention programs, there have also been several highly touted but unsuccessful efforts.

We begin by considering the pitfalls—those programmatic efforts that, despite attractive premises and promising beginnings, failed to deliver lasting improvements in violent and aggressive behavior. Some prevention and intervention programs gain considerable popularity because they sound good and offer a dramatic promise of a quick fix. Two familiar examples in the violence intervention arena are Scared Straight programs and boot camps, which have been promoted as solutions to youth crime. Scared Straight involves organized visits to prisons by youths who are newly involved with the justice system. As the name suggests, the firsthand exposure to inmates and conditions of incarceration is intended to scare these adolescents back onto the straight and narrow. Boot camps are an intensive military-style intervention that subjects young offenders to harsh discipline and living conditions, comparable to that experienced by new recruits in the military. Emphasis is on complete and immediate obedience, with swift consequences for any infraction of the rules. The media has featured both of these programs on numerous occasions, likely because they lend themselves to compelling sound bites and pictures.

The research evidence on the effectiveness of these two interventions is, in a word, dismal. The Campbell Collaboration is an international consortium of researchers who undertake systematic and critical reviews of complex research in the fields of education, justice, and social services to draw clear and meaningful conclusions about program effectiveness (see www.campbellcollaboration.org). Campbell Collaboration reviews sift through all of the research done on a topic to identify the most methodologically sound, and then use this subset to evaluate programs. Rather than averaging the results of mediocre research, their strategy is to identify the best research and use only high-quality studies to make clear statements about what works and what does not.

The consortium completed an investigation of Scared Straight and similar "juvenile awareness programs" for preventing juvenile delinquency and reported that Scared Straight programs produce effects that are more harmful than doing nothing at all. For example, these programs are more likely to increase delinquency rather than reduce or prevent its further occurrence.

The research on boot camps has been similarly discouraging. The Surgeon General's (USPHS, 2000) report on violence prevention unequivocally identified boot camps as an ineffective strategy. Boot camps can also have an adverse impact on adolescents in that youths are exposed to other, and possibly more antisocial or violent, delinquent peers in these settings, who then model and reinforce delinquent behavior (Dishion, McCord, & Poulin, 1999). If an adolescent does not know how to hotwire a car or where to access hard drugs before going to a boot camp, other inmates will likely fill in these information gaps during the period of incarceration. Combined with the learning opportunities to witness effective intimidation techniques in the name of military-style discipline, the whole experience amounts to an opportunity for young offenders and gang members to become further entrenched in their negative behavior patterns.

In contrast, effective violence-prevention programs are based on theoretically sound principles and research findings. Based on the Surgeon's General report (USPHS, 2000) and the Blueprints Violence Prevention Initiative (Elliott, 1997–2004; Mihalic, 2001), successful programs: (1) are comprehensive in nature; (2) focus on skills; (3) pick appropriate targets for change; (4) use peers; (5) include parents; and (6) attempt to change the larger environment. We expand on each of these principles of success below.

Programs that the Surgeon General's report and Blueprints identified as model or promising are *comprehensive*. Comprehensive programs recognize that risk behaviors occur in many contexts, and so successful interventions similarly need to be applicable to individual, family, peer, school, and community circumstances as much as possible. For example, all six model programs identified by Blueprints target at least three of these domains. Programs may also be comprehensive by targeting more than one particular outcome, such as violence and substance use, since these problems often co-occur. Thus, effective programs do not compartmentalize youth with respect to their environments or their behaviors. Rather, they take a more holistic approach that recognizes the complexity and interrelatedness of different settings for youth and offer knowledge and assistance that is appropriately matched.

Providing youth with opportunities to develop interpersonal skills is the most common feature of effective prevention programs. Social skills training may take numerous forms, which usually involve specific training in conflict management and problem-solving skills. This training typically incorporates a role-play component to give students opportunities to increase their ability and comfort level with their newly developed skills. For example, students may role-play strategies to deal with and/or confront instances of bullying. In other interventions, students meet in small groups to discuss and role-play positive alternatives to problem behaviors. Social skills training may also include general communication skills training, such as assertive versus passive or aggressive communication styles, social perspective taking, frustration tolerance, and anger management.

Skills training is most effective if combined with accurate information about risks and consequences. Similarly, a skills approach is action-oriented, not merely a passive discussion of behavioral options (Durlak & Wells, 1997). Model programs typically include a specific and explicit social skills "training" component, although some have mentoring components and organized social activities that allow for the informal enhancement of communication and general relationship skills, such as attending sporting events, playing catch, or going for walks. Some promising prevention programs aimed at relationship-based violence also provide training in help-seeking behavior, such as learning about and visiting with social service agencies in the community (Wolfe, Wekerle et al., 2003).

In addition to social skills, effective violence-prevention programs target antisocial attitudes and beliefs associated with aggression and violence. Activities to change attitudes can include awareness-raising activities, such as information about violence against women, and empathy-building exercises. For example, students in the Bullying Prevention Program participate in classroom activities like role-playing, writing, and small-group discussions geared toward helping them gain a better appreciation of the harm caused by bullying (Olweus, Limber, & Mihalic, 1999). In contrast to these successful strategies, programs that target issues only distally related to violence do not have much of an impact. For example, children who engage in bullying seldom suffer from low self-esteem, and so targeting poor self-esteem does not change their behavior. In contrast, empathy for victims is linked to bullying and is a viable target for reducing such behavior.

Given the significant influence that peers have on adolescent behavior, it is not surprising that effective programs commonly address the peer group factor. The Bullying Prevention Program includes regular classroom meetings about peer relations and encourages students to not condone bullying by peers. Overcoming bystander apathy is a particularly important peer-level target. Children and adolescents are encouraged to think of themselves as having a responsibility to stop others from being victimized, and inclusion of others (particularly vulnerable children) is promoted as a means for preventing bullying.

Although parents are not as actively included in school-based prevention, especially at the secondary school level, as in some other types of family-based programs, they are nonetheless important. Several of the model school-based prevention programs attempt to increase communication between home and school, which is effective in increasing parent-child connection and parental interest. In the Preventive Intervention and School Transitional Environment Program parents are regularly contacted to inform them of their child's academic progress and school attendance. Project PATHE enlists staff, students, and parents to work collaboratively to design and implement each school's particular program. Engaging these various stakeholders increases their sense of ownership of the program, which translates to investment in the success of the program.

There is increasing recognition that school-based violence prevention is not about finding the "bad kids" but rather changing the whole culture in which children learn. Effective programs specifically target aspects of school climate that are conducive to violence. Different programs address school climate by restructuring certain aspects of the school or by incorporating additional activities and services.

The School Transitional Environmental Program (STEP) is an example of a program that restructures aspects of the school in an attempt to modify school climate. The primary goals of STEP are to increase the level of social support available to students and reduce the amount of flux and complexity as students transfer to high school (Felner & Adan, 1988). To achieve these goals, STEP restructures the role of the homeroom teacher; in their expanded roles, homeroom teachers act as administrators and guidance counselors, including monitoring attendance, helping with course selection, counseling regarding school and personal problems, and communicating with parents. STEP also reduces school disorganization by having all STEP participants within the school enrolled in the same core classes, so that students spend much of their time with the same group of students as opposed to having new people in every class, and all of these core classes are located in the same wing of the school. These structural changes are intended to increase the cohesion or school connectedness of students at risk for academic and behavioral problems, which in turn raises the likelihood of school success.

Project PATHE attempts to modify the school climate by incorporating additional activities and services for students. PATHE includes an integration of services within an existing school management structure intended to produce academic gains and improved behavior. Not solely a program, it is a structure and process for managing broad school improvement, taking into account each school's strengths and needs. School-based change is central to the PATHE approach: school staff must be involved in the development and implementation of locally created plans. PATHE directs its resources toward changing student characteristics, including self-efficacy and social bonding, as well as school social organization, including sense of community and management structure. Through this integration and mobilization, PATHE seeks to increase educational attainment, reduce delinquent behavior and student misconduct, and increase postsecondary educational and career development.

Two model programs illustrate the preceding principles. Identified as a model program by Blueprints, the Bullying Prevention Program is a universal intervention for reducing and preventing bully/victim problems (Olweus et al., 1999) designed for elementary, middle, and junior high students. The second program, the Youth Relationships Project, is a dating violence–prevention program for youth considered to be at risk of violence in their intimate relationships on the basis of having witnessed or been subjected to violence in their families of origin.

In 1983, after three Norwegian adolescents committed suicide as a result of severe bullying, the country's Ministry of Education contracted Dan Olweus to develop and implement a large-scale bullying prevention program. The resulting program stands out as one of the few crisis-driven programs to achieve long-standing viability and demonstrated success with preventing violence. The Bullying Prevention Program has demonstrated significant positive results and has been implemented throughout Norway and in selected sites in the United States, Canada, Great Britain, and Germany, among others. It is a comprehensive school-based intervention that includes schoolwide, classroom, and individual components. Schoolwide components include using an anonymous questionnaire to assess the nature and prevalence of bullying at the school and a school conference day to plan interventions. In addition, the Bullying Prevention Coordinating Committee is formed to coordinate all aspects of the school's program. Schoolwide interventions are also strategic in nature and seek to restructure the existing school environment to reduce opportunities and rewards for bullying. The intervention increases supervision of bullying "hot spots," which typically include places of low monitoring or adult presence and low structure, such as locker rooms or the bus area.

Classroom components include holding regular class meetings to increase communal responsibility for individual student safety. Individual classes develop and enforce their own class rules that specifically address bullying. The program actively targets bystander apathy, that is, the tendency for those observing bullying to do nothing to stop it. Furthermore, there is an attempt to change school norms by reframing behavior viewed by students as "tattling" to a more acceptable help-seeking construct. Students are actively encouraged to talk to an adult if they are aware of an incident of bullying. At the individual level, additional services are offered to students identified as frequently having the role of bully or victim, and parent involvement is promoted through wide dissemination of information on bullying. Teachers are required to read a manual and book before undergoing training, and once the program starts teachers hold weekly classroom meetings and participate in regular discussion groups during the first year of the program. There is a clear message that adults bear the brunt of responsibility for changing bullying norms and ensuring student safety in schools.

The Bullying Prevention Program has been extensively evaluated and found to substantially reduce student reports of bullying and victimization. Findings indicate a 30 percent to 70 percent reduction in student reports of being bullied and bullying others, and peer and teacher ratings confirm these findings (Olweus et al., 1999). Although not specifically targeted, general antisocial behavior such as vandalism, fighting, theft, and truancy have also been reduced with the program. Other benefits include significant improvements in classroom order and discipline, and a more positive attitude toward schoolwork and school. These findings have been replicated in a large number of studies with a range of student populations.

Dating violence–prevention programs have a shorter history than general violence–prevention programs, and very few have been carefully evaluated. Short-term changes in attitudes and beliefs have been documented following classroom discussions or assemblies, but few have had sufficient follow-up with the participants or evaluated actual behavioral change. The Youth Relationships Project (YRP) underwent a controlled evaluation in which youths were randomly assigned to an intervention or control group (Wolfe, Wekerle et al., 2003). The YRP is an 18-session group-based intervention designed to reduce all forms of harassment, abuse, and violence by and against dating partners. It was designed particularly to address the needs of teens who had grown up with abuse and trauma experiences in their families of origin and who were thereby at greater risk for violence in their own relationships (Wolfe et al., 1996). This community-based group intervention is manual-based and instructs facilitators to help teens develop positive roles in dating by providing information, building skills, and enabling the participants to be involved in a community-service component.

There are three principal sections in the manual: education and awareness, skills building, and social action learning opportunities. Education and awareness sessions focus on helping teens recognize and identify abusive behavior across various domains including woman abuse, child abuse, sexual harassment, homophobia, and racism, with a particular focus on power dynamics in male-female relationships. To understand the responsibilities of "personal power," teens identify their own situations or privileges, such as access to resources, jobs, education, family income, race/ethnicity, sex, and so forth. Information on gender-based abuse and violence, sexual assault, and date rape is presented through guest speakers, such as a survivor of woman abuse and/or a former batterer, videos, and didactic materials regarding power and control. The skill-development aspect of the program builds on this knowledge base by exploring available choices and options to solve conflict more amicably and avoid abusive situations. Communication skills include listening, empathy, emotional expressiveness, and assertive problem solving. Students practice and apply these skills to familiar situations, such as consent and personal safety in sexual relations. Finally, social action activities provide participants with information about resources in their community that can help them manage unfamiliar, stressful issues affecting their relationships. These activities involve youth in the community in a positive way to help them overcome their prejudices or fear of community agencies such as police, welfare, and counseling. Social action projects engage youths to be actively involved in opposing attitudes and behaviors that foster gender-based violence and similar issues raised in their group.

The YRP was evaluated in a randomized trial with 158 high-risk 14–16-year-olds with histories of maltreatment (Wolfe, Wekerle et al., 2003). The control group was an existing care condition, which typically included bimonthly visits from a social worker and the provision of basic shelter and care. The teens in the study completed measures of abuse and victimization with dating partners, emotional distress, and healthy relationship skills at bimonthly intervals when dating someone. The youths were followed on average for 16 months postintervention, which showed the intervention to be effective in reducing incidents of physical and emotional abuse over time, relative to controls. An interesting adjunct finding was that symptoms of emotional distress were also lower over time compared to the control group, even though these symptoms were not directly targeted with the intervention.

Preventing Drug and Alcohol Abuse

Efforts to curb substance use have broadened considerably since U.S. Prohibition (1919–33), although controlling access remains a central part of the strategy. Contemporary substance use prevention efforts have diverged along two lines. For some approaches a moralistic quality is central to the message that deciding not to experiment with drugs or alcohol is linked to character; youths should "just say no." Other programs target the multiple pathways to substance use and abuse, from individual factors such as character to school and community influences like peers and neighborhoods, to redress risk factors and promote protective factors.

As with violence prevention, programs have had varied success in achieving their goals of abstinence and/or use reduction. One of the most widely popular, yet unequivocally unsuccessful programs, is Project DARE (Drug Abuse Resistance Education). On the surface, Project DARE seems like a good idea. One of the most widely disseminated programs, DARE uses uniformed police officers to deliver a "Just say no" and zero tolerance message to students in a school setting. DARE has now been the subject of several extensive research evaluations. The first study followed students for 5 years and found no effect (Clayton, Cattarello, & Johnstone, 1996). Critics of this study suggested that a "sleeper effect" might be present, such that the inoculation provided by Project DARE might become more evident later on. However, a recent study that followed the same participants for 10 years found the same negative results (Lynam et al., 1999). Unfortunately, there is simply no evidence that DARE is effective in preventing drug abuse.

Despite lack of effectiveness, DARE remains popular, mostly because teachers, parents, and police officers all view the program positively. To parents and teachers, having police officers talk to youths about drugs sounds like a good idea, and to police DARE is part of a good community policing strategy that helps put kids into positive contact with police officers. Although this secondary benefit of increasing positive contact between students and police is sometimes used to justify the program, critics note that this argument undermines the potential for more effective drug prevention programs to gain a foothold in the school: "Although we would allow that DARE may have beneficial effects on youth's attitudes towards the police, DARE is marketed to schools as a drug prevention program, not a program for community policing. If schools erroneously believe they are getting an effective drug prevention program in DARE, then the benefits of DARE on community-police relations are outweighed by the costs of keeping more effective drug prevention programs out of the schools" (Lynam & Milich, 2002, p. 10).

Although it is perhaps the most sensational due to its use of police officers, Project DARE is not the only ineffective program in schools. Other information dissemination programs, which use different fear tactics to emphasize the consequences of substance use, are also of little value. Similarly, affective education, which emphasizes building self-esteem, personal insight, and self-awareness with the aim of reducing substance use, does not work, largely because such programs do not address the multiple pathways to substance use and variation across individuals (Botvin, Botvin, & Ruchlin, 1998; Botvin & Kantor, 2000).

Numerous reviews and meta-analyses have identified effective components of substance abuse prevention programs in schools (Cuijpers, 2002; Ellickson, 1999; Skara & Sussman, 2003; Tobler & Stratton, 1997). Some of these characteristics are similar to those identified in the area of violence prevention, while others are more specific to substance use and abuse. For example, comprehensive programming and a focus on skills are critical ingredients, much as they are in violence prevention. In addition, successful programs tend to be grounded in a social influence theory, to use interactive techniques with students, and to focus on the effects of specific drugs.

Comprehensive programs build on the considerable progress achieved in developing effective school-based substance abuse prevention programs by extending the social environment beyond school and into the home, mass media, and the community (Flay, 2000). Effective, comprehensive approaches recognize that substance use is determined by multiple factors and therefore must target individual, peer, family, school, media, and other community influences. Furthermore, effective programs recognize the need to focus on protective factors, because some risk factors, such as family history of substance problems and availability of substances, may be difficult to change. In addition, adding community-level components to interventions and life-skills training may strengthen the effects of the prevention programs. For example, the Midwestern Prevention Project (MPP, also known as Project STAR; Pentz et al., 1989; Pentz, Mihalic, & Grotpeter, 1997) is a comprehensive prevention program that includes school, media, parent, community organizing, and health policy components designed to target use of the gateway substances, cigarettes, alcohol, and marijuana. The MPP project has resulted in significantly lower rates of substance involvement relative to comparison groups (C. A. Johnson et al., 1990). In addition, MPP is associated with much higher effect sizes than those programs with only school-based delivery (Tobler & Stratton, 1997).

Effective programs for substance use prevention also incorporate skills development as a crucial component. There are two categories of skill development: generic social competence and more specific substance use–related skills. Programs increase social competence by teaching and providing adolescents with opportunities to practice general life skills such as assertiveness, communication, social skills, problem solving, and coping strategies to deal with anxiety and stress. Programs enhance competence further by using such techniques as instruction, feedback, reinforcement, and behavioral rehearsal to strengthen skills across various settings and situations (Botvin et al., 1998). With respect to skills specifically related to substance use, students are taught techniques for resisting direct peer pressure to smoke, drink, or use drugs, including refusal skills and delay tactics. Instead of being taught to just say no, students are taught *how* to say no, or even how to say "Not right now." Youths are also taught to be assertive in situations involving pressure to use substances, not merely how to be assertive in general. In combination, these life skills, involving problem solving, decision making, refusal, and social and communication skills, have been associated with significant reductions in substance use among adolescents: prevalence rates have decreased by as much as 30 percent when a skills-based approach is used (Stoil et al., 2000).

Successful programs also incorporate the concept of social influence, based on the realization that substance use occurs in the presence of significant others such as peers and dating partners. Furthermore, this approach recognizes the social pressures to use substances and helps students develop awareness and skills to combat these pressures. Social influence-based programs include norm education and developing a personal commitment and intention not to use. Norm education is particularly important in countering the false consensus bias, which refers to students' tendency to greatly overestimate the proportion of their peers that is using substances. This false consensus raises the likelihood of individuals experimenting with substances. Students may develop more accurate perceptions about their peers' behaviors by becoming better informed of the reality that many of their friends and peers may not actually be experimenting with drugs or alcohol, especially not to the extent they imagine. Adolescents' inaccurate perceptions of peer behavior have been successfully targeted through prevention programs, and the benefits of this normative education may be sustained over several years (Donaldson et al., 2000). Successful programs also target students' awareness of external pressures by peers and media messages equating substance use with popularity. Helping youths become more critical consumers of media helps inoculate them to the persuasive techniques used by advertisers. Although peer pressure has been implicated in predicting substance use, peer dynamics can also provide a powerful countermessage to dominant popular media messages.

Interactive teaching techniques such as role-play, discussion, and small-group activities are superior to passive approaches that rely on lectures and videos alone. Interactive techniques encourage student participation and give adolescents a chance to see their peers role-play difficult situations. Having peers model appropriate solutions is much more effective than having adults model particular skills, because peer models are much more salient to adolescents. Adolescents can identify more with their peers, and the solutions that their peers generate are more realistic to them. For example, not many adolescents can imagine themselves using "I feel . . . when you . . ." statements, regardless of how many adult examples they may see! A review of school-based prevention programs also underscored the need for interaction among participants (Cuijpers, 2002). Youths need the opportunity to share ideas with each other and also to practice specific skills with their peers and try different solutions that may feel more comfortable to them.

The superiority of interactive delivery to noninteractive or instructional delivery in reducing substance use initiation is a consistent finding in the area of substance use and abuse prevention.

Finally, effective programs address the fact that students' beliefs and attitudes are highly drug specific (Johnston et al., 2003). Students need to know the accurate facts about the consequences of specific substances, since they discriminate the risks and benefits of each drug carefully. Awareness of the risks of marijuana use, for example, may have little deterrence on their alcohol consumption and vice versa. Therefore, prevention programs must target knowledge, attitudes, and beliefs about specific substances in detail to ensure adequate awareness and not attempt to deliver a blanket message that will generalize to all or most substances.

One of the most widely implemented and effective programs is the Life Skills Training (LST) program developed by Gil Botvin and his colleagues (Botvin, Mihalic, & Grotpeter, 1998). LST is a universal prevention program that targets middle/junior high school students, starting with intervention in grade 6 or 7 and following with booster sessions over the next two years. The program was developed to be implemented by classroom teachers but has also been successfully used by health professionals from outside the school and older peer leaders. LST consists of 15 sessions in year one, 10 sessions in year two, and 5 sessions in year three, with each session typically lasting about 45 minutes. The LST program is taught using a combination of traditional didactic teaching methods, facilitated group discussion, classroom demonstrations, and cognitive-behavioral skills training. Due to the skills focus of the program, intervention providers fulfill the role of trainer or coach rather than the traditional role of lecturer. This expanded role requires training and support for teachers implementing the program.

The Life Skills Training program was designed to target drug-related expectancies, teach skills for resisting social influences to use drugs, and foster personal self-management and social skills. The program includes two general skills components—personal management skills and social skills—and a specific problem-solving section targeting situations where students are faced with the choice of whether or not to engage in substance use. The personal self-management skills section of LST includes a number of objectives: to foster decision-making and problem-solving skills, teach skills to analyze and resist media influences, provide students with self-control skills for coping with anxiety and anger or frustration, and provide students with the basic principles of personal behavior change and self-management. For example, the program provides students with relaxation training to reduce anxiety and skills to reduce anger and frustration, including inhibiting impulsive reactions, reframing, and using self-statements. The social skills component is designed to increase general social competence. Communication skills, general social skills such as initiating social interactions, conversational skills, and complimenting, skills for relating to members of the opposite sex, and both verbal and nonverbal assertiveness skills are included in this section.

The drug-related information and skills section is designed to target knowledge and attitudes concerning drug use and normative expectations. In addition, this section helps students develop skills for resisting drug influences from peers and the mass media. Material in this component includes:

- The short- and long-term consequences of drug use
- Knowledge about the actual levels of drug use among adolescents and adults
- Information about the declining social acceptability of cigarette smoking and other drug use
- Information and class exercises demonstrating the immediate physiological effects of cigarette smoking
- Information about media pressures to smoke, drink, or use drugs
- Information about the techniques used by cigarette and alcoholic beverage marketers to promote the use of these drugs and skills for resisting them
- Techniques for resisting direct peer pressure to smoke, drink, or use drugs

It should be noted that while LST adheres to all of the principles about content, focus, and delivery of effective programs, it focuses only on students and has limited content for parent and community participation. Nonetheless, program evaluations have supported the long-term benefits of this theoretically derived approach to reduction of substance use among adolescents. More than a dozen studies have demonstrated the effectiveness of LST. A large-scale controlled randomized prevention trial involving nearly 6,000 students from schools in New York State has been conducted as well as numerous smaller studies. On average, the program reduces tobacco, alcohol, and marijuana use by 50 to 75 percent (Botvin et al., 1998). Long-term follow-up of students six years after participating in the intervention demonstrates that LST also reduces polydrug use by 66 percent, reduces pack-a-day cigarette smoking by 25 percent, and decreases the use of inhalants, narcotics, and hallucinogens (Botvin et al., 2000).

One of the early criticisms of school-based substance use prevention was whether or not youths with greater needs or more involvement with substances would benefit from a universal program. This criticism was surmounted by findings of a recent study in which youths were identified as being at social risk for substance use if their friends drank alcohol and smoked cigarettes and at academic risk if their grades were Cs or lower (Griffin, Botvin, Nichols, & Doyle, 2003). These at-risk youth reported lower levels of smoking, alcohol use, inhalant use, and polydrug use when assessed one year after the intervention program, compared to students who did not receive the program. A second concern about school-based programs has been the extent to which effects extend beyond the period of intervention. Fortunately, reductions in alcohol, marijuana, and tobacco use have been found six years after participation in LST. Moreover, LST can be implemented at a cost of approximately $7 per student per year, plus nominal expenses for training. Finally, culturally specific skills-based programs are as effective as the generic version of LST in reducing substance use among minority youths (Botvin, Dusenbury, Baker, James-ortiz, & Botvin, 1992; Botvin, Griffin, Diaz, & Ifill-Williams, 2001; Botvin, Schinke, Epstein, Diaz, & Botvin, 1995).

Preventing High-Risk Sexual Behavior

Sexual behavior risk-prevention programs have a range of goals. Some programs deliver an unequivocal message that abstinence is the only acceptable outcome, encouraging youth to wait until they are married before having sexual intercourse and labeling premarital sex as wrong or sinful. Other programs attempt to get youths to delay the onset of sexual intercourse and develop skills to help them wait until they are ready. Still others offer a secondary prevention approach to help teens that are sexually active lower their risk for unwanted pregnancy and sexually transmitted infections (STI). As with the other areas of experimental risk behaviors, these programs have met with various degrees of success and, in some cases, have had potentially harmful "side effects."

Under the Personal Responsibility and Work Opportunity Reconciliation Act in the United States, $50 million annually for abstinence-only programs was provided in 1995 for five years. According to the act's guidelines, key elements of abstinence education include the following premises:

- Abstinence from sexual activity outside of marriage is the expected standard for all school-age children
- Sexual activity outside of the context of marriage is likely to have harmful psychological and physical effects
- A mutually faithful monogamous relationship in the context of marriage is the expected standard of human sexual activity

This funding and legislation were developed in the context of awareness by the scientific community that despite their popularity, abstinence-only programs are ineffective in preventing pregnancy and STIs. In addition to the ineffectiveness of abstinence-only programs, some people object to the moralistic and religious undertones to these guidelines (Wiley, 2002).

Two major studies have shown that comprehensive sex education is more effective than abstinence-only education: *Emerging Answers: Research Findings on Programs to Reduce Teen Pregnancy* (Kirby, 2001a) and *Abstinence and Safer Sex: HIV Risk-Reduction Interventions for African American Adolescents* (Jemmott, Jemmott, & Fong, 1998). Another study, *Promising the Future: Virginity Pledges and First Intercourse* (Bearman & Bruckner, 2001) produced mixed results with respect to onset of sexual intercourse and safer sex practices. There was some success in delaying initiation of intercourse for some teenagers who took virginity pledges, but those who broke their pledge were one-third less likely than nonpledgers to use contraceptives once they became sexually active. Even the recent preliminary report on a study commissioned specifically by the U.S. Department of Health and Human Services found no proof that abstinence-only education programs decreased sexual activity, unwanted pregnancies, or sexually transmitted diseases among U.S. teens. The results of this report, *The Evaluation of Abstinence Education Programs Funded under Title V, Section 510: Interim Report* (Mathematica Policy Research, April 2002; http://www.mathematica-mpr.com/publications/PDFs/evalabstinence.pdf), have not dampened the enthusiasm for these programs. To the contrary, abstinence-only programs continue to be highly valued and funded by American policy makers.

Another report, titled *Ignorance Only: HIV/AIDS, Human Rights, and Federally Funded Abstinence-Only Programs in the United States* (http://hrw.org/reports) analyzed a number of programs and research findings and reached the following conclusions:

■ To date, six studies of abstinence-only programs have been published. None of these studies found consistent and significant program effects on delaying the onset of intercourse, and at least one study provided strong evidence that the program did not delay the onset of intercourse. Thus, the weight of evidence indicates that these abstinence-only programs do not delay the onset of intercourse.

■ A study of 7,326 seventh and eighth graders in California who participated in an abstinence-only program found that the program did not have a measurable impact upon either sexual or contraceptive behaviors.

■ Nearly two-thirds of teenagers think teaching "Just Say No" is an ineffective deterrent to teenage sexual activity.

■ The National Institutes of Health's Consensus Panel on AIDS said in February 1997 that the abstinence-only ap-

proach to sexuality education "places policy in direct conflict with science and ignores overwhelming evidence that
other programs [are] effective."

A final major criticism of abstinence-only programs is that they
focus exclusively on sexual intercourse. Recent surveys have reflected a
new awareness of the number of youth participating in high-risk non-
intercourse activities in early to midadolescence, and these behaviors
are not being targeted (Prinstein et al., 2003). Proponents of more
comprehensive sexual health education have also noted the need to expand research outcomes and program goals beyond the traditional foci
on sexual intercourse and condom use.

A number of reviews have been conducted in the past 10 years to
identify components of successful prevention programs in the area of
adolescent sexual behavior. Some of these reviews have focused on
school-based interventions that target a number of sexual health outcomes (Kirby et al., 1994), while others have looked at particular outcomes, such as HIV, in large community samples (Jemmott & Jemmott, 2000). One of the most stringent reviews with respect to
methodology was published by researchers affiliated with the Centers
for Disease Control (Robin et al., 2004). On the basis of these reviews
and meta-analyses, a number of components of effective programs can
be identified. Again, there is familiar overlap with violence and substance use prevention with respect to the importance of being comprehensive and focusing on skills. In addition, effective prevention programs in the sexual behavior domain include providing accurate
information, promoting abstinence as a viable option, and addressing
the social context.

Similar to the other areas of prevention, comprehensive programming is essential to ensuring successful programs. Successful programs to prevent unwanted pregnancies incorporate a combination of
interventions focused on increasing information and awareness, promoting skill development, and providing reproductive health services
(Nation et al., 2003). There has been increasing interest in school-
based health clinics to fully integrate a comprehensive range of services
into the school setting. Other successful programs emphasize improv-

ing parent-child communication, as poor communication has been implicated in the early onset of sexual intercourse.

Skills-based programs are consistently found to outperform information and counseling programs in promoting healthy sexual decision making. Effective programs have a specific behavioral focus and seek to reduce the behaviors that lead to unintended pregnancy or HIV/STI. Similar to best practices in substance use prevention, the most effective methods for developing these skills are interactive approaches that provide modeling and practice in communicating, negotiating, and refusal skills. For example, some programs provide verbal and written practice in negotiating situations that might lead to sexual intercourse (Kirby, 1997). Furthermore, participants need the opportunity to personalize the information they are learning. Value clarification exercises and activities that have students problem-solve a situation that they have encountered in the past are ways to make the information more salient.

Of our discussion of sex, drugs, and violence, the need for accurate information is perhaps most obvious in the area of sexual health. Effective programs provide basic, accurate information about the risks of unprotected sexual activity and methods of avoiding unprotected sexual intercourse. Many youths are not getting this information from their parents and may have obtained misinformation from their peers. In our program the variance of knowledge with which students enter grade 9 health classes is vast—some students lack information about basic anatomy and reproduction, while others have a much more sophisticated level of knowledge. Even within this range of knowledge, virtually all students have some misconceptions or gaps in information. Furthermore, there are several domains where accurate information is needed; adolescents need accurate information about reproduction, birth control, and sexually transmitted infections, but they also need information about more than the mechanics. Evaluating the accuracy of information portrayed by the media, for example, and whether or not sexuality portrayed in movies is realistic and healthy are also important endeavors.

Although opponents of comprehensive sexual health education worry that these programs promote sexual activity, evidence suggests they do not. Effective programs clearly identify abstinence as an appropriate and healthy choice, and teens are encouraged to delay intercourse until they are physically, cognitively, and emotionally ready for mature sexual relationships and their consequences. However, effective programs place equal emphasis on abstinence and on lowering risk behavior, rather than promoting abstinence as the only option (St. Lawrence, Jefferson, Alleyne, & Brasfield, 1995). Thus, the primary message may be to encourage youths to wait, but knowing that many will become sexually active the programs also provide information and skills to help them make safer choices if they do become sexually active.

Effective programs in sexual health also recognize that sexual decision making happens in a social context, such that teens need to recognize and counter peer and media messages about sexual behavior. A particular facet of social context in the area of sexual health is the highly divergent realities for adolescent boys and girls. Therefore, gender specificity is critical in designing information and skills that will benefit both. In research with grade 9 students, boys and girls differ both in terms of which factors predict the onset of sexual intercourse during grade 9 and also in terms of which factors predict consistent condom use (Crooks & Onyura, 2004). Tailoring programs to the specific needs of adolescent boys and girls leads to more successful outcomes, and delivering sexual health education in a gender-strategic manner can be advantageous and contribute to the comfort level of participants.

The Safer Choices program is a two-year, school-based, HIV/STI and teen pregnancy prevention program. Its primary goal is reducing unprotected sexual intercourse by encouraging abstinence and, among students who report having sex, encouraging condom use. Safer Choices consists of 20 sessions, each lasting one class period over the course of grades 9 and 10. The lessons seek to modify: (1) HIV/STI knowledge; (2) attitudes and norms about abstinence and condom use; (3) students' beliefs in their ability to refuse sex and avoid unprotected sex, to use a condom, and to communicate with partners about safer sex; (4) barriers to condom use; (5) perceptions of risk for infection with HIV or other STIs; and (6) communication with parents.

Safer Choices is a comprehensive program that has been delivered to urban and suburban youth, multiethnic populations, and sexually experienced youth. At the student level, components include an HIV/STI and teen pregnancy prevention curriculum, including experiential activities to build skills in communication and delaying sex. At the school level, there is a school health protection council and a peer-led team to host schoolwide activities. The program also includes parent and community components. Parent education is provided through the use of newsletters and some student-parent homework assignments. Links to community services are another integral component of the program, and HIV-positive speakers are an optional piece.

An evaluation of the Safer Choices program included nearly 4,000 students in grades 9 and 10, drawn from classes in 20 schools in Texas and California (Coyle et al., 2001). Positive findings with respect to behaviors, knowledge, and attitudes were found one year after the intervention. Safer Choices assisted sexually experienced youths to increase their own condom and contraceptive use as well as that of their partners. Changing condom use for sexually active teens was particularly noteworthy, given that some researchers have argued that prevention programs are ineffective with youth who are already engaging in sexual intercourse. Youths' knowledge, attitudes, and perceptions were also positively influenced by the program. For example, adolescents who participated in Safer Choices expressed significantly more positive attitudes about condoms and reported greater condom use self-efficacy, fewer barriers to condom use, and higher perceived risk of contracting HIV by engaging in unprotected sex compared to control youth. Furthermore, hearing an HIV-positive speaker was associated with participants being more likely than control youth to receive HIV testing. Due to its emphasis on safe sex the program is intended for an older adolescent population, who may benefit more from strategies designed to increase condom use rather than delaying sexual intercourse (Coyle et al., 2001). Finally, an economic analysis based on savings on medical and social costs related to unsafe sexual practices estimated a $2.65 return for every dollar invested in the program (L. Y. Wang et al., 2000).

Summary

The purpose of briefly reviewing best (and worst) practices in each of the areas was to demonstrate the considerable overlap across them. Although there are certainly some differences in emphasis (for example, compared to unsafe sexual behavior prevention, a substance abuse prevention strategy will likely have a more substantial school component), there are a lot more similarities than differences in the ingredients to successful prevention. Likewise, unsuccessful strategies in all three areas also share key features.

Ineffective programs are often oversimplified, with an implicit assumption that a particular negative behavior is caused by a single determinant. For example, the message underlying violence-prevention programs such as Scared Straight is that youth need to have a better appreciation of the negative consequences of their behavior and/or an attitude change. Similarly, a "Just say no" approach to substance use makes the implicit assumption that choosing to use substances is simply a matter of personal willpower. There is no appreciation of the range of skills, attitudes, and opportunities youth need to make healthy choices, nor of the complex social environments in which these decisions unfold. Ineffective programs may have strong media appeal and may garner public support regardless of the proven lack of effectiveness. Boot camps continue to be funded and supported, despite clear and conclusive evidence that they either have no impact or may actually make youth more likely to come into conflict with the law. One of the reasons for the popularity of these programs likely stems from their compatibility with public notions of "what's wrong with today's youth" and a growing concern with public safety.

In contrast, effective programs in substance use, sexual risk, and violence prevention are multifaceted. Even when the focus is on only one of these domains, the interventions tend to be ecologically based (that is, they address the different contexts in which youth function), emphasize the development of specific skills, and have a focus on building positive capacity in youth. There is a clear theoretical basis to the programs, often consistent with a broad Social Learning Theory perspective. Successful programs work with youth in their natural settings rather than removing them for a time-limited period to "fix" them. Furthermore, they are consistent with the research on risk factors for developing negative behavior patterns in these areas and target the areas found to increase the likelihood of engaging in these behaviors. Protective factors for specific behaviors are also developed to off-set risk behaviors that may not be as amenable to change.

Effective programs are sufficient in duration and may include booster sessions. They do not expect a one-shot deal to result in lasting behavior change. Facilitators are motivated and skilled with respect to the intervention they are delivering. Some of the programs include extensive training and implementation measures to ensure the programs are being delivered the way they were designed.

Finally, prevention programs are more likely to be successful when they offer youth a range of choices to reduce risk rather than attempt to completely eliminate particular behaviors. They provide accurate information about the consequences of particular choices but do not rely on scare tactics to steer youth away from these choices. The relative failure of abstinence-based approaches to sexual behavior compared to harm-reduction approaches emphasizing delayed onset of sexual intercourse, skills to avoid risky situations, and skills to negotiate condom use—in addition to presenting abstinence as a viable alternative—exemplifies the importance of providing teens with choice. In the next chapter these ingredients for successful prevention programs are further described.

7

The Blueprint
Best Principles for Program Design

In the previous chapter we identified what works in single-focus programs to prevent adolescents from engaging in sex, drug use, and violence. We stressed that effective programs in these areas share similar characteristics, such as being comprehensive and skills-based. In this chapter we return to issues discussed in the first half of the book: the importance of relationships, building youth capacity, and addressing multiple risk factors that co-occur in adolescence. We pull these components together into an integrated framework that represents the whole picture of what effective prevention initiatives require: a comprehensive, skills-based, relationship-focused, health-promoting and harm-reducing approach for engaging youth in harm reduction. Each of these principles was chosen because of its meaningful contribution to our intervention model.

We begin with the end in mind: How do we define success in the area of sex, drugs, and violence prevention? Specifically, what would we like to see youths gain from involvement in this type of program? We believe that many adolescents will experiment with high-risk behaviors such as drinking, and that exploring sexuality is a major aspect of their development. Consequently, we do not expect adolescents to eliminate these activities entirely. Even if we could achieve the goal of abstinence until they become adults, we would question whether this outcome was in everyone's best interests. One way or the other, adolescents need to develop their choices, values, and skills concerning these potential perils to be prepared for a successful transition to adulthood. There is much more to being ready for adult roles than avoiding drunkenness, sexual promiscuity, and violence. As such, developing relationships and social competence is critical for establishing habits to ensure their health and well-being.

Our definition of success is based on what we want adolescents to do, not merely what we want them to avoid. From this vantage point, healthy adolescent outcomes incorporate strong relationship skills, self-awareness and knowledge about one's boundaries, high levels of self-efficacy, and good citizenship skills. At the same time, we hope to see a decrease in health-damaging behaviors through a combination of delayed onset, safety strategies pertaining to particular behaviors (such as condom use and not driving if drinking alcohol), and better help-seeking strategies. Finally, we believe success is reflected by youth engagement, measured by attitudes, awareness, and involvement of youth in shaping their school climate and peer norms. In effect, we envision an outcome that incorporates healthy adolescent functioning in a range of domains and is consistent with a more holistic notion of well-being.

With this goal of preparing youth in mind, we now turn to the specifics of an integrated model: comprehensive programming, skills-based approaches, a relationships focus, and health-promotion and harm-reduction frameworks. We then return to issues of timing, in which the developmental processes outlined in the first half of the book become essential guideposts for engaging youth, including a consideration of gender.

Integrated and Comprehensive Programming

Peers, school, home, and the larger societal context all place unique demands on adolescents, requiring teens to adapt and perform under considerable pressure. At the same time these pressures and situations also provide unique opportunities for growth, as long as they remain challenges and not obstacles. Designing programs that recognize and

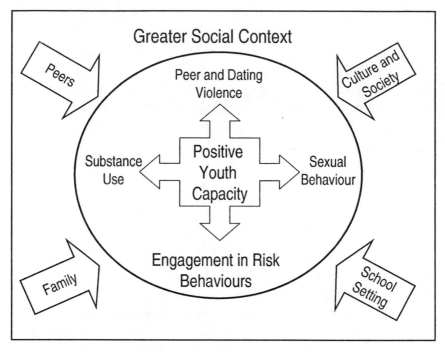

Figure 7.1. A comprehensive, integrated prevention model depicting the inter-play between youth capacity and pressures from their social surroundings.

address this complexity has emerged as a best-practice principle in all areas of prevention, and the most effective programs are sensitive to the many spheres in which adolescents function. Best-practice programs also approach adolescents in a holistic manner, avoiding a problem-fo-cused, compartmentalized message. At this level, comprehensiveness can mean addressing both risk and protective factors or targeting more than one high-risk behavior with a particular program. Comprehen-sive also refers to the need to address many domains of adolescents' lives. In effect, programs need to create opportunities for prosocial be-havior while also targeting negative behaviors (Catalano & Hawkins, 1995). This combination of simultaneously increasing the positives and targeting the negatives is more comprehensive and better matched to adolescent needs than either approach alone. Figure 7.1 above provides a visual model of how these components can be integrated into a com-prehensive prevention model.

The inner circle represents a balance between building positive youth capacity and competence as a general strategy for helping youth make healthy choices and reducing specific negative behaviors. These interactions unfold within the larger social context, in which peers, families, and schools exert both positive and negative effects on youth's choices. The developmental risk and protection literature is replete with examples:

- Involvement with an antisocial peer group provides more opportunities for delinquent behavior; prosocial peers help reaffirm attitudes and beliefs that value school achievement
- Families where there is abuse create social learning opportunities for violent behavior; families with close parent-child communication protect children from early onset of social intercourse
- Schools where violence is attributed to a handful of bad students rather than recognized as a complex, multide-termined phenomenon create norms that do not emphasize collective responsibility for ending violence; schools with teachers and administrators who are invested in the school climate create safe environments conducive to learning

Relationship Skills

Another message that emerges loud and clear from investigating successful programs in each area of the adolescent risk behaviors is the need to ground programs in skill development. Best-practice programs build competence, particularly in the social domain. Social competence, in turn, is rooted in strong relationship skills. Communication, assertiveness, refusal and resistance in the face of pressure, and conflict resolution skills are all critical for healthy adolescent adaptation (Roth & Brooks-Gunn, 2003). The skills to maintain positive relationships are not merely a feel-good domain. These skills underlie much of the success, or lack thereof, which adolescents and adults will experience in meeting the demands of their various roles.

It is now clear that these skills can be taught to children and adolescents in much the same manner as other skills, such as reading or soccer. Although ideally children would begin learning these positive social skills in healthy families and safe home environments, many families face challenges that prevent them from consistently providing these opportunities to their children. Teaching relationship skills in schools can either augment or counter the relationship lessons learned at home. Using the school environment to teach these skills offers reinforcement to children who are already learning them at home and, conversely, provides an alternate learning experience for those who have not had these experiences in their homes.

Interventions that promote healthy relationships help adolescents develop the capacity to be successful in their roles as young adults. At the heart of relationships is the notion of connection. Youths who are connected in healthy ways to their peers, families, and schools are at lower risk for health-damaging behaviors than those who feel isolated and alienated. Group norms and connectedness to others have been identified as the two most important factors in predicting and addressing adolescent risk behaviors (Kirby, 2001b). Even more than early or late adolescence, midadolescence appears to be the time when youth are most strongly influenced by their peers and hold the most rigid ideas about what constitutes normal behavior (Steinberg & Morris, 2001). Consequently, youths who are connected to prosocial peer groups and perceive their friends to be avoiding high-risk behavior are more likely to make similar choices.

Parents often feel redundant in the lives of their teens. However, the importance of parental involvement and family connection in sheltering adolescents from external pressures is well established. Youths who are connected to their parents demonstrate healthier outcomes than those who are not, regardless of race and ethnicity, the number of parents in a household, or whether families are rich or poor. They report less emotional distress and fewer suicidal thoughts, they engage in less cigarette, alcohol, and marijuana use, and they have lower rates of violent behavior and early sexual activity (Blum & Rinehart, 1998).

In addition to peer and family relationships, school connectedness has also been identified as a critical protective factor for adolescents with respect to a wide range of high-risk behaviors. School connectedness has been described in a variety of ways but includes the extent to which an individual feels that he or she is a member of the school community, identifies with that community, and feels valued by that community. Although school connectedness is a relatively recently defined and studied phenomenon, it has rapidly emerged as one of the most robust protective factors for youth. Adolescents who feel connected to their schools report more feelings of well-being and are less likely to use substances, engage in violence, or become sexually active at a young age (McNeely, Nonnemaker, & Blum, 2002).

School-based initiatives with a relationship focus address connections in several ways. First, the programs support adolescents in developing the requisite relationship skills to form healthy connections with other teens and adults. Second, the training and implementation of the program helps teachers become more connected to adolescents with a range of difficulties by providing them with more tools to engage alienated youth. Finally, a whole-school approach targets the climate of the school by working to increase students' sense of respect and safety. A more inclusive school climate creates a less hostile atmosphere for groups of youth that are traditionally excluded (Garbarino & de-Lara, 2002). Connection to the greater community is also important. Youth can be connected through caring relationships developed through mentoring, tutoring, leadership, and community service opportunities (Blum & Ellen, 2002).

Multiple Perspectives

Our philosophy incorporates the importance of approaching youth in a holistic way and recognizing the need to build positive capacity as well as reduce negative adolescent behavior. By combining elements of positive youth development and harm-reduction approaches within a health-promotion framework, the strengths of each approach can be captured. At the heart of health promotion is an understanding of health as being more than the state of being "unsick"—but rather a state of complete physical, mental, and social well-being. Health spans a continuum from disability and premature death on one end to growth and high-level wellness on the other, as depicted in the concept of a health continuum (Travis, 1988).

Health promotion is the science and art of helping people change their lifestyle to move toward a state of optimal health, analogous to helping individuals move further along the health continuum. Although initially health promotion targeted people on the healthy end of the wellness spectrum, more recently it has incorporated interventions across the entire continuum. The goals of prevention, for example, used to focus on minimizing signs, symptoms, disability, and premature death, but as the health-promotion domain has expanded, it has defined prevention more broadly. Health education in schools or primary health care settings, public health programs such as immunizations or screenings, or occupational health measures aimed at preventing disease or accidents at the workplace all constitute health-promotion activities.

Health promotion has emerged as a framework that encompasses the areas of health education, health protection, and prevention, as well as overlapping areas among these (Downie, Tannahill, & Tannahill, 1990). Applied to adolescent health, this approach refers to going beyond encouraging teens not to drink, have sex, or engage in violence, with more awareness of the need to build positive capacity and coping skills for all of the challenges that young adults require for success. Two perspectives within this health-promotion framework have emerged since the 1990s: prevention science and positive youth development (Catalano et al., 2002). These perspectives are similar in their focus on approaching children and youth in a holistic manner but differ somewhat in their emphases: prevention science focuses on specific risk and protective factors, while positive youth development takes a more global approach to building overall youth capacity.

One of the key features of a health-promotion approach is its universal nature—it offers something for everybody. There are several considerations to guide the advisability of this approach, however. First, the targeted behaviors or problems need to have sufficiently high prevalence rates: a universal health-promotion strategy to target a very rare problem may be a poor use of resources, especially if little is known about the cause of the problem. Conversely, given the skyrocketing rates of obesity among North Americans, a health-promotion approach to fitness and healthy eating is clearly warranted. The statistics on violence, substance use, and high-risk sexual behavior among adolescents indicate that these areas are sufficiently prevalent to warrant a broad health-promotion strategy.

The potential for harm must also be factored into the decision to pursue a health-promotion strategy. For example, although infants and toddlers can have adverse reactions to immunization, the belief among medical professionals is that this level of risk is acceptable given the benefits. It is a mistake to assume that because they do not involve needles psychoeducational approaches are always harmless. A striking example of psychoeducational interventions producing unintended effects occurred in the early efforts at school-based eating disorder prevention. Psychoeducational prevention efforts in the area of eating disorders emerged from the recognition that sociocultural factors play a major role in body dissatisfaction and disordered eating attitudes and behaviors, particularly among adolescent girls. It seemed logical to go into schools and classrooms and talk to young women about the perils of eating disorders. Although these programs varied in format, duration, and evaluation components, a review of published evaluations found that only four showed positive behavioral change, and another four studies revealed a worsening of symptoms and/or attitudes (Austin, 2000). There are many sound theoretical reasons for this lack of success, including the possibility that focusing on information alone exposes youth to dangerous methods of weight control without changing attitudes and behaviors. Having clear and empirically derived estimates of the potential for harm is an important piece in determining the advisability of a universal prevention approach.

During the 1990s, the focus on strengthening youth capacity versus treating problems coalesced into the *positive youth movement* (Catalano et al., 2002). This approach focuses on general competence and connection for youth rather than targeting a specific problem or set of risk factors. This approach goes beyond risk reduction and focuses on developing the positive end of the health spectrum. The logic behind this approach suggests that building overall capacity helps youth develop resiliency for a wide range of challenges they may face in the future. This model contends that youths who are competent and connected to other prosocial youths, adults, and institutions will be better able to make healthy choices in a wide range of domains and will be better prepared to face difficult situations when they encounter them.

Resilience to future stressors stems from overall competence and adjustment. Resilience is defined as the capacity to recover and maintain adaptive behavior after insult (Garmezy, 1991). In the past, the construct of resilience has sometimes been misunderstood as a characteristic inherent to an individual. The earliest description of resilient children referred to them as invulnerable or invincible and inferred that these children had some special inner ability that allowed them to withstand adversity. There was also an inherent interaction component of resiliency in these early conceptualizations, in that protective factors were initially seen as forces activated only under conditions of risk. Unfortunately, attributing resilience to an individual as if it were a trait can foster an attitude of victim blaming when someone does not exhibit resilience in the face of adversity. Resilience is better understood as an array of characteristics and supports that are derived in part from the environment and in part relate to individual capacity.

More recent work in the area has illuminated the nature of resilience as a very logical, commonsense phenomenon. In a pivotal paper aptly named "Ordinary Magic: Resilience Processes in Development," psychologist Ann Masten (2001) argued that resilience processes are not dissimilar from dynamics that typically predict positive adjustment. The same factors that increase positive child outcomes in average families also support resilience in cases of adversity. These factors can be at the individual level, such as good intellectual functioning or sociability; the family level, such as a close relationship to a caring parent figure or authoritative parenting; and within the larger community context, such as bonds to positive and caring adults outside the family or attending effective schools. It is the balance between these factors and the adversity faced by the child and family that determines outcome (Masten & Coatsworth, 1998).

From a resiliency perspective, the goal of a health-promotion and risk-prevention program is to maximize potential and build capacity in all adolescents to prepare them for future challenges. All adolescents will face difficult interpersonal situations at some point, such as ending a first dating relationship, losing childhood friends as peer allegiances shift and settle in to high school, and the ubiquitous peer pressure to engage in high-risk activities. Providing opportunities for all adolescents to acquire accurate information, engage in value clarification exercises to develop their own sense of boundaries, and build interpersonal skills can assist adolescents who are struggling with the demands of adolescence. However, these same opportunities can also promote resilience in youth who are not currently having problems and provide an inoculation effect for future stressors.

One of the ways to maximize adolescent potential is to approach adolescents as a valuable resource rather than a public health problem (Wolfe et al., 1997). Providing youth with opportunities to mentor others develops important skills and is also a rewarding experience for all involved. The Collaborative Afterschool Prevention Program, for example, is an inner city program that involved 54 youth mentors helping out with 584 elementary and middle school children in a low-income and ethnically diverse area (O'Donnell, Michalak, & Ames, 1997). The purpose of the program was to engage the adolescents as role models and leaders and to discourage the younger children from getting involved in problem behavior. The creation of these mentoring relationships was intended to provide a buffer for the younger children from some of the peer and community pressures to engage in high-risk behaviors. While adults designed the program, the teenage mentors had an active voice in program planning, and both groups were given opportunities to contribute positively to their communities. The teens were there officially to organize activities and help the children with their homework but often found themselves simply spending time with the younger children, discussing problems at home or in school. When the youth mentors were interviewed, 98 percent thought the program was effective, both for the elementary and middle school children and for the adolescent mentors. The latter group indicated improvements in social skills, bonding between the mentor and the child, and improved work habits. Some mentors even helped the younger children to deal with anger management. This program exemplifies the importance of youth empowerment, in that both the young children and the youth mentors gained a great deal from their experiences.

In a similar study focusing on peer mentoring, youths between the ages of 14 and 21 were given the task of acting as mentors to younger children between the ages of 7 and 13 to teach them about violence prevention (Sheehan, DiCara, LeBailly, & Christoffel, 1999). Again, the overall results were that the two groups—children and the young adults—gained new skills and attitudes from the program. Adolescents developed leadership abilities, became more self-confident, and learned skills that they could use for future employment. After 18 months the children changed their attitudes that previously supported violent solutions to peer conflict. These initiatives show that adolescents can be engaged as leaders and mentors in violence prevention. In addition to the benefits for the children or youth being mentored, acting as a mentor provides youth with important skills and attributes and provides what may be an unprecedented opportunity to be valued in the community.

Whereas health promotion is a universal strategy designed to decrease the incidence and prevalence of risk factors and harmful outcomes in an entire population, *selected prevention,* also known as *early intervention,* refers to focusing resources for those at risk of developing a particular problem. Efforts are begun when the early signs of difficulty or disorder are noticed. The argument behind this approach is one of efficiency: why waste valuable resources on children and adolescents who do not need the intervention? For example, critics of a universal health-promotion approach worry about adversely influencing youths who are unlikely to engage in problem behaviors; if we teach all adolescents about sexuality and substance use, are we implicitly condoning the behavior? Although early intervention makes sense, "too often we don't know when to do it, on whom to do it, and how to do it" (R. L. Johnson, 2002, p. 240). With the exception of some modest gains in areas such as teen pregnancy, the success of most early intervention efforts has not lived up to the promise. This lackluster success relates to the three necessary conditions for successful early or selected prevention (R. L. Johnson, 2002): (1) morbidities that have identifiable and detectable causal antecedents (for example, lung cancer is caused by smoking); (2) reliable tools that can effectively detect the antecedents in all populations of adolescents (for example, it is easy to determine whether or not people smoke); and (3) interventions that have the power to reliably halt the progression of these identifiable antecedents toward an undesirable goal (for example, programs that successfully help people stop smoking). To this list we would add a fourth: the need to engage youth in the situations. The best identification coupled with the most effective services will not succeed if identified youths do not participate.

It is arguable whether or not any of these criteria for successful early intervention have been met in the areas of dating violence, sexual behavior, and substance use. With respect to identifying clear-cut antecedents, the predictive models tend to be complex, interactive, and difficult to operationalize, as discussed in chapter 5. Determining risk status for any one adolescent requires a weighing and balancing of relative risk and protective factors. It is difficult to assess the specificity and sensitivity of these multidimensional models of risk, in contrast to a litmus test of medical risk, such as a genetic marker for a particular disorder. There are few successful programs that target one or two specific contributors to poor outcomes, and engaging youth in specialized service is often a struggle.

Another concern with risk identification relates to the message conveyed to those working with children and families. By identifying a child or adolescent as high risk, the source of potential problems is seen to reside in the child. This attribution influences how teachers and other professionals in the educational and mental health system respond to that child (Mash & Wolfe, 2005). Specifically, the stability of potential problems may be overestimated, as many professionals are not aware of measurement error and false positive rates associated with screening measures. In addition, by assigning the high-risk label to the child, professionals may not consider other important influences, such as previous opportunities or teaching styles. For example, an adolescent identified as being at risk for dropping out of school tends to be seen as *having* certain problems rather than viewed as being at the epicenter of a troubled system in which, perhaps, family and school factors have contributed to the adolescent's difficulties. The alternative to possibly misidentifying and labeling youth as high risk is to provide opportunities for all youth to build capacity, consistent with a positive youth development philosophy.

The universal approach of building capacity in youth has many advantages, although there are limitations to providing competency or resiliency-based education in isolation. Acknowledging that youths will respond by making a variety of choices when faced with difficult decisions concerning substance use and sexual behavior is consistent with a harm-reduction approach. Here we argue for a combination of harm reduction and health promotion and outline the reasons that neither approach may be sufficient by itself.

The strong foundation provided by a positive youth development approach sets the stage for healthy choices but does not necessarily equip an adolescent with strategies to use in particular problem situations. Although teens who are competent in one social sphere are more likely to be competent in others, there is also evidence that social competence is situation-specific. Thus, while general communication and assertiveness skills are good in theory, in practice teens need to develop these skills in different areas. For example, they need to learn how to be assertive in both peer and dating relationships, to negotiate pressure specifically around substance use and sexual behavior, and to recognize and counter abusive relationship strategies. Generic social skills training programs typically do not target these various areas with enough specificity. Furthermore, these skills need to help youth go beyond "Just say no" and give them some strategies for healthier choices when they have just said "Maybe" or even "Yes."

This extension into equipping teens with strategies for keeping themselves safer when engaging in behavior that adults would like them to avoid altogether is the domain of harm reduction. Harm reduction has been somewhat misunderstood, in part because it is used to describe a wide range of activities. Providing intravenous (IV) drug users with access to clean needles is a harm-reduction strategy but is obviously not what we are talking about with respect to universal programming with grade 9 students. The aim of any harm-reduction strategy is to minimize the harm that may occur to someone who engages in risk behavior. For IV drug users, providing clean needles minimizes the likelihood of HIV or other diseases; for sexually active adolescents, easy access to condoms has the same goal. Thus, harm reduction is not a strategy but rather a philosophy that acknowledges the reality that some individuals will engage in high-risk behavior. Instead of judging these individuals, efforts to increase safety will result in lower rates of serious negative outcomes.

The fundamental tenet of harm reduction concedes that preventing adolescents from engaging in all high-risk behavior is a futile goal; however, increasing teens' ability to keep themselves safe as they experiment with new opportunities and privileges is more manageable. Harm-reduction programs have fewer black and white goals for behavior change than do abstinence-focused or "Just say no" programs. Harm reduction recognizes that criminalization has not been effective in reducing high-risk behavior, and in some cases this approach has exacerbated the problems. For example, rigid enforcement of the minimum legal drinking age on college campuses in the United States has been implicated in injuries, and even deaths, resulting from students trying to drink quickly and in secret. Harm reduction differs from a positive youth development approach in that the former is interested in reducing a particular negative outcome (for example, adolescent pregnancy, substance dependence), while the latter focuses on building individual strengths and addressing the underlying predisposing factors that increase the likelihood of the negative outcome.

There is evidence of the effectiveness of harm-reduction approaches in the realms of sexual behavior and substance use. Effective sexual behavior risk-reduction programs place equal emphasis on abstinence and on lowering risk behavior rather than promoting abstinence as the only option (St. Lawrence et al., 1995). While it is difficult to get already sexually active teens to start using condoms, teaching about condom use raises the likelihood that adolescents not currently engaging in sex will use condoms when they become sexually active, without lowering the age of onset (Kirby & Coyle, 1997). Approaching youth who are not currently sexually active with an abstinence-only message may have some impact on delaying onset of sexual activity, but it also means that youths are less equipped to make safer choices once they become sexually active, as demonstrated by the research on virginity pledge programs. Furthermore, merely teaching about condoms will not suffice—adolescents need to practice assertive responses to pressure to engage in unsafe sex. Again, the underlying themes of skills-based programming and a focus on healthy relationships provide the context for these harm-reduction strategies.

With respect to substance use programs, harm-reduction approaches recognize that many adolescents will experiment with alcohol and some other drugs. Starting from a point where this reality is acknowledged, adolescents can be provided with appropriate education and prevention without provoking rebellious attitudes and behaviors (Mosher, 1999). The Life Skills Training program described in the previous chapter exemplifies this approach. The program focuses on reducing positive expectancies for substance use, increasing resistance skills, correcting inaccurate norms about peer substance use, and increasing overall social competency, but it does not insist that adolescents completely abstain from using substances.

Discussing harm-reduction strategies requires an important cautionary note: careful attention must be paid to the developmental stage of the youth to whom the strategies are being directed. If strategies and messages are unintentionally geared to an older stage of development, the resulting message can be overly permissive for the target audience. For example, with grade 12 students it may be appropriate to frame a message about binge drinking in a way that acknowledges that the majority of students are engaging in some substance use. The same message to 14-year-olds, the majority of whom are *not* engaging in drinking, might seem overly permissive. The appropriate harm-reduction message for 14-year-olds is not "We know you will be drinking, using drugs, and having sex, so we are going to tell you how to stay safe while doing it," but rather "We know you could end up places where some of these activities are occurring and you may find yourself pressured to try them, and we want to give you strategies to keep yourself safe." It is important to include room for abstinence as a viable and healthy alternative for youth, regardless of age. Although the majority of adolescents will at least experiment with these behaviors at some point during their teenage years, a subset of youth do not engage at all, and their choice to avoid these behaviors altogether must be framed as a positive and acceptable decision.

A study that compared rates of substance use between communities in the United States and Australia identified some of the advantages and disadvantages of the differing policies (Beyers, Toumbourou, Catalano, Arthur, & Hawkins, 2004). Most of the risk and protective factors investigated operated similarly for youth, regardless of whether they lived in the United States or Australia. At the policy level, the abstinence policy context of the United States and the harm-reduction policy of Australia exerted different influences on patterns of youth substance use. The U.S. abstinence policy context was associated with higher levels of illicit substance use, but the Australian harm-reduction policy was associated with more cigarette and alcohol use. The researchers posited that the higher cigarette and alcohol use within a social context of harm reduction might stem from exposure to normative influences that are more tolerant of youth drug use. Thus, while the abstinence-only messages clearly have their shortcomings, perhaps even more so in the area of sexual behavior than substance use, harm reduction can also send the wrong message about the acceptability of behavior choices, or it may implicitly condone use. In all likelihood, the suitability of a harm-reduction message varies depending on the age of the recipients.

Proper Timing

One of the best-practice principles in prevention programs is the idea of appropriately timed interventions (Nation et al., 2003). Interventions are not simply effective or ineffective—they are effective or ineffective under certain conditions and for certain age groups. We have considered what types of prevention approaches are most likely to be successful and have combined these crucial elements into a framework that we propose for use with youth in middle adolescence, typically grade 9. In thinking about the appropriate timing for different interventions, questions of youth's social and cognitive development and behavioral trends are pertinent. The characteristics of middle adolescence in each of these domains have implications for the comprehensive intervention we are outlining. In this section, we discuss aspects of midadolescent development that create an appropriate window for this type of intervention, referring to information we discussed in chapter 4 and how this informs our efforts.

Two major shifts occur in social behavior during this developmental period: adolescents shift toward their peer groups and away from their families as the major socializing influence in their lives, and dating and romantic relationships emerge. While these changes can frustrate parents as their children appear to withdraw from them, there is also an incredible opportunity afforded by these developments. Adolescents are fascinated by relationships and social status, as evidenced by the covers of countless magazines for teen girls that offer promising

tips for getting a boyfriend or quizzes to determine if a best friend is being loyal. This heightened awareness about relationships makes it much
easier to engage adolescents in discussion about these topics. Adolescents are actively seeking new adult identities and are willing to try out
new roles or ways of relating. By intervening with youth at this age and
introducing new relationship skills for them to practice and use, it is
possible to capitalize on this natural period of trying out new roles.

In addition to the increased interest in relationship matters, the
extent to which adolescents look to one another for cues about appropriate behavior creates a window of opportunity. The salience of the
youth's peer group at this age makes the peer group a powerful agent of
change. On one hand, the preeminence of the peer group can present
a liability: youths who think that their peers are engaging in high levels
of risk behavior are more likely to try these behaviors themselves. On
the other hand, peer dynamics can create positive momentum for
healthy choices. Youth empowerment strategies and the use of youth
leaders, especially those with high social status, can be potent strategies
for change, with much more salience than information or activities
generated by adults.

The emergence of dating relationships and pre-dating behaviors
is another feature of this age group that lends itself to a relationship-
based intervention. As adolescents begin to engage in romantic relationships, they often rely on stereotypes or images portrayed in the
media, or on advice and assumptions from their equally inexperienced
peers, to determine what is normal, healthy, and acceptable in these relationships. Providing youth with the opportunity to discuss and explore dating relationships, and also discuss the intersection between
dating and sexual intimacy, can provide an opportunity that may not
be available at home. Even in relatively healthy families, the intensity
of many adolescent-parent relationships, the independence the youths
are trying to establish, and parents' discomfort may prevent these discussions from taking place at home. Teacher-led discussions can provide an opportunity to explore these matters and equip teens with un-
biased information from an adult other than parents. In addition,
providing adolescents with the chance to discuss healthy dating relationships at the beginning of their dating careers helps them avoid
many of the dangerous pitfalls.

In chapter 4 we noted that teens become more capable of abstract thought and develop the capacity for metacognition. They are also very sensitive to hypocrisy and react negatively to being patronized by oversimplified messages. Adolescents develop a sense that they are the focus of others' attention (that is, the false audience consensus) and often show a heightened sensitivity to perceived peer norms. Indeed, the extent to which they think their peers are engaging in certain behaviors or condone certain behaviors affects their behavior, even when their perceptions are inaccurate. These changes provide an excellent opportunity to engage youth in developing healthy choices. At this age they enjoy debating and are capable of integrating more complex information. Programs that provide an opportunity for youth to wrestle with all of the available information, including both the advantages and the disadvantages of different choices, are a natural fit during this period of cognitive growth.

A final reason for timing prevention efforts around grade 9 relates to their ongoing transition to high school, which typically includes new academic challenges, a more complex environment, new social demands, and new interactions with teachers (Newman, Lohman, Newman, Mayers, & Smith, 2000). Along with this transition comes a steep rise in many risk behaviors. For example, our data from students in grades 7 to 10 reveal how shifts in dating behavior provide a backdrop for discussions of healthy and abusive dating relationships (Crooks, Wolfe, & Hutchinson-Jaffe, 2004). In grades 7 and 8 few adolescents report having started to date, but by grade 10 approximately 40 percent are dating. Binge drinking and marijuana use are relatively rare in grade 7, but then climb steadily until grade 10—when rates are four times those in grade 7. Similarly, consensual sexual intercourse is very low for grades 7–9, but jumps to about 25 percent by the end of grade 10. Taken together, these findings show that some students are already engaging in these risk behaviors in grades 7 and 8, but the vast majority is not. The picture changes quite rapidly between grades 9 and 10, at which time these concerns are relevant to a much larger group of youth. This rapidly shifting social context and peer norms provide an excellent opportunity for adolescents to explore decision making in these various areas.

These findings on the emergence of risk behaviors beg the question: Given that some youths begin to experiment with high-risk behaviors prior to grade 9, wouldn't earlier be better? One of the problems with trying to do this work with younger adolescents is that you may be addressing a largely precontemplative audience. If the behaviors you are discussing are not even on your audience's social radar, they will be unable to meaningfully engage with the process. While some high-risk adolescents will be well engaged in these behaviors by grade 9, a universal prevention program needs to be timed to meet the needs of the majority. It is not until grades 9 and 10 that there is a significant shift in rates of engagement in these behaviors. Therefore, it may be difficult to discuss some of these risks earlier due to the different social structures that exist. For example, it is difficult to meaningfully approach dating violence with adolescents who are not yet dating, nor even thinking about it. There are pre-dating violence behaviors that can be addressed earlier (such as bullying and harassment), but again, matching the content and delivery to the developmental stage is critical. Simply stated, we must strike a careful balance when planning the timing of an intervention, especially during this period of rapid transition. Interventions timed too early may lose their positive effects before teens start to experiment and conversely, if planned too late, the problem may have already begun and be difficult to control (Mrazek & Haggerty, 1994).

Ideally, children should receive developmentally matched prevention messages throughout their school years (for example, younger children are better suited to black-and-white messages about the dangers of drug use). The content and delivery should then shift dramatically to deal with the rapid emergence of experimental risk behaviors in early adolescence. For example, interventions targeting adolescent sexual behavior that fit the developmental stage of participants tend to have the best outcomes; focusing on delaying onset for younger adolescents and targeting condom use for middle and older adolescents is more effective than a one-size-fits-all message across adolescence (B. Miller & Paikoff, 1992).

Gender-Strategic Approaches

In considering the identified components of best-practice programs, one factor that does not receive attention is the importance of gender.

With the exception of some dating violence–prevention programs, most prevention programs have not taken gender into account in content or delivery decisions. Conversely, some of the dating violence–prevention programs are sometimes overly gender-focused and transpose an adult model of power and control onto adolescents, emphasizing male-to-female violence to the exclusion of other patterns of violence.

Throughout the first half of the book we emphasized the role of gender in development, and in particular the development of healthy or unhealthy adolescent relationships. The high school environment tends to magnify the gender roles for boys and girls, and abuse that occurs for this age group reflects this importance of gender. As such, we argue that gender must be taken into account in the design of prevention programs. At the same time, there are many problems with simply applying an adult model of male-to-female domestic violence. Thus, it is important to balance developing a notion of gender while avoiding blaming men and boys (Tutty et al., 2002).

We advocate a *gender-strategic* approach. We recognize that interpersonal violence has a gendered context and that the ways in which boys and girls are socialized contributes to a culture of violence against women. The high school environment is often very hostile toward girls and youths who do not fit in with mainstream ideals about masculinity and femininity. At the same time, it is essential to engage both males and females in the prevention of violence. We have coined the term gender strategic to highlight this balance between developing an awareness of gender issues among youth and not alienating adolescents from the process.

The fundamental tenets of marketing are helpful in approaching the issue of gender in program development: to sell anything, we need to know our audience. A comprehensive school-based violence-prevention program has many audiences, and each of these audiences requires a specialized message about gender. It is important to think about packaging information distinctively for students, teachers, school board personnel, and parents. For each of these audiences we need to engage them with material that seems relevant but that will also educate and move them along in their understanding of gender and violence. The implications for shaping these messages for each of the stakeholders are discussed in the next chapter.

Box 7.1
Principles of an Integrated Program

Best practices for universal health-promotion efforts to help youth avoid high-risk experimentation and learn healthy ways of coping with peer pressure are based on the following principles:

■ They are *comprehensive*, both with respect to targeting a range of behaviors and also in terms of recognizing the multiple contexts within which adolescents live

■ They are *well timed:* Information and skills are provided during midadolescence when youth are experiencing changes in social, cognitive, and physical domains and are interested in learning more about relationships, willing to try out new identities, able to approach these issues with increased cognitive sophistication, and beginning to engage in dating and risk behaviors in larger numbers

■ They involve *parents, teachers, and schools* in age-appropriate ways and increase the connection between youth and these other groups

■ They focus on *skills,* particularly social competence

■ They specifically address *communication and social competence* in different areas

■ They focus on the importance of *relationships* to underscore both the comprehensive part of an integrated model and the type of skills that should be promoted

■ They provide youth with *opportunities to develop assets* and function as valuable resources, rather than being approached as a problem

■ They increase *youth connection* to schools, which serves as a broadband protective factor for a range of potentially health-damaging behaviors

■ They emphasize *risk and harm reduction* by recognizing that youths may find themselves in difficult situations and may choose to engage in high-risk behaviors

> ■ They recognize the benefits of *delay* as an important component but also equip youth with the knowledge and skills to successfully negotiate situations if they decide to engage in sexual activity or substance use
> ■ They recognize the *gendered* nature of adolescents' world and realities, and match programming accordingly

We have combined valuable strands from the literature on youth development and best practices for addressing particular problem and risk behaviors during adolescence to develop an integrated model for prevention. There is ample overlap between the principles of best practice in the different areas of prevention to validate a model of prevention that simultaneously addresses violence, substance use, and sexual behavior. Value clarification, skills building, and peer role-playing are particularly well suited to 13- and 14-year-olds and form a central part of the principles of an integrated program, as described in box 7.1.

Summary

This chapter built on the identification of key components for effective programming by combining them into an integrated, comprehensive model. A comprehensive model provides a best-practices approach to the areas of violence, substance use, and high-risk sexual behavior prevention. Furthermore, it provides a balance between addressing areas of harm and promoting areas of strength and capacity. Comprehensive and skill-based approaches meet the best-practice criteria for prevention programs in the violence, sexual behavior, and substance use domains. Increasing adolescents' capacity to develop healthy relationships with those around them increases their resilience to peer pressure and helps prepare them for the demands of adulthood. Increasing connections between youth and their families, schools, and communities further protects adolescents from harm. These ingredients are critical components for an integrated model of preventing multiple risk behaviors.

A balance between a positive youth development approach and a harm-reduction philosophy captures the equilibrium between building positive capacity and targeting specific high-risk behaviors. The positive youth development approach recognizes youth as a societal asset whose strengths can be developed. Youth are seen as providing an important contribution to the community. Harm reduction recognizes that even well-adjusted and connected youth will face high-risk situations. In addition, there is recognition that, to some extent, experimenting with these behaviors is a hallmark of the developmental stage of adolescence. Harm reduction shifts away from the goal of total abstinence to a more realistic emphasis on minimizing risk. The combination of positive youth development and harm reduction, within a health-promotion framework, provides youth with opportunities to make safer choices across a wide spectrum of risk situations.

The issue of timing presents another consideration. The social, cognitive, and physical features of adolescence align well with an interactive and challenging approach to prevention. Nonetheless, trying to engage youth in this process too early runs the risk of reduced relevancy for them and possibly having program effects wear off before the issues become relevant for most youth.

In addition to these well-established principles, we have proposed the importance of a gender-strategic approach in shaping messages for youth. Being gender strategic means shaping messages so that they fit with adolescents' current perception of relationships and ensuring that the messages match the different experiences and realities of girls and boys. Youth are sensitive to hypocrisy and exceptions to the rule, so delivering a one-sided message that implicitly places blame on men and boys may be discarded out of hand. In their day-to-day interactions with same- and opposite-sex peers, girls as well as boys use abusive language, harassment, and sometimes violent behavior toward others. We acknowledge important gender differences in the expression of violence in adolescence and see raising this awareness with adolescents as an end goal and not a starting point.

In the next chapter, we expand on each of these areas by providing more detailed descriptions and examples of how best to put these principles into action. Specific strategies for building skills with adolescents are discussed. Appropriate ways to achieve a comprehensive approach are identified within the developmental context of adolescents' desire for autonomy. We illustrate our discussion with many of the innovative strategies that have been developed with our own school board.

8

The Delivery
Best Practices for Strengthening
Relationships and Managing Risks

We now turn to the specifics of how to operationalize the principles of an integrated and comprehensive prevention program. Information from the previous chapters on best practices for youth is used to build a picture of what a comprehensive program should look like for this age group. Because social skills are important for specific situations, we examine the most effective ways to teach them to youth in midadolescence. Similarly, because building youth capacity is critical, we consider how this should be accomplished in a school setting. We illustrate this discussion with examples from our school-based program for building healthy relationships, the Fourth R.

The Fourth R is a comprehensive school-based program designed to promote healthy relationships and prevent risk behaviors among adolescents. It grew out of the Youth Relationships Project (YRP), the dating violence–prevention program developed for youth with family backgrounds of maltreatment and violence discussed in chapter 6. The YRP's success in demonstrating changes in violence-congruent attitudes of youth at risk for violent relationships resulted in widespread interest in adapting the program for use with all youth, regardless of risk status. In 1999, we received funding from the National Institutes of Health (NIH) (in partnership with Dr. Ernest Jouriles in

Texas) for a three-year pilot project to develop the YRP into a program that could be universally implemented in high schools. The Fourth R was developed in its current form during this pilot program, and pilot findings showed significant gains in knowledge and skills relative to controls (Jaffe et al., 2004). A five-year controlled evaluation with follow-up will be completed in 2007.

The cornerstone of the Fourth R is a 21-lesson skill-based curriculum that promotes healthy relationships and targets violence, high-risk sexual behavior, and substance use among adolescents (see www.thefourthr.ca). Physical and health education teachers who deliver the curriculum receive specialized training. The contention of the Fourth R is that relationship skills can be taught in much the same way as the first three Rs (reading, 'riting, and 'rithmetic), and establishing these skills as a fundamental part of the high school curriculum is equally essential. Furthermore, given the abundance of negative relationship models available to teens, it is crucial that they be exposed to healthy alternatives and equipped with the skills to engage in healthy relationships themselves. The Fourth R is comprised of three units: "Personal Safety and Injury Prevention," dealing with peer and dating violence; "Healthy Growth and Sexuality"; and "Substance Use/Abuse." Each unit contains similar themes of value clarification, provision of information, decision making, and an extensive skill-development component. Connections among the three units are emphasized throughout.

Clarifying values allows adolescents the opportunity to think about their own boundaries and comfort levels and about the decisional balances involved in each of these behavior areas. This process is ongoing and integrated into skill development. Adolescents receive ample practice role-playing ways to resolve conflict, both as participants and in the role of bystander. In addition to practice, seeing their peers role-play solutions is an important part of the program and one of the most effective ways to increase self-efficacy (Bandura, 1977). There are three other key components in addition to the 21 curriculum lessons, addressing school, parents, and community. School interventions include staff and teacher awareness education, information about the program, and supplementary activities by the student-led Social Action Committees. Parents receive regular updates about the program through a newsletter and meetings and are provided with developmental information and strategies relevant to parenting adolescents. Student-led Social Action Committees focus on increasing links between community partners by organizing guest speakers, field trips, and agency open houses and raising the profile of violence prevention in their schools. In brief, the Fourth R was designed to operationalize the best-practice principles identified and discussed in chapters 6 and 7. It focuses on skill development within a relationship context, incorporates positive youth development initiatives, and is comprehensive.

Strengthening Relationship Skills

The importance of skills has emerged as a fundamental principle of best practice in prevention programs, regardless of the actual behavior(s) being targeted. Conceptualizing skills in adolescence is complicated—not only are skills important, but they are affected by decision-making processes that precede these skills. Teens require the behavioral ability of knowing how to do something as well as the decision-making capability of knowing and choosing when to use these skills. For example, parents may lament that although their adolescents have assertiveness skills, they use them only with their parents and not their peers or dating partners (Pipher, 1994). The challenge is to help adolescents span this gap between knowing what to do and actually doing it.

The Information-Motivation-Behavior Skills (IMB) model is particularly useful for conceptualizing how to bridge this gap between knowing what to do and doing it (J. D. Fisher, Fisher, Mischovich, Kimble, & Malloy, 1996). Initially developed to help conceptualize goal-directed behavior to avoid AIDS transmission, the model posits that AIDS risk reduction is a function of individuals' information about AIDS transmission and prevention, their motivation to reduce AIDS risk, and their behavioral skills for performing the specific acts involved in risk reduction (W. A. Fisher & Fisher, 2003). Although the model was developed specifically to address AIDS risk reduction, we see great similarity in the components needed to build useful, useable skills for adolescents in the areas of substance use and violence prevention. In simple terms, to promote the development of skills that will actually be used, adolescents need a strong foundation of accurate information, the building blocks of effective behavioral responses in difficult situations, and the blueprint of motivation to use these skills. The following sections elaborate on the importance of each of these components as well as the way they fit together.

Accurate Information

The most widely used strategies in promoting healthy living tend to be information-based. In the case of some risk behaviors such as smoking, it is clear that information about the health-damaging consequences of smoking is not sufficient to invoke individual change. Everybody knows that smoking is harmful, yet people continue to do it. In some countries, there has been a move to include increasingly graphic pictures of damaged lungs and throats on cigarette packages to illustrate the potential negative effects in the hopes of deterring smokers. If these tactics have had an impact on smokers, it has been minor. Although smoking rates overall are down slightly, the number of adolescent girls starting to smoke continues to rise, and a significant minority of North Americans continue to smoke cigarettes on a regular basis (U.S. Surgeon General, 2004).

Although not sufficient in and of itself, accurate information about the risks associated with particular behaviors is clearly an essential foundation for healthier choices. There are numerous examples of successful public health campaigns—such as those targeting seatbelt use or not drinking during pregnancy—where providing accurate information has had a significant impact on rates of use (in the former case) or abstinence (in the latter). Best practices identified for reducing risky sexual behavior include providing accurate information about the risks of unprotected intercourse and methods of avoiding unprotected intercourse (Kirby, 1999). Likewise, information about specific substances is an important part of substance use prevention (Botvin & Kantor, 2000).

Most prevention efforts aimed at preventing risk behaviors provide good information but fail to deliver other important elements of behavioral change. In Canada health education has emphasized the information aspect of health, focusing on elements such as the biology associated with sexual behavior, information about sexually transmitted infections, and the effects and consequences of alcohol and drug use. In the United States, philosophical and political perspectives at times hinder even the information-sharing piece of the puzzle, as is the case with school boards that mandate an exclusively abstinence-based approach to birth control and sexual health.

Perhaps the surprising thing in today's world of sexually sophisticated youth culture is that teens don't know as much as we think they do. A study conducted by the Kaiser Family Foundation found that young people generally feel uninformed about STIs, HIV, and contraception (2003). Campaign for Our Children, a Baltimore-based nonprofit organization that creates and executes a mass media campaign to promote abstinence in children ages 9–14, assessed this level of misinformation by compiling more than 200 questions that had been sent to their "Ask the Expert" column on their website. These questions revealed a lack of basic information about human reproduction and a lack of access to (or trust in) health care providers to share this information (Flowers-Coulson, Kushner, & Bankowski, 2000).

We had a similar experience while writing this book. The 14-year-old daughter of one of the authors asked what we were working on. When we told her, she airily told us she had learned all about that "last year." She went on to tell us that she knew, for instance, that LSD could stay in your system for years and years after you took it. "LSD is the same thing as acid, Dad," she clarified. She then told us there are some long-term health consequences associated with drugs staying in your system. According to her, this longevity is the reason so many adults suffer from "acid reflux." Amy had some of the facts, but was not as well informed as she thought! More to the point, half-accurate information alone will not keep her safe as she navigates the next few tricky years.

Information is not a passive entity merely presented to and accepted by a particular audience. The way in which information is packaged and transmitted has a significant impact on the reception it receives and the extent to which the intended audience members incorporate the information into their worldview or reject it (J. S. Brown & Duguid, 2000; Buckland, 1991). For example, interactive methods of information transfer typically have more of an impact than passive messages. In the case of violence prevention, both the cognitive authority ascribed to the information source and social inoculation play a role in whether or not information is attended to and integrated (Crooks, Goodall, Hughes, Jaffe, & Baker, 2004). Cognitive authority refers to the expertise of an information source as perceived by an individual. In contrast, social inoculation refers to the extent to which a particular message loses its salience due to oversaturation of the message. In other words, messages from people whom adolescents deem to be out of touch will lose their salience, as will repetitive messages that are easy to tune out.

The Fourth R uses a number of strategies to increase the salience and interactive nature of the information component. One of the exercises in the "Sexual Health" part of the program is a question box in which students submit anonymous questions for teachers to answer to the whole class. There is often a wide range of questions that underscore the lack of clear and accurate information common among adolescents. The issue of salience is addressed by having students themselves generate the questions. In some cases, teachers of girls' classes trade questions with teachers of boys' classes and read and answer the questions submitted by opposite-sex classes. This trading of questions is perceived very positively by the students and contributes to the material being seen as relevant. Cognitive authority is addressed by involving older adolescents in a number of ways. For example, the Teen Panel—a group of teenage parents who speak about contraception, choices, and the realities of teen parenting—is always very well received by the grade 9 students. In addition, older peers (typically grade 11 or 12 students from the Leadership Class) are used to assist in the grade 9 classes. Within the context of the high school peer hierarchy, using older students is a highly effective avenue for increasing cognitive authority and salience of information.

In sum, although accurate information is critical, it is widely recognized that information alone is not sufficient for behavior change. Furthermore, the manner in which we attempt to transmit information is critical—there is consensus that passive information and knowledge transfer, such as lectures or group discussions, should not be the main mechanism of change (Durlak, 1997). Recognizing the social context of information is also important, because the source of a message can have a significant impact on the extent to which the message is acknowledged and integrated into people's beliefs.

Behavioral Skills

Virtually every successful prevention program has a skills-building component. Improving social and emotional competence is a hallmark of effective prevention programs (Greenberg, Domitrovich, & Bumberger, 2000). Adolescents need the opportunity to learn new skills, such as assertiveness, communication, and problem solving, and to practice applying them in different situations. Without skills, accurate information by itself offers poor protection in the face of pressure from peers and dating partners.

Adolescent self-efficacy is an important target in increasing skills. Self-efficacy stems from having particular skills but also from having the *confidence* that those skills will actually work in a real situation. Four key strategies to increasing self-efficacy (Bandura, 1986) are (1) providing a successful mastery experience; (2) providing an opportunity to witness others' successful mastery experiences; (3) creating these opportunities in a way that is not overly anxiety provoking; and (4) providing immediate feedback. Simply being instructed in skills, discussing them, and even writing out responses are not likely to increase skills and self-efficacy—to foster skill development it is critical to provide realistic opportunities to practice and receive feedback. By analogy, a teen who practices layups at a basketball hoop day after day and perfects her form may have particular skills but is unlikely to feel much self-efficacy because she has not tested those skills in a game situation and is uncertain of the outcome when she tries them. By the same reasoning, an adolescent who practices being assertive in front of a mirror with no feedback from others is unlikely to have much confidence in his strategies working in a "game situation." Adolescents need to practice these skills in as realistic a situation as possible to increase their feelings of self-efficacy that these skills will actually work when called upon in situations of conflict.

This analogy can also be applied to the example of learning to intervene as a bystander when witnessing abusive behavior. Most adolescents have been in a situation where they see someone getting bullied or harassed. For youth (or adults) to attempt to intervene in such a situation, they need to have the expectation that taking action will lead to a desired outcome, that is, a resolution of the situation that does not endanger or humiliate the person intervening. Otherwise, even though they may be highly distressed by what they witness and motivated to intervene, they are unlikely to act. This example shows the importance of competence and skill building—too often it is assumed that whether or not someone takes action is simply a matter of motivation. The Family Violence Prevention Fund has a series of powerful print ads encouraging men to confront friends who are abusive in their intimate relationships. These ads have pictures of injured women, with slogans such as "It's hard to confront a friend who abuses his wife . . . but not nearly as hard as being his wife" and "If the noise coming from next door were loud music you'd do something about it." These ads have a powerful emotional impact and may be successful at motivating people to take action; however, there may still be a significant skill gap with respect to knowing what action to take. Increasing self-efficacy and competence arms individuals with the tools to intervene in such situations.

Successful programs use a range of active skill-development strategies, such as

- They provide hands-on experiences that increase participant skills
- They help participants develop assertiveness and resistance skills
- They increase communication skills
- They provide ample opportunities for written and verbal practice of these skills (Nation et al., 2003)

Role-plays can be extremely effective but they need to be carefully planned, introduced, and debriefed. A role-play activity that gets out of hand can be a failure experience and counterproductive, or so anxiety provoking that the experience is aversive. In the Fourth R students role-play a range of conflict situations relating to peer and dating relationships. Because the process of responding to a provocative situation, such as bullying or pressure to use drugs, is difficult, role-plays are broken down into small steps. Students are given actual scripts for the first few exercises to reduce their discomfort and ease them into action one step at a time. Over time students practice brainstorming solutions, trying responses, trying responses in the presence of other people, trying responses in the face of resistance, and analyzing what worked well and what did not. Importantly, they have ample opportunities to see their peers attempt to navigate similar scenarios and discuss what they liked or didn't like about particular approaches. Through feedback from their teachers and peers, they are able to handle increasingly complicated and difficult situations as the program continues.

One of the most innovative components of the Fourth R includes ways to integrate these learning opportunities into the daily fabric of high school life. Our national education coordinator (formerly the learning coordinator for violence prevention for our local school district) has been experimenting with live role-plays in sports situations. During a recent classroom visit to a grade 9 boys' physical health education class he was watching a group of young men throw footballs back and forth, and he set up a quick role-play with three of the boys. One of the boys took on the role of having been out with a girl on the weekend and wanting to talk about the sexual behavior that occurred in a way that clearly objectified the young woman. The second boy encouraged the first to tell more details and reinforced the first boy's objectification. The third boy role-played being a friend of the young woman in question, feeling uncomfortable with the situation, and trying to intervene to challenge his friends and redirect the conversation. The role-play went smoothly, with the rest of the class observing and debriefing afterward. The whole activity took less than five minutes. The success of this in vivo role-play built upon the boys' previous experience in structured classroom role-plays as part of the Fourth R— attempting a role-play like this from scratch would be difficult. The boys' feedback from the experience was positive and they indicated the situation was realistic, which increases the likelihood that learning experiences will generalize to the boys' lives. Furthermore, attempts to resolve the situation provided the rest of the class with a model for an alternate response to a common situation.

Another initiative that targets building skills with a wider audience is a form of social action theater called Forum Theatre (Jaffe et al., 2004). In Forum Theatre troupes of young actors travel to different schools and perform plays with strong themes of violence and harassment. The play is performed start to finish once, and after watching the play through the first time a teacher facilitator tells the audience members they will have the opportunity to change the situation they have just seen unfold. This time, when the play starts people in the audience are encouraged to put up their hand and yell "Stop" when they see something they find unacceptable, such as an episode of violence or harassment. When someone yells stop, the tableau freezes and the person who stopped the action replaces either the victim or the bystander (but not the perpetrator). The scene is then replayed, with the person who has intervened having the opportunity to trigger a different outcome. The interactions are very realistic, and the perpetrators do not back down simply because they are told to stop. The person who has intervened has to be creative and persistent to change the course of events, much as he or she would in real circumstances.

In this initiative individuals who volunteer to intervene have a powerful experience in trying to change the course of the interaction. They also have the opportunity to experience the stress associated with going against the flow of an incident as it unfolds. In addition, there is a clear underlying message that everybody has both the opportunity and the responsibility to stop violence, and without intervention these scenes can escalate into harmful outcomes. Students in the audience who may not have the self-confidence to volunteer to demonstrate a different solution in front of the crowd still benefit from observing their peers' well-meaning attempts.

Interpersonal skills—effective communication, assertiveness, and conflict resolution—are critical for adolescents to be able to make healthy choices, although without an accompanying sense of self-efficacy such skills are less effective. Youths need to have confidence that their skills will lead to a desired outcome. Building skills that translate to higher self-efficacy depends on them having the opportunity to practice the skills in as realistic a setting as possible, observe others practicing these skills, get feedback from adults and peers on their skills, and do all of these in a manner that is not so anxiety provoking as to be aversive.

Motivation

Even with accurate information and the behavioral skills to make healthy choices, motivation is often a critical missing piece in preventing unsafe choices. Youth can know that smoking causes cancer and have reasonably good assertiveness skills but still choose to smoke when pressured by their peers. Motivation to behave in a certain way or make specific choices is a critical determinant of outcomes. Previous attempts to motivate teens have often relied on scare tactics or emphasizing the cost of *not* changing. As we have seen this approach is rarely successful, especially for those most likely to experiment, and is particularly ill suited to adolescents' stage of cognitive development. Furthermore, adolescents are hypersensitive to adult hypocrisy (Bradley & O'Connor, 2002). Being exposed to adult role models who engage in the behaviors youth are being encouraged to avoid adds an impediment for motivation. To create motivation there needs to be a multipronged approach focusing both on the individual and on the peer culture.

Information and skills increase self-efficacy, which in turn strengthens motivation. Being aware of alternative choices and having confidence to follow through on one's choice, even in hypothetical or contrived situations, establishes a healthy pattern that is likely to be reinforced and repeated. Although scare tactics alone have not been very successful in changing risk behavior, adolescents need the opportunity to discuss in depth both the positive and negative consequences of various behaviors. Outcome expectancies, or what someone believes will happen if he or she behaves a certain way, are related to the motivation to engage in health-protective practices (National Institute of Mental Health HIV Prevention Trial Group, 2001). For example, with respect to condom use, outcome expectancies can be related to physical (pleasure), social (partner's reaction), and personal implications.

Consistent with the notion of decisional balance, teens need to be able to discuss the positive consequences of high-risk behavior. What positive physiological, social, and/or emotional benefits do adolescents get from using alcohol or other substances? They may find that alcohol helps them overcome anxiety in social situations or that it helps them gain acceptance with a particular peer group. Although adults would prefer that teens not resort to alcohol to achieve those goals, ignoring the potential benefits experienced by adolescents does not make those benefits disappear. Recognizing there are benefits experienced by teens who use alcohol and other drugs creates an environment where individuals can engage in rational decision making. Allowing individuals to consider the pros and cons of particular behaviors increases motivation, as shown in studies with resistant clients in substance abuse treatment (W. R. Miller & Rollnick, 2002). These motivational interviewing techniques empower individuals to take responsibility for their health and make decisions, rather than having the onus fall on the therapist or teacher to "talk someone into" healthy choices.

At a peer culture level there are two approaches to increase motivation. First, adolescents are motivated in part by what they perceive their peers are doing, to the extent they think "everyone is doing it." For example, in our sample of 800 teens entering grade 9 there were marked increases in the extent to which they thought their peers were engaging in a range of risk behavior over the course of their first semester of high school. These beliefs about what constituted the norm for peer behavior were in turn associated with becoming involved in the same behaviors. Indeed, behavior norms have been cited as one of the two most critical determinants of adolescent risk behavior (Kirby, 2001b).

Motivation can also stem from being part of a group that sends a positive message about violence prevention. Being part of a club or group provides youths with the inherent reinforcement of belonging as well as some protection for trying on roles that may not fit mainstream ideals, especially for boys. In an ethnographic study of young men who became involved in volunteer work concerning gender equity, several identified belonging to their schools' gender equity clubs as an important public platform for their antiviolence activities (Coulter, 2003). Having such clubs available may get a number of youth through the door who might not otherwise consider these activities. For example, one of the participants admitted that his decision to join his school's gender equity club was initially motivated by a desire to impress a young woman (Coulter, 2003). Although the initial intentions for joining were not particularly related to social action, this young man's involvement in the gender equity club came to be a meaningful and important experience for him on its own merits.

The Fourth R targets motivation at the peer level in a number of ways. First, each school has a student antiviolence club with students from different grades. Although each club has a teacher facilitator to provide supervision and support, the clubs are youth-led. These clubs serve multiple purposes: they provide a public face and forum for students interested in social action work, and they create media campaigns for the school that specifically target peer-level influences. Previous campaigns have included segments on peer pressure—some have even targeted the aforementioned gap between what students think their peers are doing and what they are actually doing. The issue of cognitive authority is addressed by using the club to develop and implement these campaigns, since youth are much more likely to see information from their peers as relevant and useful compared to messages perceived as adult-driven. Student club members also present information or assist with role-plays in younger grades in the capacity of peer leaders.

Reinforcement can also be socially constructed at the larger community level. Our local school board hosts an annual violence prevention leadership awards night for high school students who have excelled in violence prevention and gender equity activities, cosponsored by several community agencies. The leadership awards night, now in its third year, has grown from 50 parents showing up to witness their children win awards to a sold-out crowd of hundreds, with each of the 29 high schools in the district nominating two or three award winners. The concept is simple and adolescent-centered: the speeches are short, the menu is pizza, and the awards are followed by two IMAX films. It is an opportunity for the community to come together and publicly thank youth for their involvement, and the award winners take great pride in their accomplishments. Because this involvement is identified as a positive and noteworthy achievement, others have something to strive toward, much as attending a football rally may inspire those in the audience to practice their skills in the hopes of making the team next year.

Empowering Youth

Proponents of the positive youth development movement note that being problem-free is not necessarily synonymous with being prepared to meet the multitude of challenges faced by adults (Catalano, Berglund, Ryan, Lonczak, & Hawkins, 2004). When adults think of the teenagers in their lives, they typically have higher hopes for these youth than merely graduating from high school and having a drug-free, nonviolent lifestyle! While most adults are aware of wanting more for the teenagers they care about, it is difficult to articulate clearly the opposite of the problem end of the spectrum. Instead, informative initiatives and research areas take the approach that adolescents are prepared rather than problem-free (Kim et al., 1998) and are viewed as community resources rather than problems. Opportunities to meet challenges, provide leadership to peers, and mentor younger students are all activities that can foster a healthy sense of identity in teenagers. These opportunities may be particularly powerful for youths traditionally considered at risk or marginalized, because they may not have had these experiences in the past.

Far too many adolescent intervention programs are designed, led, and run by adults, with virtually no input from the very youth they are intended to help. These programs fail to provide an opportunity for youth to make any kind of positive contribution, either to their school setting or community environment. School programs in which teachers and administrators set up the entire system for dealing with conflict are ineffective because they teach students that they need adults and authority figures to be able to solve problems (D. W. Johnson & Johnson, 1996). Such strategies fail to empower students to learn conflict resolution skills as they apply to any and all parts of their lives, whether at school, in the home, or throughout the community. In our view, it is essential to thoroughly engage youth in any kind of mentoring program; the initiative must in large part belong to them for the program to be effective. Peer mediation programs are extremely effective as they empower students to share responsibility for creating a safe, secure school environment (Stomfay-Stitz, 1993). By involving youths in conflict resolution and problem solving, these programs allow them to learn the necessary skills and employ them in similar situations.

Integral to any type of youth mentoring or peer mediation program is the concept of youth empowerment that gradually increases freedom and responsibilities of young people (Moody, Childs, & Sepples, 2003). Adults can help this process by making sure youth have a voice in the decisions that will affect them. Adolescents feel empowered to the extent that they "feel valued, believe others view them as resources, make contributions to a larger whole to which they belong, and feel free of fundamental physical and emotional threats to their safety" (Moody et al., 2003, p. 264). Empowered youth generally feel more connected to adults around them and their community, which are important protective factors in reducing risk behaviors and harm. Nonetheless, empowering youth in the area of violence prevention can be difficult. Given the peer context discussed in chapters 2 and 3, and the reality that this context rewards activities most closely aligned with the male Jock, empowering youth to take on activities that do not fit the highly rigid gender scripts of adolescence can be a challenge. In Garbarino and deLara's (2002) book on emotional violence in schools, the story is told of a gifted student who identifies the irony that his school's football team won the city championships and had three pep rallies, while his science fair team was nationally ranked but received only a mention over the public announcement system. The reality of the high school environment is that very particular activities are valued, both by students and the larger adult community.

We are faced with a daunting task: How do adults make it "cool" for youth to take leadership roles in violence prevention and healthy choices? We don't. Instead, we need to support youth in creating this momentum themselves. This assistance requires a critical mass of parents and teachers who believe in the work, but the youth themselves have to take ownership and provide direction. Youth leadership and empowerment opportunities are an integral part of the Fourth R. In addition to the aforementioned youth action committees, youth have the opportunity to participate as peer leaders for younger students. One of the advantages of the raised profile of community agencies in our schools has been an increase in volunteer work at those agencies. In our province there is a mandate that every student has to perform 40 hours of volunteer work before graduating from high school. With increased community agency collaboration with school partners, youth have become aware of a wider range of agencies at which to perform those community service hours. As a result many are choosing to do their hours at one of the agencies they have come to know based on their involvement in the youth action committee or through information at an agency fair organized by the youth action committee.

One of the lessons carried forward from the Youth Relationships Project was the incredible impact of providing high-risk youth with leadership opportunities to organize and conduct social action activities. All too often leadership activities and committees include the same small circle of youth within a school. These involved youth may have excellent leadership skills, but they are typically students who are already doing quite well. Providing leadership opportunities to youth who do not usually get involved and engaging those who may feel alienated can provide them with powerful opportunities to experience success with a positive group.

In the Fourth R, we encourage the teacher facilitators of the youth action committees to put special care into how the committee will be formed. Relying on self-identification tends to lead to the same group of visible leaders comprising the committee. We encourage the teacher facilitators to identify youths—either ones they know or ones nominated by a colleague—who might be interested in the topics but who are unlikely to join the committee without encouragement. We speak to teacher facilitators about the importance of having youth on the committee who represent a range of experiences. Our experience has been that young people who would not likely volunteer to be part of the youth action committee on their own may be happy to participate if individually approached by a student or teacher with whom they have a positive relationship.

Ensuring Comprehensive Participation

We have emphasized that comprehensive programming is a best-practice principle for effective prevention strategies. Programs that address the various contexts within which youth function and the different factors that affect youth behavior are more likely to be successful than those that focus on one specific context or determinant of behavior. In the case of violence, substance use, and high-risk sexual behavior education and prevention with high school students, considerations for comprehensive programming include age-appropriate inclusion of parents, schoolwide activities, and teacher involvement.

Age-Appropriate Inclusion of Parents

A comprehensive approach dictates inclusion of parents, although deciding how to include parents is tricky in light of this developmental stage. Developing an identity autonomous from their parents is a major developmental task, but at the same time adolescents need to balance this newfound autonomy with ways of staying connected to parents. Although the individuation process is taking place, youths who maintain this connectedness tend to fare better. Another consideration for the type and extent of parent involvement is the logistics of program delivery in the school setting. Although parent-youth sessions may be feasible in programs run through community mental health agencies, there are clear limitations to the types of involvement for parents within the school setting.

In the Fourth R we have opted to use a primarily information-dissemination strategy with parents. Parents receive a presentation about the program at the orientation night for prospective high school students and their parents in the spring of grade 8. Once students are at a school that offers the Fourth R, their parents are sent an information manual designed to be a user-friendly reference covering a range of topics, including information about the changes adolescents experience, the trends for various behaviors, and what their adolescents will learn in the program. Furthermore, the manual underscores the importance of parent-adolescent communication and provides parents with many tips for increasing healthy communication with their adolescents about the sensitive areas of violence, substance use, and sexual behavior. The manual also contains many other references, such as parenting books and websites for those seeking more information on particular topics.

Another activity designed to increase parent-adolescent communication without increasing conflict or intruding on emerging adolescent autonomy is the use of student-generated newsletters. These newsletters include Frequently Asked Questions (FAQs) with a twist—

students design both the questions and the answers with parents in mind. This gives youth an opportunity to provide information they think will be helpful to their parents without having to disclose personal information. Because the FAQs are done on a class-by-class basis and compiled into a newsletter by the youth action committees, there is sufficient privacy and anonymity for youth. Our intention in implementing the FAQ newsletters is to provide a platform for parents and adolescents to communicate about the issues covered in the Fourth R while minimizing threat to either party.

Shifting School Culture

One of the underlying goals of the various activities discussed in the context of motivation and youth empowerment—clubs, award nights, media campaigns, peer leaders—is to create the momentum to shift the entire culture of a school. In some ways, we are trying to create what Malcolm Gladwell (2000) refers to as a social epidemic: ideas and behavior catching on in the same manner as a viral epidemic. In his book *The Tipping Point: How Little Things Can Make a Big Difference*, the author identifies the components necessary to make an idea reach the critical mass necessary to really take off. These components include characteristics of the message or idea being transmitted as well as characteristics of the people doing the transmitting.

Gladwell refers to the "sticky" nature of an idea or fad that takes off. Sticky ideas, similar to viruses, need to be contagious and also need to be around long enough for others to catch them. In the case of violence prevention, having activities that are designed and run by youth increases the stickiness factor. In terms of the latter part of stickiness—exposure—there is clearly a need to have ongoing activities and awareness at the school level. A one-week violence-prevention focus can raise awareness temporarily, but for school climate to tip there needs to be more sustained exposure. There are also key characteristics of people who are involved in fads that "tip." Gladwell describes two types of people that are necessary for a trend to take off—connectors and mavens. Connectors have wide spheres of social influence and a significant ability to spread information, trends, and products. Mavens (also known as early adopters) lack the social networks and impact but tend to be very well informed and like to share their knowledge in the interest of helping others. It is this combination of people that is essential. A school may have one or two teachers who attend conferences and know a lot about violence prevention but lack the impact at the school level. Opportunities for bringing mavens and connectors together—possibly through staffwide awareness and training events—can help create this synergy.

Teacher Involvement

Teachers need sufficient training to successfully implement a program such as the Fourth R. Similar to the discussion of the IMB model of behavior change for adolescents, teachers need training that addresses all three of these areas: information, motivation, and behavioral skills. Without adequate training and booster sessions for teachers, the most innovative (and effective) components of programs can get dropped. Our teacher training uses the same principles as our program: teachers are provided with sufficient background information and given opportunities to practice and receive feedback on their attempts to facilitate role-plays.

The same considerations for information transfer discussed earlier in this chapter with respect to schools apply to teacher training. Teachers must have faith in the people doing the training to attach importance to the information. We have found that training using a combination of researchers and teachers is most effective. Typically, researchers provide the background orientation to the literature and teachers do the actual training for the curriculum. Although many of us have extensive experience facilitating role-plays and training others to facilitate role-plays, experience and feedback indicate that teachers feel very strongly about nonteachers trying to tell them how to teach. In other words, we are considered credible for providing background information and explaining the research design, but we have less cognitive authority when it comes to teaching the actual skill of teaching. By partnering with experienced teachers who have extensive training skills, we are able to maximize the effectiveness of the whole training experience.

In promoting teacher motivation it is imperative to gear the message to the audience. It needs to be made clear why a particular prevention program will benefit teachers as well as students. For example, teacher and student morale and the relationship between students' feelings of school safety and their achievement scores provide a good basis for capturing teachers' interest in the Fourth R. Focusing on some of the immediate benefits of implementing such a program, such as having a ready-made curriculum that meets state or provincial guidelines, is likely to have more of an impact on teacher motivation than identifying a long-term outcome that will not directly affect their teaching experience. It is not that teachers do not care about the long-term well-being of their students; rather, in the current educational climate, in which many teachers feel overwhelmed and demoralized, immediate benefits will be much more salient. The training and implementation issues of these programs are absolutely critical to their success and are discussed in greater detail in the following chapter.

Being Gender Strategic

The importance of gender has emerged as a critical developmental theme throughout this book. In chapter 7 we proposed a gender-strategic approach to programming, which requires awareness of the audience and continual attention to the balance between presenting gender concepts and also engaging the intended audience. In this section we discuss how each of the stakeholders might be engaged in this process.

As we have noted, students are developmentally at a stage where notions of gender tend to be very rigid. The typical high school environment rewards behaviors consistent with the male "Jock" ideal, while devaluing activities seen as more feminine, leading to an aggressively homophobic culture. Furthermore, adolescents report that girls hit boys as or more often than boys hit girls in their relationships. Because they lack the gendered understanding of important differences in the nature of this violence, both boys and girls will be hypersensitive to messages that they hear as "boy bashing" (Tutty et al., 2002). The challenge is to understand this reality, yet increase awareness of adolescents' understanding of gender and societal constructs of gender. In the Fourth R we target gender awareness through media deconstruction activities, discussions about different expectations and standards for boys and girls, and sometimes using different activities for boys and girls. Opportunities to discuss these issues in single-sex groupings may also provide increased comfort while debating sensitive issues.

With respect to teachers, there is a wide range of awareness, comfort, and skill in relation to gender and violence issues. Some teachers have already sought out specialized training in the area and are skilled facilitators. Others find the topic awkward or even irrelevant. We know that statistically there will also be a subset of teachers delivering the program who perpetrate or experience violence in their own intimate relationships. Teacher buy-in is critical, and engaging them in the program requires identifying benefits to them. For example, outlining the link between safety at school and achievement is one way to engage any reluctant teachers in the process. We have piloted numerous activities and developed a program that includes detailed instructions and structure to increase teachers' comfort and competence.

The range of teacher skill also has an impact on the types of activities that are included in a program. For example, there is a powerful exercise on gender stereotypes that is used in many counselor-facilitated interventions called "Act Like a Man/Act Like a Lady." This exercise has been widely used to help youth identify gender stereotypes and was part of the Youth Relationships Project manual (Wolfe et al., 1996). The exercise involves drawing a circle or square to represent the ideal man/woman. Youths are asked to brainstorm the ideal attributes for each gender, and these characteristics are written inside the figure. For example, they may identify that the ideal man is "strong, athletic, brave, doesn't cry" and the ideal woman as "pretty, quiet, thin, ladylike." Next, facilitators ask youths to generate the derogatory terms used to describe those males or females who do not fit neatly into the boxes. Typically they are able to generate a whole list of critical terms, many of which reflect sexual or homophobic perspectives.

This exercise can be powerful for identifying stereotypes and the impact of stereotypes on those who do not meet them; however, skillful facilitation is critical. A good facilitator can contain the abusive language generated in part two of the exercise and bring the debriefing around to a powerful yet positive message. Unfortunately, in the absence of skillful facilitation, the leader may have the group identify the derogatory terms and then move too quickly to the next exercise. Our colleague Dr. Ernest Jouriles saw a wide range of skill levels with this exercise when it was implemented in schools. We decided that the potential for harm, if the exercise was poorly facilitated, outweighed the benefit and therefore we did not include it in our program. Thus, a gender-strategic approach requires consideration of who is delivering an exercise, not merely its content.

In addition to students and teachers, school board personnel and parents are critical stakeholders, if somewhat removed from the day-to-day program. These groups are strong forces in determining the success of a program and need to be engaged. At times we have been criticized for not being more directive in our written materials (such as pamphlets) about specifically targeting violence against women and homophobia. Our response is that we attempt to craft our messages with each audience in mind. Furthermore, a written pamphlet is delivered without the important opportunity to challenge and discuss the information. Conversely, in a presentation we are more likely to tackle issues directly when we have the opportunity to engage the audience, establish credibility, and answer any questions. We are sensitive to avoiding a message that alienates a group with authority, such as parents or the school board, by delivering a partial or misleading message.

Summary

This chapter built on the previous two chapters by further elucidating specific strategies that fit best-practice principles for an integrated and comprehensive prevention program. Throughout this chapter we used examples from the Fourth R to illustrate ways to build skills, empower youth, and mobilize a comprehensive approach. In discussing the most effective ways to build skills that adolescents will use, we highlighted the importance of providing information, fostering the development of behavioral skills, and increasing motivation.

We also discussed youth empowerment and leadership strategies, with the note that attempts should be made to engage a range of youth in these activities and not merely those who tend to be leaders in most domains. Providing social action and leadership opportunities for youth who may feel marginalized in the school setting creates an alternate experience for these youth and a sense of mastery in a domain in which they may not otherwise feel very successful. A comprehensive approach—involving parents, teachers, and the whole school setting —was identified. Parents' involvement requires thoughtful consideration of the developmental task of individuation. That is, adolescents will not welcome perceived overinvolvement and interference by parents. Information dissemination to parents may provide an effective balance between excluding them, on the one hand, and involving them to the extent that adolescents feel resentful, on the other hand. Teachers and other school personnel need support to fully engage in prevention initiatives and create a social epidemic based on promotion of healthy relationships and youth involvement.

Building skills that support adolescents to make healthy choices is a multidimensional endeavor. We used Fisher et al.'s Information-Motivation-Behavior Model to highlight the importance of these various components. Although information is the component that tends to be targeted most often, it is typically presented in a way that fails to appreciate issues such as cognitive authority of the information source, social inoculation, and the importance of interactive delivery. Effective behavioral skills training requires practice and opportunities to see others practice to increase both competence and self-efficacy. Motivation, which can be targeted individually or through the use of peers, helps adolescents put all the pieces together to make healthy choices in their peer and dating relationships. Most of all, adolescents require ongoing opportunities to practice resolving difficult situations in a range of areas as well as in the face of realistic resistance.

Youth empowerment and leadership opportunities are central to the notion of positive youth development. These opportunities help youth go beyond preventing negative behaviors to help develop abilities that will provide youth with important skills for adulthood. Furthermore, this approach uses youth as an important resource in preventing negative health behaviors. To truly engage adolescents, an understanding of their gender development is critical. The goal of a gender-strategic approach is to engage them on issues of gender and challenge their perceptions without alienating them at the outset. Chapter 9 extends this theme of comprehensive programming and explores barriers and solutions for implementing sustainable, integrated programming.

9

The Context
Overcoming Barriers and Engaging Schools

In the previous chapters we described emerging research on the critical aspects of adolescence and promising prevention approaches. This information was integrated into a model of intervention that combines best practices in building youth capacity while addressing specific risk behaviors. Given the underlying theme of relationships, it is possible to integrate substance use and sexual health programs into a larger safety and violence-prevention framework for this age group. We also identified the natural fit between these activities and the school setting, which is an ideal forum for promoting healthy relationships when all partners collaborate in this process.

The systems pieces that are necessary to implement the strategies discussed in the previous three chapters are the focus of this chapter. We review ways in which this ideal can become a reality by helping students, teachers, parents, administrators, and community partners make a commitment to work toward the same goals. We start by identifying a number of barriers that prevent successful and sustainable implementation of comprehensive violence-prevention programs in the schools. We discuss the need for a paradigmatic approach to violence prevention in schools and introduce the Stage-Based School Change Model, using examples of innovative stage-based strategies.

Schools are increasingly being called on to help students develop good citizenship and character in addition to providing a foundation of academic skills. There are many advantages inherent in school-based prevention programming. The universal nature of the school experience allows for repeated opportunities over time to provide a foundation of relationship skills and nonviolent conflict resolution tactics. In addition, a comprehensive health-promotion approach that extends beyond a prevention model can be used: all youth can be taught these core skills, instead of addressing only those deemed to be at risk. The school setting is also the crucible in which peer socialization takes place. The inevitable peer conflicts provide the chance to foster adaptive or challenge maladaptive patterns that may have germinated in the home environment. Although the importance of school-based relationship skills promotion and violence prevention is widely accepted, there is a significant gap between the ideal prevention model and what currently exists in most schools.

The Barriers

The past decade witnessed a sharp rise in the number of programs developed to foster the skills-based approaches to reducing risk behaviors such as violence, binge drinking, and unsafe sex. Despite the availability of these programs, widespread adoption has not been achieved. Many of these programs have been short-lived, and their success has often depended on the enthusiasm and vision of a handful of dedicated staff. In some cases, a program lasts as long as the accompanying evaluation, then fizzles after the research team withdraws. In our experience, many motivated and committed teachers and administrators have worked to implement prevention programs, but despite their best efforts these programs often do not live up to their potential. We have identified nine barriers that limit the success and longevity of these programs.

Overlooking the Obvious: Violence in Relationships

Recent episodes of lethal violence in schools have made every parent, teacher, and student more aware of violence in schools and much more conscious of safety. Numerous initiatives have arisen, ranging from an attempt by the FBI to create a profile of a school shooter to specific inquests such as the one following the tragedy at Columbine High School in Littleton, Colorado. As questions of accountability and liability are raised, it is increasingly clear that school violence is being taken extremely seriously. Unfortunately, there is still much confusion about how to address this concern, and some efforts clearly miss the mark. The Columbine incident, in particular, led to a widespread feeling of "If it can happen there, it can happen anywhere." Columbine High School is an upper-middle-class suburban school with high scholastic standards. It is well known for the success of its athletic teams, and a large majority of its graduates go on to college. According to the commission report, the Columbine incident mirrored previous incidents of school shootings in that the perpetrators were students who had been bullied at school and who were seeking to kill students and teachers they knew (Erickson, 2001). The focus on seeking out pathological or deviant school shooters overlooks the importance of the day-to-day school climate and context in which the majority of violence is perpetrated.

This reality that youth are more likely to experience violence at the hands of somebody they know is at the heart of the Fourth R concept. The Fourth R is intended to draw attention to the importance of relationships, both in understanding violence and knowing how to prevent it. The majority of violence is inherently relational in nature: surveys in many countries indicate that children and youth are victimized by people they know and trust, not by strangers (Wolfe & Jaffe, 2001). Changing the norms and climate about relationships and providing students and teachers with the skills to foster healthy relationships is the most viable way to shift from a crisis orientation to one of prevention in response to school violence and similar concerns. Unfortunately, relationships remain the neglected "R" in most school settings.

Seeking the Quick Fix

For many years police departments and shelters for abused women have faced resistance as to the legitimacy of their involvement in schools. The good news is that now the role of schools is no longer debated; many educators want to be leaders in the effort against violence. The bad news is that people are still looking for quick solutions: find the bad kids and suspend or expel them and increase physical security and monitoring. The emphasis continues to be on extreme and stranger-perpetrated violence rather than the daily reality of bullying, harassment, and abuse in the context of peer and romantic relationships.

There has never been greater awareness of, and anxiety surrounding, the issue of violence. At the same time, we have never been more polarized in deciding how to respond—reactively or proactively. This controversy is mirrored in the highly politicized debate in the youth justice arena on rehabilitation and prevention versus getting tough with boot camps and stricter sanctions. Countless documents, such as the American Psychological Association Commission on Violence and Youth, recognize the potential for schools to become a leading force in providing programs to reduce and prevent violence in adolescence (American Psychological Association, 1993). However, this potential has not been fulfilled despite unprecedented funding in the area of violence prevention. Far from being at the cutting edge of promoting healthy relationships proactively, many school boards have become increasingly entrenched in reactive, security-driven approaches.

The Columbine Commission Report reflects this tension between reactivity and prevention (Erickson, 2001). On the one hand, the report dedicates large sections to providing guidelines for crisis response, including improving communication during a crisis, advanced planning for critical emergencies, and assigning police officers to schools. Other recommendations are more proactive in nature, and recognize that preventing violence will be an intensive, ongoing process. In particular, the report speaks to the need to encourage students to break the code of silence and to implement violence-prevention programs in all schools. The universal use of metal detectors, video surveillance, and other security equipment was unequivocally rejected as a way to deter school violence. While many of the recommendations center around a more effective response in critical emergencies, the report acknowledges that tighter security alone will not prevent further critical incidents from occurring.

Planting Seeds in Rock

Violence-prevention and health-promotion efforts need to have roots in the day-to-day life and general climate of the school. Schools cannot start a successful program on healthy eating to address obesity when the vending machines are full of pop and cake and there are no regular opportunities for physical activity. Similarly, a violence-prevention program may be futile in a school that tolerates daily acts of racism, sexism, and homophobia. Violence prevention is more than an assembly where kids "just say no to violence"; programs have to operate at all levels in the life of a school to ensure policies, practices, and daily activities are aligned with the spirit and content of the program messages.

Incorporated in this idea is adolescents' extreme sensitivity to perceived hypocrisy. Adolescents often take new learning experiences and apply them to the adults in their lives. For example, a comprehensive and integrated alcohol-prevention program will be undermined by a group of teachers talking about their drinking on the weekend. Similarly, presentations on violence against women are quickly undone by teachers' jokes or sexist comments. For far too many schools, the totality of their prevention efforts is receiving a binder of material, watching an entertaining video, or listening to an inspirational speaker. Our position is simply that any prevention program, even in a seedling stage, needs to target multiple levels to ensure fertile soil for long-term benefits to be realized.

Relying on the Charismatic Leader

Often one highly skilled and motivated person is responsible for programs brought into a school to prevent violence and other high-risk behaviors. This person may have sought additional training in the area and often works tirelessly to bring a particular program or set of activities to the school. Although having a leader in violence prevention and healthy relationships is an excellent idea, reliance on one key person may undermine success for several reasons. First, someone who excels in this area is a likely candidate for promotion to an administrative role. He or she might have an excellent program in a particular school, but once recruited to work at a larger level the program in the initial school may falter. Second, the burden on any one person trying to change a school climate and culture alone is overwhelming and raises the likelihood of burnout. Finally, the impact of one person, even if that person is talented and committed to making changes, will be limited as long as there are other teachers or staff in the school who are sending out opposing messages. Returning to the idea of a tipping point, early adopters are essential to serve as the vanguard of a new movement, but a critical mass of people who share the same ideas is what tips an idea from a fad to a sustainable reality.

Getting Rid of the Bad Kids

The term "zero tolerance" evokes a get-tough sentiment that has been politically well received. This concept has been widely applied in a number of campaigns to reduce and eliminate high-risk behaviors at a societal level, such as antidrug campaigns and drinking and driving efforts. The application of the term in relation to violence was introduced to the Canadian public in 1993 in the final report of the Canadian Panel on Violence against Women (Marshall & Vaillancourt, 1993). Adopting a zero tolerance policy was defined as "making a firm commitment to the philosophy that no amount of violence is acceptable, and that adequate resources must be made available to eliminate violence and achieve equality" (p. 25). It is clear from this definition that zero tolerance was meant as an end goal, not simply as a reactive punishment-oriented stance. The concept of accountability is an inherent part of zero tolerance, but zero tolerance was also envisioned to encapsulate a proactive strategy. The misapplication of zero tolerance has been brought to the forefront by front-page stories of 8-year-old students being suspended from school for trying to kiss a girl or bringing a war relic to class for show-and-tell. A better application of zero tolerance would be for adults to respond in an age-appropriate manner to any incident of abuse or violence, gauging their response to the circumstances and the seriousness of the incident. For example, a teacher in the classroom would rebuke inappropriate language and behavior and respond to even minor incidents with firm conviction and respectful language.

The adoption of zero tolerance language in school systems has focused on the first part of the definition (a commitment that violence is unacceptable), while largely ignoring the second part (the commitment of resources to a proactive, wide-scale behavior-change strategy). The ideal application of zero tolerance to violence has to include all aspects of society, including schools, parenting, interpersonal conflict resolution, and the media and entertainment industries (Sudermann, Jaffe, & Schieck, 1996). Unfortunately, this vision of accountability and mobilization on the part of all segments of society has been reduced to a policy of expulsions and sanctions, despite evidence against such strategies as deterrents of violent behavior (USPHS, 2000). Furthermore, there is evidence from the ADD Health Study in the United States that zero tolerance exacts a cost on school connectedness. An analysis of 127 schools from the ADD Health database demonstrated that students in schools with zero tolerance policies (as defined by harsh punishments for first infractions) felt *less* safe and *less* connected to their schools than students in schools without these policies (McNeely et al., 2002).

Collateral Damage—The Cost of Insufficient Follow-Through

Schools are asked to take on many social problems. The average high school in North America is bombarded with requests from educators and community members to address issues ranging from eating disorders to suicide. Most requests are founded on the premise that one inspirational speaker or classroom presentation will go a long way to solving complex problems. Although well intentioned, most presentations fall short of their goals because they lack a thoughtful plan on how this material will be integrated over the long haul through repeated presentations, integration into curriculum, teacher preparation, administrative and school resource support, and school policies.

Several years ago an outstanding play on dating violence and sexual abuse was touring Ontario. A neighboring school district, anxious not to miss out on the opportunity, scheduled the play as a last event on a Friday afternoon. However, there was no opportunity for students to debrief with staff or specialized counselors about this emotionally provocative experience and no preparation for the parents to deal with adolescents' reactions and discussion at the dinner table. A wonderful opportunity turned into painful experience for many adolescents and the significant adults in their lives. In other words, poor planning and integration of prevention efforts can result in limited success or adverse consequences.

Although the school community might assume that any prevention activities are better than none, the potential for unintended negative effects must be kept in mind. Unfortunately, these negative experiences can be powerful deterrents for future initiatives. School personnel may prematurely conclude that such programs don't work, instead of realizing that the particular program was not implemented with enough planning, integration, and follow-through to be successful. Prevention efforts need to begin with the end goals in mind, which include sustained efforts by educators, parents, and students to carry the message into the future.

Teacher Morale and Mandate

There has never been greater pressure on teachers and school systems to maximize success of all students in academic areas. Many states and provinces have made education a priority and have enhanced accountability through standardized testing, despite decreasing funding and support. As a result, the morale in many staff rooms has suffered, and the threat of strikes, work to rule, and conflicts among education partners has become the norm. Within this climate it is not surprising that teachers are resistant to take on new challenges, such as prevention programs, and that they may feel overwhelmed with their existing mandate.

Many prevention programs have a limited understanding of the education system and the struggles within individual schools. Without such an understanding programs cannot take root. The gap between the focus of prevention and teachers' mandate is particularly pronounced in high school, when educators focus most on individual subject areas and implementing challenging new curricula. Solutions include listening to teachers and the reality of their jobs, finding ways to implement programs within existing initiatives and curricula rather than making everything a new add-on, producing teacher-friendly material, and promoting the benefits of such materials in creating safe, effective learning environments.

Lack of Community Involvement, Parental Support, and Student Ownership

Teachers are most likely to be supportive when they feel prevention programs are part of an overall community plan. A program that is dumped on a teacher's lap as a new responsibility will likely have limited success. Conversely, a program that represents a community interest and is supported by committed parents, enthusiastic students, and community organizations has a high probability of success. Engagement is a process, rather than a one-time event or meeting. This process has to recognize the varying stages of change on social issues, which may range from denial that a problem exists to a deep commitment to sustained action. Prevention programs based on a one-size-fits-all model fail to recognize the need for engaging each of the partners with individualized strategies. In contrast, an approach that assesses the progress and needs of each of the partners and matches these unique circumstances will be more successful at meaningfully engaging all of a community's relevant resources. Aside from the concern that a program will fall flat, there may be backlash to these fledgling efforts that creates animosity for future efforts. For example, a program on violence against women that fails to recognize the different challenges in engaging boys and men may engender hostility and resistance to future related activities. Although discomfort may be part of the process of shifting attitudes and behaviors, adverse reactions at the outset ruin potential partnerships that may represent the foundation for future program accomplishments.

Overcompartmentalization

Many early prevention efforts were driven by external groups or community agencies bringing their message to students, and as such represented specific agendas. For example, the local council on antiracism may have begun efforts for tolerance in parallel with a women's shelter introducing a program on violence against women. Although early efforts were critical forerunners in bringing social issues to the school setting, the result was sometimes a series of disjointed, compartmentalized awareness-raising activities. It is not uncommon for schools to have separate antihate weeks, sexual harassment activities, bullying programs, and date rape education, each totally disconnected from the others. The result both minimizes the impact of any one campaign and overwhelms teachers and students with the demands of each event. With research-based projects, the compartmentalization has another component—university versus school-based—further diminishing a sense of ownership for projects by the school community. There is a need for an integrated, comprehensive approach that provides a background context for all of these other activities. Our position is that the theme of healthy relationships underscores all of these other domains and can be used as the unifying ingredient.

The Solutions

There are many challenges to implementing meaningful and sustainable programs. Although many well-intentioned educators or parents try to initiate innovative programs, without a thoughtful analysis of how to approach schools and communities in the change process they are doomed to a short shelf life. It is clear that the issue is not simply one of resources or programs—within a particular school board there may be considerable disparity in the extent to which individual schools embrace available opportunities for violence prevention. What accounts for these differences among schools, and why is it such a struggle to get violence-prevention and other risk-reduction initiatives incorporated into school systems in an ongoing, self-sustaining manner? We think there are six main ingredients to achieving this long-term success: understanding how systems change, matching strategies to stage of change, differentiated programming, teacher training, mobilizing the community, and engaging and empowering students.

Understanding the Change Process

Change is not one step but a series of transitions, each of which requires particular strategies. One of the most empirically supported models for explaining change is the Transtheoretical Model of Change (TTM), which was developed to provide a framework for explaining the way that individuals make significant behavioral change, particularly in health-related behaviors (J. O. Prochaska & DiClemente, 1983). The TTM was founded on the premise that individuals move through predictable stages when undertaking behavioral change. Each stage is different from the others in terms of an individual's "readiness" to take action. In addition, individuals are expected to move through the stages with intermittent regression to previous stages before progressing onward; thus the process is seen as somewhat iterative in nature. Research demonstrates that matching particular change strategies to each individual stage of change increases success and decreases dropout rates across a wide range of targeted behaviors (J. O. Prochaska & Velicer, 1997).

Briefly, these stages include a precontemplation stage, in which individuals are not planning to act in the foreseeable future. They may be insufficiently informed about the consequences of their behavior or deny that the behavior poses a problem. During the contemplation stage, individuals recognize they have a problem and intend to change within the next six months. When they reach the preparation stage, persons intend to take action in the immediate future and have likely already taken some significant action within the past year. By the action stage, people make specific, observable changes in their overt behavior, and in the final maintenance stage, they are less tempted to relapse and more confident of their ability to sustain their behavioral change.

The Transtheoretical Model arose as a conceptual model for charting change primarily in health-related behavior such as smoking, exercise, and diet, and it has been expanded to include change in social issues such as violence perpetration through validation of the model with men involved in batterer treatment (Levesque, Gelles, & Velicer, 2000; Scott & Wolfe, 2003). The success of the TTM to explain change in a wide range of problem domains suggests a robustness of the model independent of the problem under consideration. Most efforts at change within organizations are unsuccessful because they are attempted without recognition of the principles of change (J. M. Prochaska, Prochaska, & Levesque, 2001).

While the Transtheoretical Model of Change provides a useful framework for change in general, it requires some adaptation and elaboration to fit the case of school-based prevention initiatives. We de-

Table 9.1 Readiness to address school violence: Comparison of stage characteristics in the Stage-Based School Change Model and the Transtheoretical Model of Change

Stage-Based School Change Model	Transtheoretical Model	Generic prototype in Transtheoretical Model	Unique characteristics in school-based violence prevention
Inertia	Precontemplation	Denial of problem Lack of acceptance of negative consequences associated with *not* changing	Silence (can exist at all levels of stakeholders) Hopelessness, helplessness Ignorance: violence seen as random, discrete acts by bad individuals
Naming the problem	Contemplation	Awareness that problem exists Realization of need for change	Articulated commitment to address violence in school community Perception of violence broadens to concept of it as a widespread community problem Recognition that schools play an integral role in perpetuating or addressing violence in the larger community Awareness that remedies exist and change is possible
Understanding the problem	Preparation	Preparing to make change in immediate future	Three components to understanding how to address violence: Role of behavioral expectations and sanctions Reality that most violence occurs in relationships

Program and policy development	Action	Phase where observable action and attempts to change are evident	Violence as a complex, multiply determined social issue (role of family, media, peers) Directly linked to how violence is understood Obedience model Skill-based healthy relationship–promotion model for all students; appropriate services for victims and perpetrators Need to influence multiple systems and intervene before problems are entrenched Recognition of need for differential interventions by gender, cultural groups, experience with violence, community realities
Integration and accountability	Maintenance	Relapse prevention	Integrated policies and goals Community collaboration among parents, community agencies, students, and school staff Clearly articulated responsibilities at both school and system levels Evaluation of programs Ongoing cycle of feedback and refinements Annual report cards documenting progress and needs for improvement

Sources: Jaffe et al. (2004). Used with permission. The Stage-Based School Change Model is from Sudermann et al. (1996); the Transtheoretical Model of Change is from J. O. Prochaska & DiClemente (1983).

vised the Stage-Based School Change Model, which delineates the steps that a school must navigate to effectively target violence: inertia, naming the problem, understanding the problem, program and policy development, and integration and accountability (Jaffe et al., 2004; Sudermann et al., 1996). The characteristics of each step are described in table 9.1. The importance of this stage-based model lies in the problems that emerge when one attempts to implement a complex, best-practices model with a system that is not ready. The comprehensive approach that is described in the previous three chapters requires substantial investment from a wide range of people. A school that is not ready for this type of commitment will not have success trying to implement such an intensive program and might be better served by attempting some smaller activities initially to build momentum. Different strategies are indicated based on the stage of readiness to change. However, before the appropriate strategies can be chosen, the processes of change need to be further described.

Applying the Stage-Based School Change Model provides two clear advantages over the current one-size-fits-all approach to school-based intervention. First, the model leads to a theoretically informed assessment tool to categorize schools into the different readiness-to-change stages. A second advantage of the model is that it provides clear guidelines and empirical support for working with resistance to change, based on two decades of research with the TTM. Application of this model, in combination with a validated assessment tool, increases our capacity to meet schools at their current place on the change continuum. By developing the flexibility to meet individual schools' needs in a systematic, theoretically informed manner, there is less likelihood of overwhelming schools and inadvertently feeding their resistance to change. The model consists of five phases:

Inertia. In this phase, there is silence about violence as a problem, and stakeholders at all levels may be overwhelmed by feelings of helplessness or hopelessness. The inertia phase is different from the standard precontemplation phase in that the latter is defined by the lack of awareness that a problem exists. In the case of violence, schools are largely past the stage where they do not recognize the problem exists. Another characteristic of the inertia phase is recognizing that violence exists but conceptualizing it as random, discrete acts on the part of individuals who are either mentally ill or inherently bad. Schools that focus all of their resources on detecting troublemakers are usually in the inertia phase. Such schools might react swiftly and severely to transgressions but minimize their own role in promoting healthy relationships and preventing violence.

Naming the problem. In this phase a school's perception of violence broadens to the concept of violence as a widespread community problem rather than the acts of a few disturbed individuals. This stage would also be the point at which a given school becomes aware that remedies exist and change is possible and makes a commitment to address violence in the school community. Inherent to this stage is recognizing that schools play an integral role in perpetuating or addressing violence in the larger community. One feature identified as a necessary prerequisite for schools ready to change is the presence of a leader, often the principal, who is committed to the process (Stephens, 1998). Without someone willing to take a leadership role, a school would get stuck in the inertia phase, perhaps making brief, vague attempts to move forward.

Understanding the problem. This phase includes developing three types of understanding: (1) school staff and administration need to understand the role of behavioral expectations and sanctions in preventing violence; (2) staff and administration need to recognize that most violence occurs in relationships; and (3) a school must conceptualize violence as a complex, multiply determined social issue, with an appreciation of the roles played by family, media, and peers. Schools in this phase may be developing an awareness of the overlap of the links between violence and other risk behaviors. Schools collect information about different programs and attempt to determine a suitable course of action. Committees, focus groups, and teams are hallmarks of this stage, and these groups ideally include members of the different systems such as students, teachers, administrators, and parents. The multiple components of understanding serve as the foundation for this preparatory work; if a school understands only the role of sanctions in deterring behavior, then it will prepare a program focusing only on the implementation of such sanctions.

Program and policy development. This phase is characterized by overt activity, including psychoeducational components, policy review, poster competitions, displays, newsletters, and a high degree of teacher, administrator, parent, and student involvement. By definition this stage is time-limited; even though there will be ongoing effort, the intensity of the activity level characteristic of this phase cannot be maintained indefinitely. The type of actions that a school chooses to engage in during the program and policy development phase stems directly from the complexity of understanding achieved previously. For example, a school that understands violence simply as an act of aggression that should be punished will focus on developing sanction protocols but perhaps miss the opportunity for skill development and the promotion of healthy, positive relationships.

Integration and accountability. Schools in this phase still participate in special events such as those mentioned above, but most of the activities are self-sustaining. Skill-building activities integrated into a curriculum or regular meetings of a social action club are examples of activities in this category. In comparison with schools in the previous phases, these schools might not appear as outwardly busy in their pursuit of violence prevention primarily because many of the activities are seamlessly integrated into the everyday routine of the school. In addition to program integration, there is integration between parties such as parents, teachers, and the school board, and among policies for related issues such as sexual harassment and bullying. Inherent to the accountability part of this phase is the notion that success in this area has to be measured and it has to matter. Schools have a strong commitment to ongoing surveillance and reassessment of their status with respect to violence prevention. Annual report cards document progress and needs for improvement, comparable to standardized testing in core academic areas, and provide a mechanism for this accountability. Finally, these schools provide a supportive role for schools that are in an earlier stage in the change process.

Matching Interventions to the Stage of Change

The strength of a stage-based theory of change lies in its prescriptive nature. In other words, program developers are offered a framework to enhance the likelihood their initiatives will be successful by matching strategies to the particular stage. Schools at different phases of the change process require different types of interventions. Below we provide examples of innovative strategies to illustrate the types of interventions required at each phase of the Stage-Based School Change Model.

The processes required of a school in the inertia phase include dramatic relief, self-reevaluation, and thinking about commitment. Dramatic relief is described as the process wherein emotional arousal, such as fear about failure to change or excitement about possibility of change, is targeted to increase motivation (J. M. Prochaska et al., 2001). It is essentially the process of helping a school see that it cannot afford *not* to change. A variety of performing arts–based activities can be used to evoke these emotions. Students perform plays written by students and teachers to challenge people to think about violence, followed by discussion groups led by trained university student facilitators. Another activity is to have students view a film, such as *A Love That Kills* (National Film Board of Canada, 1999), accompanied by facilitated discussion. *A Love That Kills* is based on the true story of a young woman in an abusive relationship who was eventually murdered by her boyfriend. The young woman's mother, Dawna Speers, has developed six lesson plans to complement the video and help youth identify warning signs of abusive relationships and make responsible choices (www.speerssociety.org). Both the drama presentations and the video tend to stimulate emotional reactions in students and staff, and in this capacity help to generate momentum regarding the need to change.

During the understanding the problem phase, the core need is to shift people's thinking about violence away from an emphasis on violent individuals who must be punished and more toward an understanding of the numerous factors involved. One way to approach this phase is to present people who are further along the readiness-to-act spectrum with opportunities to think about plans and share ideas with others. Participation in major conferences is one way to achieve this aim. We hosted a recent conference that attracted over 950 delegates, with 170 individuals presenting from 19 countries. Concurrent with this conference a special initiative for grade 11 students was organized to allow students to meet and discuss domestic and dating violence as well as to develop a plan for violence prevention. Developing these plans demanded a higher level of insight about the causes of violence and the multiple factors that are involved.

Most schools have a safe-schools policy document that outlines pertinent policies and procedures to ensure student safety. However, schools in the program and policy development phase often require additional resources and strategies that seek to balance the focus on rule compliance with a greater focus on student skills development. One of the hallmarks of this transition is developing programs of suffi-cient dosage and duration—these activities need to be more than one-time events. At the same time there has to be an alignment of school policies with the new learning material being developed. For example, violence occurring off school property or after school hours should re-main a concern of educators.

The integration part of the final phase refers to collaboration among the different systems and stakeholders, including parents, teachers, students, police, community agencies. Policies and programs need to be integrated with each other and into the fabric of the school community. This type of integration means shifting away from ad-dressing different types of issues as separate policies or one-day events, such as sexual harassment, bullying, racism, and dating violence, and moving toward a comprehensive program to build a school climate of respect and positive relationships. One indication of the level of inte-gration is the provision of a full-time violence-prevention coordinator for the school board and a dedicated link on the school board website to update people about current violence-prevention initiatives. These indications of an infrastructure to support violence prevention facili-tate ongoing progress and convey a permanency and commitment to the violence-prevention effort. Integration also includes networking between schools and community agencies and between schools that are at different points along the change continuum. The Forum The-atre program discussed in chapter 8 is one vehicle for students' ability in a particular school to help raise awareness at other schools.

The accountability facet of the final phase stresses that a commit-ment to violence prevention must be monitored. Clearly articulated spheres of responsibility throughout the whole system are necessary, and an annual report card outlining progress and remaining weak-nesses should be implemented. For example, having violence-prevention curricula that are credit courses is one way of attaching value to student endeavors. In keeping with the health-promotion concept, schools that go beyond the bare minimum deserve extra recognition. Although the concept of a scorecard can be threatening to school administrators, the idea is more palatable if the audit is linked to solutions. A school board recently struck a committee to develop a school-based audit to track the progress of individual schools with respect to violence prevention. Based on this audit, schools were identified as being at a particular stage of change, and recommendations for programming were suggested (Crooks, Hughes, Dale, & Homuth, 2004). This audit process serves an accountability function (that is, schools can be monitored over time) and also provides practical suggestions for improving violence-prevention programming at a particular school.

Differentiated Programs

Schools are not homogeneous, and the variety of audiences within a school community requires differentiated strategies. For example, we have noted the pervasive differences in the ways boys and girls are socialized, which become more exaggerated during adolescence when youth adhere to rigid gender roles. Boys are socialized to be more accepting of abusive and violent behavior and maintain a code of silence around victimization experiences, while girls are socialized to value relationships and provide supportive networks (Pollack, 1998). If programs ignore these critical differences in basic socialization, the message may not be heard or active resistance may ensue.

Although adolescent girls enjoy the opportunity to explore and discuss relationships, extra effort is often required to engage boys. Important ways to engage boys include providing them with more action-oriented activities, structuring opportunities for them to be socially reinforced for engaging in roles that do not follow the rigid gender code (for example, social action committees and awards events), and being prepared to work with them at whatever stage they are in terms of thinking about gender roles and violence (Crooks, Goodall et al., 2004). Adolescent boys may be alienated by the traditional feminist approach that focuses on power and control and the need to recognize male privilege as a starting point. Although we aspire to have all adolescents develop an appreciation of larger societal and systemic gender inequalities, we also recognize the need to engage students by making the material relevant to their current level of understanding. It is important to create an environment in which issues of gender and violence can be openly discussed and explored. A punitive environment that discourages questions may result in youth staying quiet and losing the opportunity to develop insight into these important issues.

As vital as gender is to understanding cultural diversity within and between schools, emerging research examines how various cultures identify social problems and what types of strategies are most acceptable to these different groups. A youth empowerment approach must provide opportunities to develop in ways consistent with their values and culture. For example, in schools with a significant number of First Nation students, prevention and promotion strategies have to be holistic in their approach and engage the larger community, including elders. In addition, materials can be adapted so the innovative components remain intact, while the content changes accordingly. In other words, while role-plays are an integral part of the Fourth R approach, the *content* of the role-plays can be adapted to be more relevant to different cultural and geographically defined groups of students. This type of adaptation has already been successfully demonstrated with the Life Skills Training (LST) program. In LST, role-play scenarios, language, and graphics were adapted for various groups of youth without affecting the significant positive impact of the program (Botvin et al., 1995).

In addition to the cultural makeup of a school and the importance of gender-specific programming, there is also a diversity of needs with respect to the level of problems individual students are already experiencing. Universal prevention provides an excellent foundation on which to build future resilience for all students. However, for some students their needs already surpass the limitations of a universal prevention approach. The extent to which universal programs have a positive impact on youths already engaging in high levels of risk behavior or struggling with clinical levels of psychopathology has been a subject of debate. Regardless of whether or not these youths benefit from universal prevention, it is doubtful that this approach would meet the needs of everyone. Schools need to have a strong universal prevention program as a foundation, coupled with additional services for those at various levels of risk. These services should range from early identification of problems that require additional resources to help for troubled students who need an array of services or alternative classrooms to meet their needs. These systems should be integrated so the universal program can provide a screening and identification process.

Finally, successful adaptation also requires engaging the wider community as the project is disseminated. In our experience violence-prevention programs take on a life of their own beyond initial printed materials and videos. Programs stimulate active discussion about local needs and unique issues within different cultural communities. A successful program can flourish when there is investment by students, parents, educators, and community services dedicated to youth. For example, as the Fourth R is disseminated to other school boards across the country, we have developed partnerships with research and education representatives. These representatives are themselves associated with dozens of other individuals and organizations committed to harm reduction and youth safety. Engaging these partners so they are able to make a significant contribution to the adaptations of the program to their local community leads to more meaningful collaboration.

Teacher Preparation and Training

Many program developers naively assume that a new initiative will be met with enthusiasm as it is parachuted into the school. In reality, educators need a strong foundation of understanding and collaboration to support the success of any new program. The cornerstones for this foundation include orientation to raise awareness about the role and relevance of prevention in the school setting, training to enhance skills and comfort level, developing champions within the school to deal with the critics, and building partnerships with community agencies and researchers to share the burden.

The Fourth R begins with an orientation and motivational session that includes clear links to government-mandated curricula, background information about experimental risk behaviors, and the manner in which these behaviors may exert a negative impact on learning. It is critical to link the aims of the program to the audience's mandate. By sharing such results with teachers, healthy relationships and school safety are elevated from the vague realm of mental health professionals to that of a core academic issue. Information needs to target each audience specifically and engage the various stakeholders through issues important to that particular group. Skills-based training provides teachers with opportunities to practice the activities they will be required to implement. Teachers are much more comfortable teaching the substance use and sexual health components of our program, largely because they have been teaching versions of this for a number of years. Their comfort level with the violence-prevention and more interactive components appears to increase with opportunities for practice and feedback. Furthermore, practicing the interactive components, such as role-play facilitation, is critical because these interactive and innovative components are the ones most likely to be dropped in an unmonitored implementation (Ennett et al., 2003).

The success of any program requires leaders in the school to develop a sense of ownership and commitment. Schools that have a program champion tend to implement programs with more fidelity than those without (Fagan & Mihalic, 2003). In our previous systemwide violence-prevention efforts, we identified two key staff members in every school who received specialized training. As part of this training they were given strategies to respond to the naysayers who actively undermine new initiatives in their schools (Sudermann et al., 1996). This leadership role is validated when community partners arrive at the school to support new programs with funding, expertise, and high levels of enthusiasm.

Researchers and community agency representatives trying to develop supportive working relationships with professionals in the education system should be vigilant for opportunities to provide service back to the school system. Researchers in particular have at times engendered resentment for engaging in "drive-by" research (Denner, Cooper, Lopez, & Dunbar, 1999). School-based professionals can be left feeling exploited or undervalued when the focus of the relationship is on the opportunities that school systems can provide researchers. There are many simple ways for researchers to be good partners. Our team regularly accepts speaking engagements at the request of teachers, and when we collect data from a school we generate an attractive report of tables and graphs for administrators, providing them with a snapshot of what is going on at their schools. We also organize and sponsor social events to honor the contributions made by teachers and administrators. Most important, we try to convey an air of respect for the numerous demands that teachers have on their time. We keep meetings short, stick to an agenda, and try to keep correspondence to a minimum.

Mobilizing the Community

Although there is tremendous pressure on schools to go back to the basics in student achievement that can be measured across states and countries, there are also competing forces encouraging educators to look at the whole student and recognize his or her complex needs. Some argue that to ignore these needs puts students at risk for later social and emotional adjustment problems, at a cost to society (Bennett & Offord, 1998; Zins, Weissberg, Wang, & Walberg, 2004). At the forefront of this argument are community agencies that work with at-risk youth in the justice, mental health, social service, and health systems. The professionals in these agencies recognize the value of prevention and early identification efforts as well as the ideal forum that schools offer for these initiatives. Fueling this trend are parents who are increasingly anxious about the headlines they read about date rape, drugs, bullying, and school shootings.

The success of mobilizing communities lies in aligning the interests of parents, students, and community service providers with those of forward-thinking educators. The enthusiasm for this involvement by community agencies can be overwhelmingly positive. In one of our first attempts to increase the presence of community agencies in schools, we made a request for service providers to help facilitate programs on dating violence in five schools. Although we were warned we would likely not find enough facilitators, we received over 80 volunteers from 25 agencies and were forced to turn away many others. It is not the enthusiasm or even mandate that is lacking; rather, specific activities and opportunities are needed to provide a focus and a structure for these fledgling cooperative events.

Engaging and Empowering Students

It is hard to conceive of any successful prevention program directed toward adolescents that does not look to them for leadership. Adolescents turn to their peers first for any problem. As soon as they get the impression that programs are lectures from adults about how to live their lives, the message and the messenger are lost. Accordingly, prevention is not something that is done *to* adolescents, nor is adolescence a public health problem that should be prevented. Rather, we need to find meaningful ways to engage adolescents, helping them to develop leadership skills and to use these skills to promote health and safety among their peers. One way to engage students in the area of violence prevention is having older students write plays and perform them for grade 7 and 8 students who visit the high school. The older students are trained to facilitate discussions with the younger ones on the topics raised by the performance, such as bullying, sexual harassment, and dating violence. The grade 7 and 8 students are raptly attentive to the words of wisdom dispensed by their older peers. The mentors develop higher levels of awareness by virtue of writing and performing a play, and they become part of the solution and ongoing agents of social change.

Summary

As the missing piece in current educational approach, relationships (the Fourth R) are crucial both to understanding violence and to countering violence in our schools. In this chapter we identified existing barriers to achieving integrated and sustainable programs that are based on empirical evidence.

Implementing comprehensive prevention programs in schools and communities is very new, and many important barriers need to be recognized and addressed. Many schools and educators suffer from significant problems related to funding and competing priorities. There are debates about the role of schools in this area and whether sticking to the basics is all that is appropriate for the educational environment. Too many school districts define violence prevention as simply providing cameras and security guards, to the exclusion of a proactive approach. Many individuals seek a quick fix or ride the tail of an enthusiastic leader for a short period of time. These are not programs built for success. We believe that success has to begin with an understanding that schools and school districts range in their preparation and readiness to take on prevention programs.

We proposed the Stage-Based School Change Model as a helpful framework to examine the programs most likely to work in different circumstances. The paradigm's ability to match particular interventions to the needs of different stages along the change continuum underscores its usefulness. The Stage-Based School Change Model approach to linking the needs of schools to specific types of interventions is merely the first step in customized intervention. The next step in this pursuit of flexible and responsive interventions will be the provision of a menu of options for different segments within a school body that may have unique requirements based on differences in culture, experience with violence, or gender. A careful needs assessment that identifies different groups within a school that may be at different stages along the readiness-to-act spectrum will lead to a multitiered approach that meets the prevention and intervention needs of each of these groups.

In our view, the keys to overcoming barriers are clear. Beyond the framework offered by the change model, prevention programs need teachers who are invested and prepared for this endeavor. There is a fundamental need for teacher training and the fostering of leadership opportunities as much in this area as in other aspects of the school's life. The community needs to be mobilized in its commitment, both by parents and by the many volunteers in community agencies eager to collaborate with educators. Finally, programs have to engage youth's energies and beliefs that these issues belong to them and future generations and are not adults imposing themselves on the adolescent's world.

10

The Evolution of Universal Efforts to Reduce Adolescent Risk Behaviors

We approached this book from a developmental perspective that informs prevention strategies for youth. In the first half of the book, we traced the importance of relationship development from infancy to adolescence, describing the continuity in how relationships evolve and become an essential centerpiece of how children and youth develop. The importance of gender identity and gender role expectations in the development of both healthy and abusive relationships was emphasized and reemerged in our discussion of the pressures to conform during early adolescence. Major theories were examined to understand why some adolescents develop risky behavior and others are more successful at keeping themselves safe. We then shifted the focus to pulling together these theories into practical strategies, drawing on innovative approaches that are integrated and comprehensive. The how-to focus in the second half of the book included ways to motivate youth and caring adults in learning successful ways to manage the known risks of adolescence.

Adolescence is a critical stage of development for strengthening interpersonal skills and learning to navigate more challenging pressures and responsibilities. The changes that occur during adolescence—socially, physically, and cognitively—make it a valuable window of opportunity for teaching about healthy relationships and establishing a foundation for informed decision making. Much like the well-validated finding that the first few years of development are extremely important in learning to relate to others, early adolescence offers similar opportunities for growth and adjustment to new demands. Relationship patterns are shaped from an early age, but they remain flexible and adaptable throughout adolescence. The manner in which children and youth look to others for support and advice, and relate to others in positive or negative ways, can be significantly altered during the trials and tribulations of adolescence. Accordingly, adolescence is an ideal time to provide various opportunities to learn about the central role of relationships in helping youth cope with unfamiliar pressures and enjoy new prospects. Building the skills necessary for youth to develop these healthy relationships must be the centerpiece of prevention efforts. Furthermore, building on strengths for those who already have strong relationship skills will help them develop further capacity for later challenges.

In approaching solutions to the risks associated with adolescent experimentation, we argued for integrated strategies that address such behaviors more realistically. A fundamental point is that risk behaviors share common causes and coexist in the context of peer and romantic relationships. Therefore, harm reduction and healthy choices involve engaging the adolescent holistically in seeking ways to manage the vast amount of peer pressure and expectations. This view opposes addressing each problem area as if it were independent, advocating a more integrated, comprehensive education strategy. The underlying context of peer and dating relationships provides the crucial link among risk behaviors and must be a part of a more comprehensive approach to addressing the complexity of adolescents' lives.

As societal institutions come to understand that most forms of abuse and violence occur within the context of relationships, considerable progress is being made in identifying risk factors that are amenable to change or elimination, such as gender rigidity, bullying, and early sexual activity. Yet, policies and actions still remain overly focused on controlling adolescent behavior through scare tactics, zero tolerance policies, and harsh consequences for violations. Although rules and enforcement are necessary and important, they must be ac-

companied by developmentally relevant and proactive education to assist youth in healthy decision making and harm avoidance. Such education needs to involve youth in all aspects of planning and implementation and exploit the strengths of youth culture and their eagerness
to seek reasonable solutions. Contemporary approaches to engaging
youth identify risk factors and strive to reduce their potency rather
than waiting for signs of trouble. They place a stronger emphasis on
helping youth succeed and draw upon the resources of youth and their
important institutions to maximize their chances of success.

Thirty Years into a Hundred-Year Process of Change

One of the founders of the domestic violence movement in the United
States, Minnesota's Ellen Pence, often reminds her audiences that
changes in the field are analogous to being at the 30-year mark in a 100-
year process of social change. This insight is an important reminder in
dealing with both the frustration and elation in developing prevention
strategies for youth. We have the accumulated wisdom that comes
from years of successes and failures. This wisdom gives us a sense of historical perspective in abandoning a search for simple or quick solutions
and instead embracing a commitment for social change in the com-
pany of a community of partners. We have attempted to capture this
process in this book by blending the burgeoning literature on adolescent development with the most recent findings on key ingredients for
effective prevention efforts.

Almost 30 years ago we began our careers in searching for ways to
end violence in the family. We had thought that by working with abusive parents and children exposed to domestic violence we could develop sustainable strategies to prevent such occurrences. We quickly
learned that these problems were part of a much larger social context.
These families had much in common with families not yet identified
by official agencies in charge of child protection and domestic violence. A meaningful approach to addressing these issues had to involve
the entire community and actively engage future generations in establishing broad-based education and prevention programs. Although we
are not alone in our commitment to prevention, we remain close to the
starting gate in terms of developing the best strategies, tools, and fund-

ing sources. Prevention and health promotion, unfortunately, lag far behind in priority to current crises and needs. It is our hope that the prevention ideas offered throughout this book will become a greater priority for every community.

Early adolescence is a key point in development because of the transition from the family to the peer group. Adolescents seek information and skills to make choices that will keep them connected to both, but they are sensitive to messages that are blaming or judgmental. Early adolescence is an ideal time to introduce positive alternatives to teens when they are faced with the competing pressures from families and peers and help them make healthy, positive choices. Helping all teens navigate this critical transition period is a worthy goal, regardless of their past experiences with violence or abuse. Adolescence is a perfect time to introduce education and skills that promote healthy relationships, and most teens are interested in learning alternatives to violence and ways of counteracting strong negative messages from their peer culture.

The most effective prevention programs empower young people to be involved in the work and include a commitment to helping them to develop the necessary skills to succeed as adults. Youths need developmentally appropriate knowledge and education delivered in a nonjudgmental and highly salient format that emphasizes their choices, responsibilities, and consequences. Youth, especially youth at risk, need education and skills to promote healthy relationships, to develop peer support, and to establish social action aimed at ending violence in relationships. They need to feel connected not only to their peers but also to their school, family, and community.

Risk behaviors occur in the context of a relationship. Therefore, the foundation for the approaches described in this book is predicated on the importance of relationships and their protective and supportive role in dealing with the situations youth face. Youths' relationships and their peer culture play a significant role in understanding many of the motives and beliefs underlying their healthy or harmful choices. Relationships include past and present interactions with parents and family members, which shape many of their current attitudes and provide the foundation for making safe versus risky choices. It often comes down to the individual's skill at negotiating relationship issues, particularly with parents, peers, and romantic partners, that determines his or her degree of risk.

The importance of gender roles in the formation of relationships from early childhood through adolescence was highlighted throughout this book. Gender identification is one of the earliest ways that children can make some sense of a complex world. They see the world initially in terms that they can easily discriminate, such as male and female, and the subsequent assignment of activities and characteristics to these categories appears to be universal. Children in many cultures prefer to play with their same-sex peers, although there is a broad range in terms of how rigidly children may adhere to gender boundaries. Children who do not manage the boundaries between males and females face social repercussions from their peers and possibly adults as well, so the salience of gender remains well into adolescence. Gender role expectations reemerge with considerable force during early adolescence, perhaps again in response to their need to simplify a changing world. As their peer networks rapidly expand, teens are caught in the middle between their family and peer values. They often face considerable pressure to conform to peer expectations while at school or in the community, while maintaining allegiance to family values while at home.

Separating from the family is a normal and healthy part of development. Nonetheless, it is often a difficult time as teens adapt to peer expectations while maintaining or modifying their family connection. As youths become more engaged with their peers, they rely once again on familiar gender role expectations to improve their chances of fitting in and being accepted. This reliance on familiar roles and expectations once again provides some structure to this demanding situation, although this time the process of learning to relate is more challenging than ever. Bullying, harassment, dating violence, gay baiting, lethal violence, and gang involvement are just some of the dangers they face in attempting to connect with their peer culture, and once again relationships play a crucial role.

We described how rigid gender role expectations are at the root of many forms of adolescent risk behavior. Youths often stick to the familiar and adhere carefully to gender role expectations that are communicated to them from many angles. Adhering to what is widely believed to be popular, attractive, or normal makes it easier to be accepted by peers and avoid some of the hazards of this tricky period of development. Gender role beliefs are policed by disparaging others who fail to match such expectations, examples of which abound in the homophobic taunting that is common among adolescents. Such taunting and abuse play a particularly significant role in the different forms of relationship violence that emerge.

Youth do not avoid experimenting with sex, drugs, and violence simply because there are risks involved, no matter how clearly these risks are communicated to them. Most teens experiment with substance use and sexual behavior, and some mimic the abusive and violent language and actions of peer and adult role models. Studies of emotional violence and harassment experienced by the majority of youth point to the need to address this form of behavior universally and at an early age. Moreover, involvement in one risk behavior greatly increases involvement in others. The overlap between alcohol, sexual behavior, and abusive or violent acts is of concern because these behaviors often co-occur and magnify the risk of harm.

In chapter 5 we examined the myriad of factors that influence adolescents' choices and the extent to which normal experimentation may result in undesirable health outcomes and behavior patterns. Trying to make sense of why some teens choose to engage in risky behaviors, even in the face of overwhelming evidence of harm or danger, requires a good understanding of typical and atypical adolescent development. The field has moved well beyond single-factor explanations of why teens engage in high-risk behaviors, embracing the importance of multiple layers of influence affecting adolescent decision making. Rather than enter the early adult years ready for new challenges, some adolescents make life-altering choices that impose significant limits or impairments on their future.

Explanations as to why many youth make poor decisions that pose harm to themselves and others raise the importance of family, school, peer, and community experiences. These explanations involve cognitive factors, such as beliefs about norms and pressures, costs and benefits, and their ability to engage in or avoid such risk behaviors; behavioral factors, such as refusal skills and interpersonal and academic competence; and social factors, such as attachment to high-risk peers and alienation from or limited exposure to healthy role models and positive socialization agents. For example, an adolescent may choose to drink alcohol after weighing the risks and benefits, derived from his or her perception of how others handle such choices. Their behavior is further determined by teens' feelings of self-efficacy, which reflects the extent to which they believe they can obtain alcohol or resist social pressure to do so. Importantly, these decisions are shaped by relationships with influential role models, past and present, which influence one's current beliefs, intentions, and self-efficacy. The role of parental monitoring, the quality of the parent-adolescent relationship, and the extent of parent-adolescent communication about risks and responsibilities are all significant factors in promoting safe choices and reducing harm. Similarly, school climate, including safety, connectedness, academic standards, and clear behavioral expectations, emerged as a critical determinant of positive, responsible choices.

A universal strategy that strengthens relationship skills and addresses their importance in reducing risk is a key conclusion from the literature on adolescent risk behaviors. Rather than targeting risk behaviors or high-risk peers directly, this strategy argues for the necessity of providing fundamental education and skills to all youth regardless of risk, with additional services for those found to be in greater need. Such efforts range from family-focused approaches aimed at positive, healthy parent-child or parent-teen relationships to school-based programs that improve success and connection to school to community-based efforts to improve neighborhood safety and foster commitment to conventional standards of behavioral conduct. School-based programs that address youth risk and health-promoting behaviors more comprehensively are replacing problem-based strategies that address one or two risk behaviors. The important role of teachers and other school personnel is increasing among programs for adolescents, as are ways to incorporate healthy messages and positive skills into the regular curriculum.

Best Practices

Successful and unsuccessful approaches to preventing adolescent risk behaviors both have important lessons to share. Ineffective programs focus on one or two primary causes or correlates that are believed to be responsible for a problem behavior and usually provide a simple message or approach that can be readily implemented with little training or cost. The most familiar example is a "Just say no" approach to substance use, which assumes that teens can or will avoid alcohol and drugs if they are told to and if they exercise willpower. There is no appreciation for the range of skills, attitudes, and opportunities youth need to make healthy choices, nor of the complex social environments in which these decisions unfold. In addition, ineffective programs may have strong media appeal and may garner public support regardless of the proven lack of effectiveness.

In contrast, effective programs in substance use, sexual risk, and violence prevention are multifaceted. Even when the focus is on one problem at a time, these interventions are sensitive to the various situations that youth face, emphasize the development of specific skills, and have a focus on building positive youth capacity. Successful programs, simply stated, target the known risk factors associated with each problem behavior or the commonly shared risk factors of two or more problem areas. They build on known protective factors that offset risk behaviors and that are amenable to change, such as healthy relationship skills, conflict resolution, and decision making. Moreover, effective programs operate within an adequate time frame and do not involve brief interventions that cannot provide adequate information and skills for lasting change. Most of these programs include extensive training and implementation measures to ensure the programs are being delivered the way they were designed.

Prevention programs are more likely to be successful when they are properly timed to development and offer youth a range of choices to reduce risk rather than attempt to completely eliminate particular behaviors. They provide accurate information about the consequences of particular choices but do not rely on scare tactics to steer youth away from these choices. The relative failure of abstinence-based approaches to sexual behavior compared to harm-reduction approaches emphasizing delayed onset of sexual intercourse, skills to avoid risky situations, and skills to negotiate condom use—in addition to presenting abstinence as a viable alternative—exemplifies the importance of providing teens with choice. We also raised the importance of being gender strategic in delivering the right messages to youth. Being gender strategic means shaping messages so that they fit with adolescents' current perception of relationships and ensuring that the messages match the different experiences and realities of girls and boys. In particular, important gender differences in the expression of violence in adolescence need to be acknowledged so that teens engage in the process of learning about the dynamics of abuse in relationships rather than reject this out of hand.

We examined the successful elements shared by programs addressing each of the three risk behaviors of sex, drugs, and violence and came to similar conclusions: they focus on changing attitudes and behaviors to lead to positive and safe choices. Effective substance use prevention programs, for example, address a range of behaviors and attitudes related to the onset of substance use and target the larger social context within which youth live. The role of peers in promoting or avoiding risk behaviors is also addressed in these programs along with the skills adolescents need to assert themselves in the face of peer pressure. In short, successful programs teach ways to develop positive relationships, not merely how to avoid negative outcomes.

Comprehensive and skill-based approaches meet the best-practice criteria for prevention programs in the violence, sexual behavior, and substance use domains. Increasing adolescents' capacity to develop healthy relationships with those around them increases their resilience to peer pressure and helps prepare them for the demands of adulthood. Increasing connections between youth and their families, schools, and communities further protects adolescents from harm. In short, critical ingredients for an integrated model of preventing multiple risk behaviors include providing accurate information and teaching useful skills for handling conflict and pressure, interventions that are timed properly to the developmental level of the audience, an integrated and comprehensive program, and gender-strategic ways of delivering the messages.

We used examples from the Fourth R to illustrate ways to build skills, empower youth, and mobilize a comprehensive approach to healthy relationships. We highlighted the importance of providing information, fostering the development of behavioral skills, and increasing motivation. Effective behavioral skills training requires practice and opportunities to see others practice in order to increase both competence and self-efficacy. Motivation, which can be targeted individually or through the use of peers, helps adolescents make healthy choices in their peer and dating relationships. We also discussed youth empowerment and leadership strategies. Providing social action and leadership opportunities for youth who may feel marginalized in the school setting creates an alternate experience for these youth and a sense of mastery in a domain in which they may not otherwise feel very successful. Strategies for a comprehensive approach—involving parents, teachers, and the whole school setting—are essential.

Sex, Drugs, and Violence: Shifting from Fear to Effective Education

Throughout this book we have offered a challenge to parents and educators of adolescents not to become overly fearful and confrontational during this critical stage of development but rather to seek meaningful connection and engagement in helping youth navigate these turbulent years. The paradox of adolescence lies in teens' strong desire to be free of adult supervision while at the same time seeking information and guidance from these same adults. This process can be so delicate that many parents and teachers feel they are walking a tightrope on a windy day: the winds are a certainty; the only issue is whether the adults can maintain their balance. Adult guidance and support that is developmentally sensitive is critical to adolescents' growth and responsibility, much as it was throughout earlier stages of development.

Relationships both protect and endanger children and youth. Accordingly, we have emphasized the critical importance of learning to relate to others and how this transforms throughout adolescence. The process of relationship development in early adolescence is fraught with diamonds and land mines. The diamonds provide new opportunities for self-awareness and positive identity that can provide the foundation for personal growth and contribution to the community. The land mines are omnipresent and often difficult to avoid. They include strong gender-biased expectations as to dress and behavior that can pose powerful limits on this process of self-discovery. Pressure to reject the values and influences of parents and other adults may simply

lead to the adoption of adolescent peer culture. What causes alarm is
the dark side of peer culture and the uncertainty and fragility of maintaining positive relationships with adults during this transition. The
invisible force creating fear and tension stems from ignorance on the
part of both teens and adults: teens keep their parents in the dark under the assumption that they will be judgmental and harsh rather than
understanding; likewise, parents are provoked by fear of a peer culture
that is very foreign to their own past experiences.

Experimenting with adult privileges and unfamiliar territory is a
cornerstone of adolescent development—and also the number one
concern of adults. This experimentation may involve a range of activity, from seeking meaningful information about risks and consequences of engaging in certain behaviors to more harmful involvement
in health-compromising activities. Although not all forms of experimentation and exposure are necessarily harmful, every adolescent
needs the information and skills necessary to avoid harm and make
safe choices. Sooner or later, everyone needs to call into action his or
her knowledge, values, and skills to manage the increasing challenges
of adolescence and young adulthood; avoiding potential risk and harm
is an ongoing, ever-changing endeavor.

An important message woven throughout this book is that risk
behaviors cannot be suitably addressed in a piecemeal, disconnected
manner. Sex, drugs, and violence cannot be easily separated into neat
categories—they coexist in the context of peer and dating relationships and are part of the fabric of youth culture. Therefore, teens need
a comprehensive message to guide choices and behavior concerning
the reality of their life situations rather than oversimplified messages
conveying fear and reprimand. Not only do teens need to understand
how these risk behaviors are interconnected, they need relevant information and skills that prepare them for real-life situations. These real-
life situations most often involve their close friends, romantic partners,
and other peers, which brings us back to the importance of healthy relationships in building strengths and reducing risk.

Adolescents also need parents and educators as primary partners
in promoting healthy relationships in all aspects of their lives. This important mission cannot be undertaken without the commitment and
involvement of the most important socialization influence outside of

the family: the school. Schools are an ideal forum to develop prevention programs that matter, especially when they adhere to best practices derived from prevention science. These principles include strengthening relationship skills; empowering youth; ensuring comprehensive participation of parents, teachers, and schools; and being gender strategic. We discussed how this undertaking has to be more of a process than a one-time event and one that adapts to the changing needs of adolescents in their community, rather than a prescription for a quick fix. Programs that are successfully integrated into the milieu of a school and manage to mobilize all the stakeholders have the opportunity to create safe and caring learning environments while preparing the students for their adult roles. Furthermore, the universal nature of school attendance eliminates the stigma associated with indicated programming.

Although there are many barriers to developing effective school-based prevention programs, there is considerable momentum to tackle these remaining barriers and bolster involvement of schools and communities in positive adolescent development. In our experience in developing the Fourth R program, we have seen a high level of enthusiasm from educators and parents. We envision a future when the success of schools is measured not only by math and reading scores but also by the nature and quality of the relationships shown throughout the school environment. With this vision parents and educators can move from fear of adolescent development to embracing creative strategies that reduce harm, foster healthy relationships, and maximize successful transition to adulthood.

References

Abma, J. C., Chandra, A., Mosher, W. D., Peterson, L., & Piccinino, L. (1997). Fertility, family planning, and women's health: New data from the 1995 national survey of family growth. *Vital Health Statistics, Series 23, 19,* 1–114.

Adlaf, E. M., Paglia, A., & Ivis, F. (2003). Drug use among Ontario students, 1977–1999: Findings from the Ontario Drug Use Survey. In *Research Document Series.* Toronto: Center for Addiction and Mental Health.

Ajzen, I., & Fishbein, M. (1980). *Understanding attitudes and predicting social behavior.* Englewood Cliffs, NJ: Prentice Hall.

Alderman, E. M., & Shine, W. A. (1998). Affluence. In S. K. Schonberg (Ed.), *Comprehensive adolescent health care* (pp. 743–745). St. Louis, MO: Mosby.

American Association of University Women. (2001). *Hostile hallways: Bullying, teasing, and sexual harassment in school.* Washington, DC: American Association of University Women Educational Foundation.

American Psychological Association. (1993). *Commission on youth and violence summary report: Vol. 1. Violence and youth: Psychology's response.* Washington, DC: Author.

Armstrong, T. D., & Costello, J. E. (2002). Community studies on adolescent substance use, abuse, or dependence and psychiatric comorbidity. *Journal of Consulting and Clinical Psychology, 70*(6), 1224–1239.

Arthur, M. W., Hawkins, J. D., Pollard, J. A., Catalano, R. F., & Baglioni, A. J., Jr. (2002). Measuring risk and protective factors for substance use, delinquency, and other adolescent problem behaviors: The Communities That Care Youth Survey. *Evaluation Review, 26,* 575–601.

Austin, S. B. (2000). Prevention research in eating disorders: Theory and new directions. *Psychological Medicine, 30*(6), 1249–1262.

Avery-Leaf, S., Cascardi, M., O'Leary, K. D., & Cano, A. (1997). Efficacy of a dating violence prevention program on attitudes justifying aggression. *Journal of Adolescent Health, 21,* 11–17.

Aydt, H., & Corsaro, W. A. (2003). Differences in children's construction of gender across culture: An interpretive approach. *American Behavioral Scientist, 46*(10), 1306–1325.

Bakken, L., & Romig, C. (1992). Interpersonal needs in middle adolescence: Companionship, leadership, and intimacy. *Journal of Adolescence, 15*(3), 301–316.

Bandura, A. (1977). *Social learning theory.* Englewood Cliffs, NJ: Prentice Hall.

Bandura, A. (1986). *Social foundations of thought and action: A social cognitive theory.* Upper Saddle River, NJ: Prentice Hall.

Bank, L., & Burraston, B. (2001). Abusive home environments as predictors of poor adjustment during adolescence and early adulthood. *Journal of Community Psychology, 29*(3), 195–217.

Bar-on, M. E., Broughton, D. D., Buttross, S., Corrigan, S., Gedissman, A., de Rivas, M. R. G., et al. (2001). Media violence. *Pediatrics, 108*(5), 1222–1226.

Basow, S. A., & Rubin, L. R. (1999). Gender influences on adolescent development. In N. G. Johnson, M. C. Roberts, & J. Worell (Eds.), *Beyond appearance: A new look at adolescent girls* (pp. 25–52). Washington, DC: American Psychological Association.

Bearman, P. S., & Bruckner, H. (2001). Promising the future: Virginity pledges and first intercourse. *American Journal of Sociology, 106*(4), 859–912.

Beebe, T. J., Asche, S. E., Harrison, P. A., & Quinlan, K. B. (2004). Heightened vulnerability and increased risk-taking among adolescent chat room users: Results from a statewide school survey. *Journal of Adolescent Health, 35*(2), 116–123.

Bennett, K. J., & Offord, D. R. (1998). Schools, mental health, and life quality. In *Canada Health Action: Building on the legacy* (Vol. 3, pp. 45–86). Ste. Foy, QC: Editions Multimondes.

Berman, H., & Jiwani, Y. (Eds.). (2002). *In the best interests of the girl child.* Ottawa: Health Canada.

Bernstein, D. P., Ahluvalia, T., Pogge, D., & Handelsman, L. (1997). Validity of the Childhood Trauma Questionnaire in an adolescent psychiatric population. *Journal of the American Academy of Child & Adolescent Psychiatry, 36*(3), 340–348.

Bethke, T. M., & Dejoy, D. M. (1993). An experimental-study of factors influencing the acceptability of dating violence. *Journal of Interpersonal Violence, 8*(1), 36–51.

Beyers, J. M., Loeber, R., Wikstrèom, P.-O. H., & Stouthamer-Loeber, M. (2001). What predicts adolescent violence in better-off neighborhoods? *Journal of Abnormal Child Psychology, 29*(5), 369–381.

Beyers, J. M., Toumbourou, J. W., Catalano, R. F., Arthur, M. W., & Hawkins, J. D. (2004). A cross-national comparison of risk and protective factors for adolescent substance use: The United States and Australia. *Journal of Adolescent Health, 35*(1), 3–16.

Biglan, A. (2004). Contextualism and the development of effective prevention science. *Prevention Science, 5*(1), 15–21.

Biringen, Z., Robinson, J. L., & Emde, R. N. (1994). Maternal sensitivity in the 2nd year: Gender-based relations in the dyadic balance of control. *American Journal of Orthopsychiatry, 64*(1), 78–90.

Birns, B., Cascardi, M., & Meyer, S. L. (1994). Sex-role socialization: Develop-

mental influences on wife abuse. *American Journal of Orthopsychiatry,*
64(1), 50–59.

Blakemore, J. E. O. (2003). Children's beliefs about violating gender norms:
Boys shouldn't look like girls, and girls shouldn't act like boys. *Sex Roles,*
48(9–10), 411–419.

Blum, R. W., & Ellen, J. (2002). Work group V: Increasing the capacity of
schools, neighborhoods, and communities to improve adolescent health
outcomes. *Journal of Adolescent Health, 31*(6), 288–292.

Blum, R. W., & Rinchart, P. M. (1998). *Reducing the risk: Connections that make
a difference in the lives of youth.* Minneapolis: Division of General Pediatrics, & Adolescent Health Department of Pediatrics, University of
Minnesota.

Borawski, E. A., Ievers-Landis, C. E., Lovegreen, L. D., & Trapl, E. S. (2003).
Parental monitoring, negotiated unsupervised time, and parental trust:
The role of perceived parenting practices in adolescent health risk behav-
iors. *Journal of Adolescent Health, 33*(2), 60–70.

Botvin, G. J., Botvin, E. M., & Ruchlin, H. (1998). School-based approaches to
drug abuse prevention: Evidence for effectiveness and suggestions for determining cost-effectiveness. In W. J. Bukoski & R. I. Evans (Eds.), *Cost-bene-
fit/cost-effectiveness research of drug abuse prevention: Implications for programming and policy (NIH Publication No. 98–4021, NIDA Research Monograph
176, pp. 59–82).* Rockville, MD: National Institute on Drug Abuse.

Botvin, G. J., Dusenbury, L., Baker, E., Jamesortiz, S., & Botvin, E. M. (1992).
Smoking prevention among urban minority youth: Assessing effects on
outcome and mediating variables. *Health Psychology, 11*(5), 290–299.

Botvin, G. J., Griffin, K. W., Diaz, T., & Ifill-Williams, M. (2001). Preventing
binge drinking during early adolescence: One- and two-year follow-up of
a school-based preventive intervention. *Psychology of Addictive Behaviors,*
15(4), 360–365.

Botvin, G. J., Griffin, K. W., Diaz, T., Scheier, L. H., Williams, C., & Epstein,
J. A. (2000). Preventing illicit drug use in adolescents: Long-term follow-
up data from a randomized control trial of a school population. *Addictive
Behaviors, 25*(5), 769–774.

Botvin, G. J., & Kantor, L. W. (2000). Preventing alcohol and tobacco use
through life skills training: Theory, methods, and empirical findings. *Alcohol Research & Health, 24*(4), 250–257.

Botvin, G. J., Mihalic, S. F., & Grotpeter, J. (1998). *Life Skills Training* (Vol. 5).
Boulder: Center for the Study and Prevention of Violence, Institute of
Behavioral Science, University of Colorado at Boulder.

Botvin, G. J., Schinke, S. P., Epstein, J. A., Diaz, T., & Botvin, E. M. (1995). Effectiveness of culturally focused and generic skills training approaches to
alcohol and drug-abuse prevention among minority adolescents: 2-year
follow-up results. *Psychology of Addictive Behaviors, 9*(3), 183–194.

Bowlby, J. (1980). *Attachment and loss.* New York: Basic.

Boyle, D. E., Marshall, N. L., & Robeson, W. W. (2003). Gender at play: Fourth-grade girls and boys on the playground. *American Behavioral Scientist, 46*(10), 1326–1345.

Bradley, M. J., & O'Connor, C. (2002). *Yes, your teen is crazy! Loving your kid without losing your mind.* Gig Harbor, WA: Harbor Press.

Brener, N. D., Simon, T. R., Krug, E. G., & Lowry, R. (1999). Recent trends in violence-related behaviors among high school students in the United States. *Jama: Journal of the American Medical Association, 282*(5), 440–446.

Bretherton, I. (1995). Attachment theory and developmental psychopathology. In D. Cicchetti & S. L. Toth (Eds.), *Emotion, cognition, and representation* (Vol. 6, pp. 231–260). Rochester, NY: University of Rochester Press.

Brown, B. B. (1999). "You're going out with who?" Peer group influences on adolescent romantic relationships. In W. Furman, B. B. Brown, & C. Feiring (Eds.), *The development of romantic relationships in adolescence* (pp. 291–329). New York: Cambridge University Press.

Brown, J. S., & Duguid, P. (2000). *The social life of information.* Boston: Harvard Business School Press.

Brown, L. M., & Gilligan, C. (1993). Meeting at the Crossroads: Women's Psychology and Girls' Development. *Feminism & Psychology, 3*(1), 11–35.

Brown, S. A., & Abrantes, A. M. (in press). Substance use disorders. In E. J. Mash & D. A. Wolfe (Eds.), *Behavioral and emotional disorders in adolescence.* New York: Guilford.

Buckland, M. K. (1991). Information as thing. *Journal of the American Society for Information Science, 42*(5), 351–360.

Bugental, D. B. (1993). Communication in abusive relationships: Cognitive constructions of interpersonal power. *American Behavioral Scientist, 36*(3), 288–308.

Burt, M. R., Zweig, J. M., & Roman, J. (2002). Modeling the payoffs of interventions to reduce adolescent vulnerability. *Journal of Adolescent Health, 31*(1), 40–57.

Byers, E. S., Sears, H. A., Voyer, S. D., Thurlow, J. L., Cohen, J. N., & Weaver, A. D. (2003). An adolescent perspective on sexual health education at school and at home: II. Middle school students. *Canadian Journal of Human Sexuality, 12,* 19–33.

Capaldi, D. M., Crosby, L., & Stoolmiller, M. (1996). Predicting the timing of first sexual intercourse for at-risk adolescent males. *Child Development, 67*(2), 344–359.

Capaldi, D. M., DeGarmo, D., Patterson, G. R., & Forgatch, M. (2002). Contextual risk across the early life span and association with antisocial behavior. In J. B. Reid, G. R. Patterson, & J. Snyder (Eds.), *Antisocial behavior in children and adolescents: A developmental analysis and model for intervention* (pp. 123–145). Washington, DC: American Psychological Association.

Capaldi, D. M., Dishion, T. J., Stoolmiller, M., & Yoerger, K. (2001). Aggression toward female partners by at-risk young men: The contribution of male adolescent friendships. *Developmental Psychology, 37*(1), 61–73.

Cascardi, M., Avery-Leaf, S., O'Leary, K. D., & Slep, A. M. S. (1999). Factor structure and convergent validity of the Conflict Tactics Scale in high school students. *Psychological Assessment, 11*(4), 546–555.

Catalano, R. F., Berglund, M. L., Ryan, J. A. M., Lonczak, H. S., & Hawkins, J. D. (2004). Positive youth development in the United States: Research findings on evaluations of positive youth development programs. *Annals of the American Academy of Political and Social Science, 591,* 98–124.

Catalano, R. F., & Hawkins, J. D. (1995). The social development model: A theory of antisocial behavior. In J. D. Hawkins (Ed.), *Delinquency and crime: Current theories* (pp. 149–197). New York: Cambridge University Press.

Catalano, R. F., Hawkins, J. D., Berglund, M. L., Pollard, J. A., & Arthur, M. W. (2002). Prevention science and positive youth development: Competitive or cooperative frameworks? *Journal of Adolescent Health, 31*(6), 230–239.

Cauffman, E., Feldman, S. S., Jensen, L. A., & Arnett, J. J. (2000). The (un)acceptability of violence against peers and dates. *Journal of Adolescent Research, 15*(6), 652–673.

Centers for Disease Control and Prevention (CDC). (1997). Youth risk behavior surveillance. *MMWR Surveillance Summaries, 47,* 1–89.

Centers for Disease Control and Prevention (CDC). (2001). Youth risk behavior surveillance. *MMWR Surveillance Summaries, 51,* 1–64.

Centers for Disease Control and Prevention (CDC). (2002). Surveillance summaries: MMWR (Vol. 51). Atlanta: Author.

Chassin, L., Pitts, S. C., & Prost, J. (2002). Binge drinking trajectories from adolescence to emerging adulthood in a high-risk sample: Predictors and substance abuse outcomes. *Journal of Consulting and Clinical Psychology, 70*(1), 67–78.

Chassin, L., & Ritter, J. (2001). Vulnerability to substance use disorders in childhood and adolescence. In R. E. Ingram & J. M. Price (Eds.), *Vulnerability to psychopathology: Risk across the lifespan* (pp. 107–134). New York: Guilford.

Cicchetti, D., & Cohen, D. J. (Eds.). (1995). *Developmental psychopathology: Vol. 1. Theory and methods.* Oxford: John Wiley & Sons.

Cicchetti, D., & Toth, S. L. (Eds.). (1997). *Developmental perspectives on trauma: Theory, research, and intervention.* Rochester, NY: University of Rochester Press.

Cicchetti, D., Toth, S. L., & Lynch, M. (1995). Bowlby's dream comes full circle: The application of attachment theory to risk and psychopathology. *Advances in Clinical Child Psychology, 17,* 1–75.

Clark, C. M. (1992). Deviant adolescent subcultures: Assessment strategies and clinical interventions. *Adolescence, 27*(106), 283–293.

Clayton, R. R., Cattarello, A. M., & Johnstone, B. M. (1996). The effectiveness of Drug Abuse Resistance Education (Project DARE): 5-year follow-up results. *Preventive Medicine, 25*(3), 307–318.

Coid, J., Petruckevitch, A., Feder, G., Chung, W. S., Richardson, J., & Moorey, S. (2001). Relation between childhood sexual and physical abuse and risk of revictimisation in women: A cross-sectional survey. *Lancet, 358*(9280), 450–454.

Collins, W. A., & Sroufe, L. A. (1999). Capacity for intimate relationships: A developmental construction. In W. Furman, B. B. Brown, & C. Feiring (Eds.), *The development of romantic relationships in adolescence* (pp. 125–147). New York: Cambridge University Press.

Connolly, J., Craig, W., Goldberg, A., & Pepler, D. (2004). Mixed-gender groups, dating, and romantic relationships in early adolescence. *Journal of Research on Adolescence, 14*(2), 185–207.

Connolly, J., Furman, W., & Konarski, R. (2000). The role of peers in the emergence of heterosexual romantic relationships in adolescence. *Child Development, 71*(5), 1395–1408.

Connolly, J., & Goldberg, A. (1999). Romantic relationships in adolescence: The role of friends and peers in their emergence and development. In W. Furman, B. B. Brown, & C. Feiring (Eds.), *The development of romantic relationships in adolescence* (pp. 266–290). New York: Cambridge University Press.

Connolly, J., & Johnson, A. M. (1996). Adolescents' romantic relationships and the structure and quality of their close interpersonal ties. *Personal Relationships, 3*(2), 185–195.

Connolly, J., Pepler, D., Craig, W. M., & Taradash, A. (2000). Dating experiences of bullies in early adolescence. *Child Maltreatment: Journal of the American Professional Society on the Abuse of Children, 5*(4), 299–310.

Corsaro, W. A. (1997). *The sociology of childhood.* Thousand Oaks, CA: Pine Forge Press.

Cote, S., Vaillancourt, M. A., Farhat, A., & Tremblay, R. E. (2002). *Childhood physical and indirect aggression: Sex difference in developmental trends.* Paper presented at the biannual meeting of the International Society for Research on Aggression, Montreal.

Coulter, R. P. (2003). Boys doing good: Young men and gender equity. *Educational Review, 55*(2), 135–145.

Coyle, K., Basen-Engquist, K., Kirby, D., Parcel, G., Banspach, S., Collins, J., et al. (2001). Safer choices: Reducing teen pregnancy, HIV, and STDs. *Public Health Reports, 116,* 82–93.

Crawford, A. M., Pentz, M. A., Chou, C. P., Li, C. Y., & Dwyer, J. H. (2003). Parallel developmental trajectories of sensation seeking and regular substance use in adolescents. *Psychology of Addictive Behaviors, 17*(3), 179–192.

Crick, N. R., & Grotpeter, J. K. (1995). Relational aggression, gender, and social-psychological adjustment. *Child Development, 66*(3), 710–722.

Crockett, L. J., & Petersen, A. C. (1993). Adolescent development: Health risks and opportunities for health promotion. In S. G. Millstein & A. C. Petersen (Eds.), *Promoting the health of adolescents: New directions for the twenty-first century* (pp. 13–37). London: London University Press.

Crooks, C. V., Goodall, G. R., Hughes, R., Jaffe, P. G., & Baker, L. (2004). *Engaging men and boys in preventing violence against women: Applying a cognitive-behavioral model.* Unpublished manuscript, London, ON.

Crooks, C. V., Hughes, R., Dale, S., & Homuth, D. (2004). *A continuum for safe schools to assist program planning.* Unpublished manuscript, London, ON.

Crooks, C. V., & Onyura, B. (2004). *Sex differences in predictors of onset of sexual intercourse and consistent condom use among adolescents.* Unpublished manuscript, London, ON.

Crooks, C. V., Wolfe, D. A., & Hutchinson-Jaffe, A. (2004). *Relationship-related risk behaviors in early adolescence: Developmental trends, patterns of risk, and windows of opportunity. Report prepared for the Ontario Women's Directorate.* London, ON: CAMH Centre for Prevention Science.

Cuijpers, P. (2002). Effective ingredients of school-based drug prevention programs: A systematic review. *Addictive Behaviors, 27*(6), 1009–1023.

Currie, D. H. (1998). Violent men or violent women? Whose definition counts? In B. Kennedy and R. K. Bergen (Eds.), *Issues in intimate violence* (pp. 97–111). Thousand Oaks, CA: Sage.

Darroch, J. E., Singh, S., & Frost, J. J. (2001). Differences in teenage pregnancy rates among five developed countries: The roles of sexual activity and contraceptive use. *Family Planning Perspectives, 33*(6), 244–250.

Davies, P. T., & Windle, M. (2000). Middle adolescents' dating pathways and psychosocial adjustment. *Merrill-Palmer Quarterly Journal of Developmental Psychology, 46*(1), 90–118.

DeLahunta, E. A., & Baram, D. A. (1997). Sexual assault. *Clinical Obstetrics and Gynecology, 40*(3), 648–660.

Denner, J., Cooper, C. R., Lopez, E. M., & Dunbar, N. (1999). Beyond "giving science away": How university-community partnerships inform youth programs, research, and policy (No. 8–1). Ann Arbor, MI: Society for Research on Child Development.

Diamond, L. M., Savin-Williams, R. C., & Dube, E. M. (1999). Sex, dating, passionate friendships, and romance. In W. Furman, B. B. Brown, & C. Feiring (Eds.), *The development of romantic relationships in adolescence.* New York: Cambridge University Press.

DiClemente, R. J. (1992). Psychosocial determinants of condom use among adolescents. In R. J. DiClemente (Ed.), *Adolescents and AIDS: A generation in jeopardy* (pp. 34–51). Thousand Oaks, CA: Sage.

Dietz, T. L. (1998). An examination of violence and gender role portrayals in video games: Implications for gender socialization and aggressive behavior. *Sex Roles, 38*(5–6), 425–442.

Dishion, T. J., McCord, J., & Poulin, F. (1999). When interventions harm: Peer groups and problem behavior. *American Psychologist, 54*(9), 755–764.

Dobash, R. E., & Dobash, R. P. (1992). *Women, violence, and social change.* New York: Routledge.

Dodge, K. A., Coie, J. D., & Brakke, N. P. (1982). Behavior patterns of socially rejected and neglected preadolescents: The roles of social approach and aggression. *Journal of Abnormal Child Psychology, 10*(3), 389–409.

Dodge, K. A., Pettit, G. S., & Bates, J. E. (1994a). Effects of physical maltreatment on the development of peer relations. *Development and Psychopathology, 6*(1), 43–55.

Dodge, K. A., Pettit, G. S., & Bates, J. E. (1994b). Socialization mediators of the relation between socioeconomic status and child conduct problems. *Child Development, 65*(2), 649–665.

Donaldson, S. I., Thomas, C. W., Graham, J. W., Au, J. G., & Hansen, W. B. (2000). Verifying drug abuse prevention program effects using reciprocal best friend reports. *Journal of Behavioral Medicine, 23*(6), 585–601.

Downie, R. S., Tannahill, C., & Tannahill, A. (1990). *Health promotion: Models and values.* Oxford: Oxford University Press.

Dryburgh, H. (2000). Teenage pregnancy. *Health Reports, 12*(1), 9–19.

Dryfoos, J. G. (1990). *Adolescents at risk: Prevalence and prevention* (Vol. 9). New York: Oxford University Press.

DuRant, R. H., Smith, J. A., Kreiter, S. R., & Krowchuk, D. P. (1999). The relationship between early age of onset of initial substance use and engaging in multiple health risk behaviors among young adolescents. *Archives of Pediatrics & Adolescent Medicine, 153*(3), 286–291.

Durlak, J. A. (1997). Primary prevention programs in schools. *Advances in Clinical Child Psychology, 19*, 283–318.

Durlak, J. A., & Wells, A. M. (1997). Primary prevention mental health programs for children and adolescents: A meta-analytic review. *American Journal of Community Psychology, 25*(2), 115–152.

Ellickson, P. (1999). School-based substance abuse prevention: What works, for whom, and how? In S. B. Kar (Ed.), *Substance abuse prevention: A multicultural perspective.* Amityville, NY: Baywood.

Ellickson, P. L., Saner, H., & McGuigan, K. A. (1997). Profiles of violent youth: Substance use and other concurrent problems. *American Journal of Public Health, 87*(6), 985–991.

Ellickson, P. L., Tucker, J. S., & Klein, D. J. (2001). High-risk behaviors associated with early smoking: Results from a 5-year follow-up. *Journal of Adolescent Health, 28*(6), 465–473.

Elliott, D. S. (1997–2004). *Blueprints for violence prevention.* Boulder, CO: Center for the Study and Prevention of Violence.

Elliott, D. S., Hamburg, B. A., & Williams, K. R. (1998). *Violence in American schools: A new perspective.* New York: Cambridge University Press.

Elliott, D. S., Huizinga, D., & Menard, S. (1989). *Multiple problem youth: Delinquency, drugs, and mental health problems.* New York: Springer-Verlag.

Elze, D. E. (2003). Gay, lesbian, and bisexual youths' perceptions of their high school environments and comfort zone. *Children and Schools, 25*(4), 225–239.

Emde, R. N., & Spicer, P. (2000). Experience in the midst of variation: New horizons for development and psychopathology. *Development & Psychopathology, 12*(3), 313–331.

Ennett, S. T., Ringwalt, C. L., Thorne, J., Rohrbach, L. A., Vincus, A., Simons-Rudolph, A., et al. (2003). A comparison of current practice in school-based substance use prevention programs with meta-analysis findings. *Prevention Science, 4*(1), 1–14.

Epstein, D. (1997). Boyz' own stories: Masculinities and sexualities in schools. *Gender and Education, 9*(1), 105–115.

Epstein, D., & Johnson, R. (1998). *Schooling sexualities.* Berkshire, UK: Open University Press.

Erickson, W. H. (2001). *The report of Governor Bill Owens' Columbine Review Commission.* Denver: Governor of Colorado.

Erikson, E. (1968). *Identity: Youth and crisis.* New York: Norton.

Esbensen, F., & Deschenes, E. P. (1998). A multisite examination of gang membership: Does gender matter? *Criminology, 36*(4), 799–827.

Fabes, R. A. (1994). Physiological, emotional, and behavioral correlates of gender segregation. In C. Leaper (Ed.), *Childhood gender segregation: Causes and consequences* (pp. 19–34). San Francisco: Jossey-Bass.

Fagan, A. A., & Mihalic, S. F. (2003). Strategies for enhancing the adoption of school-based prevention programs: Lessons learned from the Blueprints for Violence Prevention replications of the Life Skills Training Program. *Journal of Community Psychology, 31*(3), 235–253.

Fagot, B. I. (1994). Peer relations and the development of competence in boys and girls. In C. Leaper (Ed.), *Childhood gender segregation: Causes and consequences* (pp. 53–65). San Francisco: Jossey-Bass.

Farrell, A. D., & White, K. S. (1998). Peer influences and drug use among urban adolescents: Family structure and parent-adolescent relationship as protective factors. *Journal of Consulting and Clinical Psychology, 66*(2), 248–258.

Farrington, D. P. (1989). Early predictors of adolescent aggression and adult violence. *Violence and Victims, 4*(2), 79–100.

Federal Interagency Forum on Child and Family Statistics. (2004). *America's children in brief: Key national indicators of well-being.* Vienna, VA: Health Resources and Services Administration Center.

Feiring, C. (1996). Concepts of romance in 15-year-old adolescents. *Journal of Research on Adolescence, 6*(2), 181–200.

Felner, R. D., & Adan, A. M. (1988). The school transitional project: An ecological intervention and evaluation. In R. H. Price, E. L. Cowen, R. P. Lorion, & J. Ramos-McKay (Eds.), *14 ounces of prevention: A casebook for practitioners* (pp. 111–122). Washington, DC: American Psychological Association.

Ferguson, T. J., Eyre, H. L., & Ashbaker, M. (2000). Unwanted identities: A key variable in shame-anger links and gender differences in shame. *Sex Roles, 42*(3–4), 133–157.

Fergusson, D. M., & Horwood, L. J. (1999). Prospective childhood predictors of deviant peer affiliations in adolescence. *Journal of Child Psychology & Psychiatry, 40*(4), 581–592.

Fisher, J. D., Fisher, W. A., Mischovich, S. J., Kimble, J. D., & Malloy, T. E. (1996). Changing AIDS behavior: Effects of an intervention emphasizing AIDS risk reduction information, motivation, and behavioral skills in a college population. *Health Psychology, 15*(2), 114–123.

Fisher, W. A., & Boroditsky, R. (2000). Sexual activity, contraceptive choice, and sexual and reproductive health indicators among single Canadian women aged 15–29: Additional findings from the Canadian Contraception Study. *Canadian Journal of Human Sexuality, 9*(2), 79–93.

Fisher, W. A., & Fisher, J. D. (2003). The Information-Motivation-Behavior Skills model: A general social psychological approach to understanding and promoting health behavior. In J. Suls & K. Wallston (Eds.), *Social psychological foundations of health* (pp. 82–106). London: Blackwell.

Flay, B. R. (2000). Approaches to substance use prevention utilizing school curriculum plus social environment change. *Addictive Behaviors, 25*(6), 861–885.

Florsheim, P. (2003). *Adolescent romantic relations and sexual behavior: Theory, research, and practical implications.* Mahwah, NJ: Lawrence Erlbaum Associates.

Flowers-Coulson, P. A., Kushner, M. A., & Bankowski, S. (2000). The information is out there but is anybody getting it? Adolescent misconceptions about sexual education and reproductive health and the use of the Internet. *Journal of Sex Education and Therapy, 25*(2–3), 178–188.

Floyd, F. J., & Stein, T. S. (2002). Sexual orientation identity formation among gay, lesbian, and bisexual youths: Multiple patterns of milestone experiences. *Journal of Research on Adolescence, 12*(2), 167–191.

Follingstad, D. R., Wright, S., Lloyd, S., & Sebastian, J. A. (1991). Sex-differences in motivations and effects in dating violence. *Family Relations, 40*(1), 51–57.

Foshee, V. A., Linder, F., MacDougall, J. E., & Bangdiwala, S. (2001). Gender differences in the longitudinal predictors of adolescent dating violence. *Preventive Medicine, 32*(2), 128–141.

Funk, J. B., Baldacci, H. B., Pasold, T., & Baumgardner, J. (2004). Violence exposure in real-life, video games, television, movies, and the Internet: Is there desensitization? *Journal of Adolescence, 27*(1), 23–39.

Furman, W., & Buhrmester, D. (1992). Age and sex-differences in perceptions of networks of personal relationships. *Child Development, 63*(1), 103–115.

Furman, W., & Shaffer, L. A. (1999). A story of adolescence: The emergence of other-sex relationships. *Journal of Youth and Adolescence, 28*(4), 513–522.

Furman, W., & Shaffer, L. (2003). The role of romantic relationships in adolescent development. In P. Florsheim (Ed.), *Adolescent romantic relations and sexual behavior: Theory, research, and practical implications* (pp. 3–22). Mahwah, NJ: Lawrence Erlbaum Associates.

Furman, W., & Simon, V. A. (1998). Advice from youth: Some lessons from the study of adolescent relationships. *Journal of Social and Personal Relationships, 15*(6), 723–739.

Furman, W., Simon, V. A., Shaffer, L., & Bouchey, H. A. (2002). Adolescents' working models and styles for relationships with parents, friends, and romantic partners. *Child Development, 73*(1), 241–255.

Furman, W., & Wehner, E. A. (1997). Adolescent romantic relationships: A developmental perspective. In S. Shulman & W. Collins (Eds.), *Romantic relationships in adolescence: Developmental perspectives* (Vol. 78, pp. 21–36). San Francisco: Jossey-Bass.

Gagné, M.-H., & Lavoie, F. (1993). Young people's views on the causes of violence in adolescents' romantic relationships. *Canada's Mental Health, 41*(3), 11–15.

Garbarino, J., & deLara, E. (2002). *And words can hurt forever: How to protect adolescents from bullying, harassment, and emotional violence.* New York: Free Press.

Garmezy, N. (1991). Resilience and vulnerability to adverse developmental outcomes associated with poverty. *American Behavioral Scientist, 34*(4), 416–430.

Gillmore, M. R., Butler, S. S., Lohr, M. J., & Gilchrist, L. (1992). Substance use and other factors associated with risky sexual behavior among pregnant adolescents. *Family Planning Perspectives, 24*(6), 255–261.

Gladwell, M. (2000). *The tipping point: How little things can make a big difference* (1st ed.). Boston: Little, Brown.

Gondolf, E. W. (2002). *Batterer intervention systems: Issues, outcomes, and recommendations.* Thousand Oaks, CA: Sage.

Goodwin, M. H. (1998). Games of stance: Conflict and footing in hopscotch. In S. Hoyle & C. T. Adger (Eds.), *Kid's talk: Strategic language use in later childhood* (pp. 23–46). New York: Oxford University Press.

Goodwin, M. H. (2001). Organizing participation in cross-sex jump rope: Situating gender differences within longitudinal studies of activities. *Research on Language and Social Interaction, 34,* 75–106.

Grant, B. F., & Dawson, D. A. (1997). Age at onset of alcohol use and its association with DSM-IV alcohol abuse and dependence: Results from the National Longitudinal Alcohol Epidemiologic Survey. *Journal of Substance Abuse, 9,* 103–110.

Grant, B. F., Stinson, F. S., & Harford, T. (2001). The 5-year course of alcohol abuse among young adults. *Journal of Substance Abuse, 13*(3), 229–238.

Gray, H. M., & Foshee, V. (1997). Adolescent dating violence: Differences between one-sided and mutually violent profiles. *Journal of Interpersonal Violence, 12*(1), 126–141.

Gray, M. R., & Steinberg, L. (1999). Adolescent romance and the parent-child relationship: A contextual perspective. In W. Furman, B. B. Brown, & C. Feiring (Eds.), *The development of romantic relationships in adolescence* (pp. 235–262). New York: Cambridge University Press.

Greenberg, M. T., Domitrovich, C., & Bumberger, B. (2000). *Preventing mental disorders in school-aged children: A review of the effectiveness of prevention programs.* Washington, DC: Substance Abuse and Mental Health Services Administration, U.S. Department of Health and Human Services.

Griffin, K. W., Botvin, G. J., Epstein, J. A., Doyle, M. M., & Diaz, T. (2000). Psychosocial and behavioral factors in early adolescence as predictors of heavy drinking among high school seniors. *Journal of Studies on Alcohol, 61*(4), 603–606.

Griffin, K. W., Botvin, G. J., Nichols, T. R., & Doyle, M. M. (2003). Effectiveness of a universal drug abuse prevention approach for youth at high risk for substance use initiation. *Preventive Medicine, 36*(1), 1–7.

Griffin, K. W., Scheier, L. H., Botvin, G. J., & Diaz, T. (2000). Ethnic and gender differences in psychosocial risk, protection, and adolescent alcohol use. *Prevention Science, 1*(4), 199–212.

Grigsby, C., & Julian, K. (2002). *How to get your teen to talk to you.* Sisters, OR: Multnomah.

Grossman, D., & DeGaetano, G. (1999). *Stop teaching our kids to kill: A call to action against TV, movie, & video game violence* (1st ed.). New York: Crown.

Grunbaum, J. A., Kann, L., Kinchen, S. A., Williams, B., Ross, J. G., Lowry, R., et al. (2002). Youth risk behavior surveillance: United States, 2001. *Journal of School Health, 72*(8), 313–328.

Guo, J., Chung, I. J., Hill, K. G., Hawkins, J. D., Catalano, R. F., & Abbott, R.

D. (2002). Developmental relationships between adolescent substance use and risky sexual behavior in young adulthood. *Journal of Adolescent Health, 31*(4), 354–362.

Guterman, N. B., Hahm, H. C., & Cameron, M. (2002). Adolescent victimization and subsequent use of mental health counseling services. *Journal of Adolescent Health, 30*(5), 336–345.

Halpern, C. T., Oslak, S. G., Young, M. L., Martin, S. L., & Kupper, L. L. (2001). Partner violence among adolescents in opposite-sex romantic relationships: Findings from the National Longitudinal Study of Adolescent Health. *American Journal of Public Health, 91*(10), 1679–1685.

Halpern-Felsher, B. L., Millstein, S. G., & Irwin, C. E. (2002). Work group II: Healthy adolescent psychosocial development. *Journal of Adolescent Health, 31*(6), 201–207.

Hammock, G., & O'Hearn, R. (2002). Psychological aggression in dating relationships: Predictive models for males and females. *Violence & Victims, 17*(5), 525–540.

Hampton, M., Jeffery, B., Smith, P., & McWatters, B. (2001). Sexual experience, contraception, and STI prevention among high school students: Results from a Canadian urban centre. *Canadian Journal of Human Sexuality, 10*(3–4), 111–126.

Haninger, K., Thompson, K. M., & Ryan, M. S. (2004). Violence in teen-rated video games. *Medscape General Medicine, 6*(1).

Harper, G. W., & Robinson, W. L. (1999). Pathways to risk among inner-city African-American adolescent females: The influence of gang membership. *American Journal of Community Psychology, 27*(3), 383–405.

Hawkins, J. D., Catalano, R. F., & Miller, J. Y. (1992). Risk and protective factors for alcohol and other drug problems in adolescence and early adulthood: Implications for substance abuse prevention. *Psychological Bulletin, 112*(1), 64–105.

Hawkins, J. D., Herrenkohl, T. I., Farrington, D. P., Brewer, P., Catalano, R. F., Harachi, T. W., et al. (2000). *Predictors of youth violence.* Washington, DC: Substance Abuse and Mental Health Services Administration, U.S. Department of Health and Human Services.

Hawkins, J. D., & Weis, J. G. (1985). The social development model: An integrated approach to delinquency prevention. *Journal of Primary Prevention, 6*(2), 73–97.

Health Canada. (2004). *Canadian Tobacco Use Monitoring Survey: Results for 2003.* Ottawa: Health Canada.

Herrenkohl, T. I., Maguin, E., Hill, K. G., Hawkins, J. D., Abbott, R. D., & Catalano, R. F. (2000). Developmental risk factors for youth violence. *Journal of Adolescent Health, 26*(3), 176–186.

Hill, K. G., White, H. R., Chung, I. J., Hawkins, J. D., & Catalano, R. F. (2000). Early adult outcomes of adolescent binge drinking: Person- and variable-centered analyses of binge drinking trajectories. *Alcoholism: Clinical and Experimental Research, 24*(6), 892–901.

Huesmann, L. R., Moise-Titus, J., Podolski, C., & Eron, L. D. (2003). Longitudinal relations between children's exposure to TV violence and their aggressive and violent behavior in young adulthood: 1977–1992. *Developmental Psychology, 39*(2), 201–221.

Huff, C. R. (1997). Life in the gang: Family, friends, and violence. *American Journal of Sociology, 103*(2), 512–513.

Hussong, A. M. (2000). The settings of adolescent alcohol and drug use. *Journal of Youth and Adolescence, 29*(1), 107–119.

Irwin, C. E., Burg, S. J., & Cart, C. U. (2002). America's adolescents: Where have we been, where are we going? *Journal of Adolescent Health, 31*(6), 91–121.

Jackson, S. M., Cram, F., & Seymour, F. W. (2000). Violence and sexual coercion in high school students' dating relationships. *Journal of Family Violence, 15*(1), 23–36.

Jaffe, P. G., Crooks, C. V., & Goodall, G. R. (2004). The role of affluence in child development: Implications for child support guidelines. *Canadian Family Law Quarterly, 22,* 319–336.

Jaffe, P. G., & Reitzel, D. (1990). Adolescents' views on how to reduce family violence. In R. Roesch, D. Dutton, & V. Saccol, (Eds.), *Family violence: Perspectives on treatment research and policy.* Vancouver: British Columbia Institute on Family Violence.

Jaffe, P. G., Sudermann, M., Reitzel, D., & Killip, S. (1992). An evaluation of a secondary school primary prevention program on violence in intimate relationships. *Violence & Victims, 7*(2), 129–146.

Jaffe, P. G., Wolfe, D. A., Crooks, C. V., Hughes, R., & Baker, L. (2004). The Fourth R: Developing healthy relationships in families and communities through school-based interventions. In P. G. Jaffe, A. Cunningham, & L. Baker (Eds.), *Innovative strategies to end domestic violence for victims, perpetrators, and their children.* New York: Guilford.

Jaffe, P. G., Wolfe, D. A., & Wilson, S. K. (1990). *Children of battered women.* Thousand Oaks, CA: Sage.

Janovsky, J. (2004, August 9). When kids turn cyberbullies. *Newsday.*

Jemmott, J. B., & Jemmott, L. S. (2000). HIV behavioral interventions for adolescents in community settings. In J. L. Peterson & R. J. DiClemente (Eds.), *Handbook of HIV prevention* (pp. 103–127). Dordrecht, NL: Kluwer Acadamic.

Jemmott, J. B., Jemmott, L. S., & Fong, G. T. (1998). Abstinence and safer sex HIV risk-reduction interventions for African American adolescents: A randomized controlled trial. *Jama: Journal of the American Medical Association, 279*(19), 1529–1536.

Jessor, R., Costa, F., Jessor, L., & Donovan, J. E. (1983). Time of 1st intercourse:

A prospective-study. *Journal of Personality and Social Psychology, 44*(3), 608–626.

Jessor, R., Donovan, J. E., & Costa, F. M. (1991). *Beyond adolescence: Problem behavior and young adult development.* New York: Cambridge University Press.

Jessor, R., van den Bos, J., Vanderryn, J., Costa, F. M., & Turbin, M. S. (1995). Protective factors in adolescent problem behavior: Moderator effects and developmental change. *Developmental Psychology, 31*(6), 923–933.

Johnson, C. A., Pentz, M. A., Weber, M. D., Dwyer, J. H., Baer, N., Mackinnon, D. P., et al. (1990). Relative effectiveness of comprehensive community programming for drug-abuse prevention with high-risk and low-risk adolescents. *Journal of Consulting and Clinical Psychology, 58*(4), 447–456.

Johnson, D. W., & Johnson, R. T. (1996). Teaching all students how to manage conflicts constructively: The peacemakers program. *Journal of Negro Education, 65*(3), 322–335.

Johnson, R. L. (2002). Pathways to adolescent health: Early intervention. *Journal of Adolescent Health, 31,* 240–250.

Johnston, L. D., & O'Malley, P. M. (2003). Tobacco, alcohol, and other drug use in adolescence: Modern-day epidemics. In R. P. Weissberg (Ed.), *Long term trends in the well-being of children and youth: Issues in children's and families' lives* (pp. 77–102). Washington, DC: CWLA Press.

Johnston, L. D., O'Malley, P. M., & Bachman, J. G. (2003). *Monitoring the future: National results on adolescent drug use. Overview of key findings.* Bethesda, MD.: National Institute on Drug Abuse, U.S. Department of Health and Human Services, Public Health Service, National Institutes of Health.

Jordan, K. M., Vaughn, J. S., & Woodworth, K. J. (1997). I will survive: Lesbian, gay, and bisexual youths' experience of high school. In M. B. Harris (Ed.), *School experiences of gay and lesbian youth: The invisible minority* (pp. 17–33). Binghamton, NY: Haworth.

Kaiser Family Foundation. (1996). *Kaiser Family Foundation survey on teens and sex: What they say teens need to know and who they listen to* (No. 1159). Menlo Park, CA: Author.

Kaiser Family Foundation. (2003). *National survey of adolescents and young adults: Sexual health knowledge, attitudes, and experiences.* Menlo Park, CA: Author.

Kaplan, E. B. (1997). Women's perceptions of the adolescent experience. *Adolescence, 32*(127), 715–734.

Kilpatrick, D. G., Acierno, R., Saunders, B., Resnick, H. S., Best, C. L., & Schnurr, P. P. (2000). Risk factors for adolescent substance abuse and dependence: Data from a national sample. *Journal of Consulting and Clinical Psychology, 68*(1), 19–30.

Kim, S., Crutchfield, C., Williams, C., & Helper, B. (1998). Toward a new paradigm in substance abuse and other problem behavior prevention for youth: Youth development and empowerment. *Journal of Drug Education, 28*(1), 1–17.

Kimmel, M. S., & Mahler, M. (2003). Adolescent masculinity, homophobia, and violence: Random school shootings, 1982–2001. *American Behavioral Scientist, 46*(10), 1439–1458.

Kindlon, D. J. (2001). *Too much of a good thing: Raising children of character in an indulgent age* (1st ed.). New York: Hyperion.

Kirby, D. (1997). *No easy answers: Research findings on programs to reduce teen pregnancy.* Washington, DC: National Campaign to Prevent Teen Pregnancy.

Kirby, D. (1999). Reflections on two decades of research on teen sexual behavior and pregnancy. *Journal of School Health, 69*(3), 89–94.

Kirby, D. (2001a). *Emerging answers: Research findings on programs to reduce teen pregnancy.* Washington, DC: National Campaign to Prevent Teen Pregnancy.

Kirby, D. (2001b). Understanding what works and what doesn't in reducing adolescent risk-taking. *Family Planning Perspectives, 33*(6), 276–281.

Kirby, D., & Coyle, K. (1997). School-based programs to reduce sexual risk-taking behavior. *Children and Youth Services Review, 19*(5–6), 415–436.

Kirby, D., Short, L., Collins, J., Rugg, D., Kolbe, L., Howard, M., et al. (1994). School-based programs to reduce sexual risk behaviors: A review of effectiveness. *Public Health Reports, 109*(3), 339–360.

Klinteberg, B. A., Andersson, T., Magnusson, D., & Stattin, H. (1993). Hyperactive behavior in childhood as related to subsequent alcohol problems and violent offending: A longitudinal study of male subjects. *Personality and Individual Differences, 15*(4), 381–388.

Kodluboy, D. W. (1997). Gang-oriented interventions. In A. P. Goldstein & J. C. Conoley (Eds.), *School violence intervention: A practical handbook* (pp. 198–214). New York: Guilford.

Kosciw, J. G. (2004). *The 2003 National School Climate Survey: The school-related experiences of our nation's lesbian, gay, bisexual, and transgender youth.* New York: GLSEN.

Kyratzis, A., & Guo, J. S. (2001). Preschool girls' and boys' verbal conflict strategies in the United States and China. *Research on Language and Social Interaction, 34*(1), 45–74.

LaFreniere, P. (1999). *Emotional development: A biosocial perspective* (1st ed.). New York: Wadsworth.

Langille, D. B., & Curtis, L. (2002). Factors associated with sexual intercourse before age 15 among female adolescents in Nova Scotia. *Canadian Journal of Human Sexuality, 11*(2), 91–99.

Laursen, B., & Collins, W. A. (1994). Interpersonal conflict during adolescence. *Psychological Bulletin, 115*(2), 197–209.

Lavoie, F., Hebert, M., Tremblay, R. E., Vitaro, F., Vezina, L., & McDuff, P. (2002). History of family dysfunction and perpetration of dating violence by adolescent boys: A longitudinal study. *Journal of Adolescent Health, 30*(5), 375–383.

Lempers, J. D., & Clark-Lempers, D. S. (1993). A functional comparison of same-sex and opposite sex friendships during adolescence. *Journal of Adolescent Research, 8*(1), 89–108.

Lerner, R. M. (2002). *Adolescence: Development, diversity, context, and application.* Upper Saddle River, NJ: Prentice Hall.

Lerner, R. M., & Galambos, N. L. (1998). Adolescent development: Challenges and opportunities for research, programs, and policies. *Annual Review of Psychology, 49,* 413–446.

Lever, J. (1978). Sex differences in the complexity of children's play and games. *American Sociological Review, 43*(4), 471–483.

Levesque, D. A., Gelles, R. J., & Velicer, W. F. (2000). Development and validation of a stages of change measure for men in batterer treatment. *Cognitive Therapy and Research, 24*(2), 175–199.

Lewinsohn, P. M., Rohde, P., & Seeley, J. R. (1996). Alcohol consumption in high school adolescents: Frequency of use and dimensional structure of associated problems. *Addiction, 91*(3), 375–390.

Litrownik, A. J., Elder, J. P., Campbell, N. R., Ayala, G. X., Slymen, D. J., Parra-Medina, D., et al. (2000). Evaluation of a tobacco and alcohol use prevention program for Hispanic migrant adolescents: Promoting the protective factor of parent-child communication. *Preventive Medicine: An International Journal Devoted to Practice & Theory, 31*(2,Pt.1), 124–133.

Luthar, S. S. (2003). The culture of affluence: Psychological costs of material wealth. *Child Development, 74,* 1581–1593.

Luthar, S. S., & D'Avanzo, K. (1999). Contextual factors in substance use: A study of suburban and inner-city adolescents. *Development & Psychopathology, 11,* 845–867.

Lynam, D. R., & Milich, R. (2002). An empirical look at Project DARE. *National Association of School Psychologists (NASP) Communique, 31*(4), 10.

Lynam, D. R., Milich, R., Zimmerman, R., Novak, S. P., Logan, T. K., Martin, C., et al. (1999). Project DARE: No effects at 10-year follow-up. *Journal of Consulting and Clinical Psychology, 67*(4), 590–593.

MacMillan, H. L., Fleming, J. E., Streiner, D. L., Lin, E., Boyle, M. H., Jamieson, E., et al. (2001). Childhood abuse and lifetime psychopathology in a community sample. *American Journal of Psychiatry, 158*(11), 1878–1883.

Maney, D. W., Higham-Gardhill, D. A., & Mahoney, B. S. (2002). The alcohol-related psychosocial and behavioral risks of a nationally representative sample of adolescents. *Journal of School Health, 72,* 157–163.

Marshall, P. F., & Vaillancourt, M. A. (1993). *Changing the landscape: Ending violence, achieving equality, final report.* Ottawa: Canadian Panel on Violence against Women.

Martin, C. L. (1994). Cognitive influences on the development and maintenance of gender segregation. In C. Leaper (Ed.), *Childhood gender segregation: Causes and consequences* (pp. 35–51). San Francisco: Jossey-Bass.

Martino, W. (1999). "Cool boys," "party animal," "squids," and "poofters": Interrogating the dynamics and politics of adolescent masculinities in school. *British Journal of Sociology, 20*(2), 239–263.

Mash, E. J., & Wolfe, D. A. (2005). *Abnormal child psychology* (3rd ed.). Pacific Groves, CA: Wadsworth.

Masten, A. S. (2001). Ordinary magic: Resilience processes in development. *American Psychologist, 56*(3), 227–238.

Masten, A. S., & Coatsworth, J. D. (1998). The development of competence in favorable and unfavorable environments: Lessons from research on successful children. *American Psychologist, 53*(2), 205–220.

Maticka-Tyndale, E. (2001). Sexual health and Canadian youth: How do we measure up? *Canadian Journal of Human Sexuality, 10*(1–2), 1–17.

McEvoy, A., & Welker, R. (2000). Antisocial behavior, academic failure, and school climate: A critical review. *Journal of Emotional & Behavioral Disorders, 8*(3), 130–140.

McHale, S. M., Crouter, A. C., & Whiteman, S. D. (2003). The family contexts of gender development in childhood and adolescence. *Social Development, 12*(1), 125–148.

McIntyre-Smith, A. (2004). *Patterns of adolescent risk behaviour: Sex, drugs, and violence.* Unpublished master's thesis, University of Western Ontario, London.

McMaster, L. E., Connolly, J., Pepler, D., & Craig, W. M. (2002). Peer to peer sexual harassment in early adolescence: A developmental perspective. *Development and Psychopathology, 14*(1), 91–105.

McNeely, C. A., Nonnemaker, J. M., & Blum, R. W. (2002). Promoting school connectedness: Evidence from the national longitudinal study of adolescent health. *Journal of School Health, 72*(4), 138–146.

Media Awareness Network. (2000). *YTV tween report, 2000.* Retrieved July 6, 2004, from www.media-awareness.ca/eng/issues/stats/usenet2000.htm #tweens.

Melnick, S. M., & Hinshaw, S. P. (2000). Emotion regulation and parenting in AD/HD and comparison boys: Linkages with social behaviors and peer preference. *Journal of Abnormal Child Psychology, 28*(1), 73–86.

Meschke, L. L., Bartholomae, S., & Zentall, S. R. (2002). Adolescent sexuality and parent-adolescent processes: Promoting healthy teen choices. *Journal of Adolescent Health, 31,* 264–279.

Mezzich, A. C., Tarter, R. E., Giancola, P. R., Lu, S., Kirisci, L., & Parks, S.

(1997). Substance use and risky sexual behavior in female adolescents. *Drug and Alcohol Dependence, 44*(2–3), 157–166.

Mihalic, S. F. (2001). *Blueprints for violence prevention.* Washington, DC: U.S. Department of Justice, Office of Justice Programs, Office of Juvenile Justice and Delinquency Prevention.

Miller, B., & Paikoff, R. L. (1992). Comparing adolescent pregnancy programs. In B. Miller, J. J. Card, R. L. Paikoff, & J. L. Peterson (Eds.), *Preventing adolescent pregnancy* (pp. 265–284). Newbury, CA: Sage.

Miller, B. C. (2000). Family influences on adolescent sexual and contraceptive behavior. *Journal of Sex Research, 39*(1), 22–26.

Miller, W. R., & Rollnick, S. (2002). *Motivational interviewing: Preparing people for change.* New York: Guilford.

Mitchell, K. J., Finkelhor, D., & Wolak, J. (2001). Risk factors for and impact of online sexual solicitation of youth. *Jama: Journal of the American Medical Association, 285*(23), 3011–3014.

Modzeleski, W., Small, M. L., & Kann, L. K. (1999). Alcohol and other drug prevention policies and education in the United States. *Journal of Health Education, 30*(5), S42–S49.

Moffitt, T. E., Caspi, A., Dickson, N., Silva, P., & Stanton, W. (1996). Childhood-onset versus adolescent-onset antisocial conduct problems in males: Natural history from ages 3 to 18 years. *Development and Psychopathology, 8*(2), 399–424.

Moody, K. A., Childs, J. C., & Sepples, S. B. (2003). Intervening with at-risk youth: Evaluation of the youth empowerment and support program. *Pediatric Nursing, 29*(4), 263–273.

Morales, A. T. (1992). Therapy with Latino gang members. In L. A. Vargas & J. Koss-Chioino (Eds.), *Working with culture: Psychotherapeutic interventions with ethnic minority children and adolescents* (pp. 129–154). San Francisco: Jossey-Bass.

Mosher, J. F. (1999). Alcohol policy and the young adult: Establishing priorities, building partnerships, overcoming barriers. *Addiction, 94*(3), 357–369.

Mrazek, P. B., & Haggerty, R. J. (1994). *Reducing risks for mental disorders: Frontiers for preventive intervention research.* Washington, DC: National Academy Press.

Murphy, C. M., & Blumenthal, D. R. (2000). The mediating influence of interpersonal problems on the intergenerational transmission of relationship aggression. *Personal Relationships, 7*(2), 203–218.

Murphy, S. (2000). *Deaths: Final data for 1998. National vital statistics report* (Vol. 48, No. 11). Centers for Disease Control and Prevention, National Center for Health Statistics, National Vital Statistics System.

Musher-Eizenman, D. R., Holub, S. C., & Arnett, M. (2003). Attitude and peer influences on adolescent substance use: The moderating effect of age, sex, and substance. *Journal of Drug Education, 33*(1), 1–23.

Nation, M., Crusto, C., Wandersman, A., Kumpfer, K. L., Seybolt, D., Morris-sey-Kane, E., et al. (2003). What works in prevention: Principles of effective prevention programs. *American Psychologist, 58*(6–7), 449–456.

National Center for Education Statistics. (2000). *Dropout rates in the United States.* Washington, DC: U.S. Department of Education.

National Center on Addiction and Substance Abuse at Columbia University. (1999). *Dangerous liaisons: Substance abuse and sex.* New York: Author. Available from http://www.casacolumbia.org/supportcasa/item.asp?cID =12&PID=115.

National Children's Home. (2002). Survey. Retrieved March 18, 2004, from www.nch.org/uk/news.

National Film Board of Canada. (1999). A love that kills. Montreal.

National Highway Traffic Safety Administration. (2003). *Traffic safety facts, 2002* (No. DOT HS 809 612). Washington, DC: National Center for Statistics and Analysis.

National Institute of Mental Health HIV Prevention Trial Group. (2001). Social cognitive theory mediators of behavior change in the National Institute of Mental Health Multisite HIV Prevention Trial. *Health Psychology, 20*(5), 369–376.

National Research Council. (1996). *Understanding violence against women.* Washington, DC: National Academy Press.

Neemann, J., Hubbard, J., & Masten, A. S. (1995). The changing importance of romantic relationship involvement to competence from late childhood to late adolescence. *Development and Psychopathology, 7*(4), 727–750.

Neumark-Sztainer, D., Story, M., French, S. A., & Resnick, M. D. (1997). Psychosocial correlates of health compromising behaviors among adolescents. *Health Education Research, 12*(1), 37–52.

Newman, B. M., Lohman, B. J., Newman, P. R., Mayers, M. C., & Smith, V. L. (2000). Experiences of urban youth navigating the transition to ninth grade. *Youth & Society, 31*(4), 387–416.

Odgers, C. L., & Moretti, M. M. (2002). Aggressive and antisocial girls: Research update and challenges. *International Journal of Forensic Mental Health, 1*(2), 103–119.

O'Donnell, J., Michalak, E., & Ames, E. (1997). Inner-city youths helping children: After-school programs to promote bonding and reduce risk. *Social Work in Education, 19,* 231–241.

Office of Applied Statistics. (2002). *Results from the 2001 National Household Survey on Drug Abuse: Vol. 1. Summary of national findings* (DHHS Publication No. SMA 02–3758, NHSDA Series H-17). Rockville, MD: Substance Abuse and Mental Health Administration.

O'Hara, P., Parris, D., Fichtner, R. R., & Oster, R. (1998). Influence of alcohol and drug use on AIDS risk behavior among youth in dropout prevention. *Journal of Drug Education, 28*(2), 159–168.

O'Keefe, M. (1997). Predictors of dating violence among high school students. *Journal of Interpersonal Violence, 12*(4), 546–569.

O'Keefe, M., & Treister, L. (1998). Victims of dating violence among high school students: Are the predictors different for males and females? *Violence against Women, 4*(2), 195–223.

Olds, D., Henderson, C. R., Jr., Cole, R., Eckenrode, J., Kitzman, H., Luckey, D., et al. (1998). Long-term effects of nurse home visitation on children's criminal and antisocial behavior: 15-year follow-up of a randomized controlled trial. *Jama: Journal of the American Medical Association, 280*(14), 1238–1244.

Olweus, D., Limber, S., & Mihalic, S. F. (1999). *Bullying prevention program.* Boulder: Center for the Study and Prevention of Violence, Institute of Behavioral Science, University of Colorado at Boulder.

Orpinas, P., Murray, N., & Kelder, S. (1999). Parental influences on students' aggressive behaviors and weapon carrying. *Health Education & Behavior, 26*(6), 774–787.

Parker, E. L. (2001). Hungry for honor. *Interpretation, 55,* 148–161.

Parrott, D. J., Adams, H. E., & Zeichner, A. (2002). Homophobia: Personality and attitudinal correlates. *Personality and Individual Differences, 32*(7), 1269–1278.

Pascoe, C. J. (2003). Multiple masculinities? Teenage boys talk about jocks and gender. *American Behavioral Scientist, 46*(10), 1423–1438.

Patterson, G. R., & Yoerger, K. (1997). A developmental model for late-onset delinquency. In D. W. Osgood & J. McCord (Eds.), *Motivation and delinquency* (Vol. 44). Lincoln: University of Nebraska Press.

Pentz, M. A., Dwyer, J. H., Mackinnon, D. P., Flay, B. R., Hansen, W. B., Wang, E. Y. I., et al. (1989). A multicommunity trial for primary prevention of adolescent drug-abuse: Effects on drug-use prevalence. *Jama: Journal of the American Medical Association, 261*(22), 3259–3266.

Pentz, M. A., Mihalic, S. F., & Grotpeter, J. K. (1997). *The midwestern prevention project* (Vol. 1). Boulder: Center for the Study and Prevention of Violence, Institute of Behavioral Science, University of Colorado at Boulder.

Pepler, D. J., Craig, W. M., Connolly, J., & Henderson, K. (2002). Bullying, sexual harassment, dating violence, and substance use among adolescents. In C. Wekerle & A.-M. Wall (Eds.), *The violence and addiction equation: Theoretical and clinical issues in substance abuse and relationship violence* (pp. 153–168). New York: Brunner-Routledge.

Perry, C. L., Williams, C. L., Komro, K. A., Veblen-Mortenson, S., Forster, J. L., Bernstein-Lachter, R., et al. (2000). Project Northland high school interventions: Community action to reduce alcohol use. *Health Education & Behavior, 27*(1), 29–49.

Petraitis, J., Flay, B. R., & Miller, T. Q. (1995). Reviewing theories of adolescent substance use: Organizing pieces in the puzzle. *Psychological Bulletin, 117*(1), 67–86.

Phinney, J. (1990). Ethnic identity in adolescents and adults: A review of the research. *Psychological Bulletin, 108,* 99–514.

Phoenix, A., Frosh, S., & Pattman, R. (2003). Producing contradictory masculine subject positions: Narratives of threat, homophobia, and bullying in
11–14 year old boys. *Journal of Social Issues, 59*(1), 179–195.

Pipher, M. B. (1994). *Reviving Ophelia: Saving the selves of adolescent girls.* New
York: Putnam.

Pollack, W. (1998). *Real boys: Rescuing our sons from the myth of boyhood.* New
York: Henry Holt.

Pollak, S. D., Cicchetti, D., Hornung, K., & Reed, A. (2000). Recognizing
emotion in faces: Developmental effects of child abuse and neglect. *Developmental Psychology, 36*(5), 679–688.

Prinstein, M. J., Meade, C. S., & Cohen, G. L. (2003). Adolescent oral sex, peer
popularity, and perceptions of best friends' sexual behavior. *Journal of Pediatric Psychology, 28*(4), 243–249.

Prochaska, J. M., Prochaska, J. O., & Levesque, D. A. (2001). A transtheoretical
approach to changing organizations. *Administration and Policy in Mental
Health, 28*(4), 247–261.

Prochaska, J. O., & DiClemente, C. C. (1983). Stages and processes of self-
change of smoking: Toward an integrative model of change. *Journal of
Consulting and Clinical Psychology, 51*(3), 390–395.

Prochaska, J. O., & Velicer, W. F. (1997). The transtheoretical model: Introduc-
tion. *American Journal of Health Promotion, 12*(1), 6–7.

Rai, A. A., Stanton, B., Wu, Y., Li, X. M., Galbraith, J., Cottrell, L., et al.
(2003). Relative influences of perceived parental monitoring and perceived peer involvement on adolescent risk behaviors: An analysis of six
cross-sectional data sets. *Journal of Adolescent Health, 33*(2), 108–118.

Randall, H. E., & Byers, E. S. (2003). What is sex? Students' definitions of having sex, sexual partner, and unfaithful sexual behaviour. *Canadian Journal of Human Sexuality, 12,* 87–96.

Reitzel-Jaffe, D., & Wolfe, D. A. (2001). Predictors of relationship abuse among
young men. *Journal of Interpersonal Violence, 16*(2), 99–115.

Resnick, M. D., Bearman, P. S., Blum, R. W., Bauman, K. E., Harris, K. M.,
Jones, J., et al. (1997). Protecting adolescents from harm: Findings from
the National Longitudinal Study on Adolescent Health. *Jama: Journal of
the American Medical Association, 278*(10), 823–832.

Resnick, M. D., Harris, L. J., & Blum, R. W. (1993). The impact of caring and
connectedness on adolescent health and well-being. *Journal of Paediatrics
and Child Health, 29,* S3–S9.

Riggs, D. S., & O'Leary, K. D. (1989). A theoretical model of courtship aggression. In M. A. Pirog-Good & J. E. Stets (Eds.), *Violence in dating relationships: Emerging social issues* (pp. 3–32). New York: Praeger.

Riggs, D. S., & O' Leary, K. D. (1996). Aggression between heterosexual dating partners: An examination of a causal model of courtship aggression. *Journal of Interpersonal Violence, 11*(4), 519–540.

Roberts, D. F., Foehr, U. G., Rideout, V. J., & Brodia, M. (1999). *Kids and media and the new millennium: A comprehensive national analysis of children's media use.* Menlo Park, CA: Kaiser Family Foundation.

Roberts, D. F., Henriksen, L., & Christenson, P. (1999). *Substance use in popular movies and music* (No. BKD305). Rockville, MD: National Clearinghouse for Alcohol and Drug Information.

Robin, L., Dittus, P., Whitaker, D., Crosby, R., Ethier, K., Mezoff, J., et al. (2004). Behavioral interventions to reduce incidence of HIV, STD, and pregnancy among adolescents: A decade in review. *Journal of Adolescent Health, 34*(1), 3–26.

Rogosch, F. A., Cicchetti, D., & Aber, J. L. (1995). The role of child maltreatment in early deviations in cognitive and affective processing abilities and later peer relationship problems. *Development and Psychopathology, 7*(4), 591–609.

Romer, D. (2003). *Reducing adolescent risk: Toward an integrated approach.* Thousand Oaks, CA: Sage.

Rosenfeld, A., & Wise, N. (2000). *The over-scheduled child: Avoiding the hyper-parenting trap.* New York: St. Martin's Griffin.

Roth, J. L., & Brooks-Gunn, J. (2003). Youth development programs: Risk, prevention, and policy. *Journal of Adolescent Health, 32*(3), 170–182.

Rouner, D., Slater, M. D., & Domenech-Rodriguez, M. (2003). Adolescent evaluation of gender role and sexual imagery in television advertisements. *Journal of Broadcasting & Electronic Media, 47*(3), 435–454.

Ruble, D. N., & Martin, C. L. (1998). Gender development. In W. Damon and N. Eisenberg (Eds.), *Handbook of child psychology: Vol. 3. Social, emotional, and personality development* (pp. 933–1016). New York: John Wiley & Sons.

Rutter, M., & Sroufe, L. A. (2000). Developmental psychopathology: Concepts and challenges. *Development and Psychopathology, 12*(3), 265–296.

Sameroff, A. J., & Fiese, B. H. (2000). Models of development and developmental risk. In C. H. Zeanah, Jr. (Ed.), *Handbook of infant mental health* (2nd ed., pp. 3–19): New York: Guilford Press.

Samet, N., & Kelly, E. W. (1987). The relationship of steady dating to self-esteem and sex-role identity among adolescents. *Adolescence, 22*(85), 231–245.

Savin-Williams, R. C., & Berndt, T. J. (1990). Friendship and peer relations. In S. S. Feldman & G. R. Elliott (Eds.), *At the threshold: The developing adolescent* (pp. 277–307). Cambridge, MA: Harvard University Press.

Schuster, M. A., Bell, R. M., & Kanouse, D. E. (1996). The sexual practices of adolescent virgins: Genital sexual activities of high school students who have never had vaginal intercourse. *American Journal of Public Health, 86*(11), 1570–1576.

Scott, K. L., Wekerle, C., & Wolfe, D. A. (1997). *Considered sex differences in youth self-reports of violence and their implications for the development of violence relationships.* Paper presented at the biennial meeting of the Society for Research in Child Development, Washington, DC.

Scott, K. L., & Wolfe, D. A. (2003). Readiness to change as a predictor of outcome in batterer treatment. *Journal of Consulting and Clinical Psychology, 71,* 879–889.

Scott, K. L., Wolfe, D. A., & Wekerle, C. (2003). Maltreatment and trauma: tracking the connections in adolescence. *Child and Adolescent Psychiatric Clinics of North America, 12*(2), 211–230.

Serbin, L. A., Moller, L. C., Gulko, J., Powlishta, K. K., & Colburne, K. A. (1994). The emergence of gender segregation in toddler playgroups. In C. Leaper (Ed.), *Childhood gender segregation: Causes and consequences* (pp. 7–17). San Francisco, CA: Jossey-Bass.

Serbin, L. A., Powlishta, K. K., & Gulko, J. (1993). The development of sex typing in middle childhood. *Monographs of the Society for Research in Child Development, 58*(2), 5–74.

Sewell, T. (1997). *Black masculinities and schooling: How black boys survive modern schooling.* Stoke on Trent, UK: Trentham.

Shakib, S. (2003). Female basketball participation: Negotiating the conflation of peer status and gender status from childhood through puberty. *American Behavioral Scientist, 46*(10), 1405–1422.

Shapiro, J. P., Baumeister, R. F., & Kessler, J. W. (1991). A 3-component model of children's teasing: Aggression, humor, and ambiguity. *Journal of Social and Clinical Psychology, 10*(4), 459–472.

Sharpe, D., & Taylor, J. K. (1999). An examination of variables from a social-developmental model to explain physical and psychological dating violence. *Canadian Journal of Behavioural Science, 31*(3), 165–175.

Sheehan, K., DiCara, J., LeBailly, S., & Christoffel, K. K. (1999). Adapting the gang model: Peer mentoring for violence prevention. *Pediatrics, 104,* 50–54.

Shrier, L. A., Emans, S. J., Woods, E. R., & DuRant, R. H. (1996). The association of sexual risk behaviors and problem drug behaviors in high school students. *Journal of Adolescent Health, 20*(5), 337–383.

Shrier, L. A., Goodman, E., & Emans, S. J. (1999). Partner condom use among adolescent girls with sexually transmitted diseases. *Journal of Adolescent Health, 24*(5), 257–361.

Sieving, R. E., Maruyama, G., Williams, C. L., & Perry, C. L. (2000). Pathways to adolescent alcohol use: Potential mechanisms of parent influence. *Journal of Research on Adolescence, 10*(4), 489–514.

Sieving, R. E., Perry, C. L., & Williams, C. L. (2000). Do friendships change behaviors, or do behaviors change friendships? Examining paths of influence in young adolescents' alcohol use. *Journal of Adolescent Health, 26*(1), 27–35.

Signorella, M. L., Bigler, R. S., & Liben, L. S. (1993). Developmental differences in children's gender schemata about others: A meta-analytic review. *Developmental Review, 13,* 147–183.

Silbereisen, R. K., & Kracke, B. (1997). Self-reported maturational timing and adaptation in adolescence. In J. Schulenberg, J. L. Maggs, and Hurrelmann, K. (Eds.), *Health risks and developmental transitions during adolescence* (pp. 85–109). New York: Cambridge University Press.

Silverman, J. G., Raj, A., Mucci, L. A., & Hathaway, J. E. (2001). Dating violence against adolescent girls and associated substance use, unhealthy weight control, sexual risk behavior, pregnancy, and suicidality. *Jama: Journal of the American Medical Association, 286*(5), 572–579.

Simons-Morton, B. (2004). Prospective association of peer influence, school engagement, drinking expectancies, and parent expectations with drinking initiation among sixth graders. *Addictive Behaviors, 29*(2), 299–309.

Singh, S., & Darroch, J. E. (2000). Adolescent pregnancy and childbearing: Levels and trends in developed countries. *Family Planning Perspectives, 32*(1), 14–23.

Skara, S., & Sussman, S. (2003). A review of 25 long-term adolescent tobacco and other drug use prevention program evaluations. *Preventive Medicine, 37*(5), 451–474.

Skroban, S. B., Gottfredson, D. C., & Gottfredson, G. D. (1999). A school-based social competency promotion demonstration. *Evaluation Review, 23*(1), 3–27.

Snyder, H., & Sickmund, M. (1999). *Juvenile offenders and victims: 1999 national report.* Washington, DC: Office of Juvenile Justice and Delinquency Prevention.

Spoth, R., Goldberg, C., & Redmond, C. (1999). Engaging families in longitudinal preventive intervention research: Discrete-time survival analysis of socioeconomic and social-emotional risk factors. *Journal of Consulting and Clinical Psychology, 67*(1), 157–163.

Spoth, R., Redmond, C., & Lepper, H. (1999). Alcohol initiation outcomes of universal family-focused preventive interventions: One- and two-year follow-ups of a controlled study. *Journal of Studies on Alcohol,* 103–111.

Sroufe, L. A. (1979). The coherence of individual development: Early care, attachment, and subsequent developmental issues. *American Psychologist, 34*(10), 834–841.

Sroufe, L. A. (2000). Early relationships and the development of children. *Infant Mental Health Journal, 21*(1–2), 67–74.

Sroufe, L. A., Bennett, C., Englund, M., Urban, J., & Shulman, S. (1993). The significance of gender boundaries in preadolescence: Contemporary correlates and antecedents of boundary violation and maintenance. *Child Development, 64*(2), 455–466.

Stanton, B., Li, X. M., Pack, R., Cottrell, L., Harris, C., & Burns, J. (2003). Longitudinal influences of perceptions of peer and parental factors on African-American adolescent risk involvement. *Journal of Urban Health, 79*, 536–548.

Stattin, H., & Magnusson, D. (1990). *Pubertal maturation in female development.* Hillsdale, NJ: Lawrence Erlbaum Associates.

Stedman, L. C. (2003). U.S. educational achievement in the 20th century: Brilliant success and persistent failure. In R. P. Weissberg & H. J. Walberg (Eds.), *Long-term trends in the well-being of children and youth: Issues in children's and families' lives* (pp. 53–76). Washington, DC: Child Welfare League of America.

Steinberg, L. (2004). Risk taking in adolescence: What changes, and why? *Annals of the New York Academy of Sciences, 1021*, 51–58.

Steinberg, L., & Morris, A. S. (2001). Adolescent development. *Annual Review of Psychology, 52*, 83–110.

Steinberg, L., & Scott, E. S. (2003). Less guilty by reason of adolescence: Developmental immaturity, diminished responsibility, and the juvenile death penalty. *American Psychologist, 58*(12), 1009–1018.

Stephens, R. D. (1998). Safe school planning. In D. S. Elliott, B. A. Hamburg, & K. R. Williams (Eds.), *Violence in American schools: A new perspective.* New York: Cambridge University Press.

St. Lawrence, J. S., Jefferson, K. W., Alleyne, E., & Brasfield, T. L. (1995). Comparison of education versus behavioral skills training interventions in lowering sexual HIV-risk behavior of substance-dependent adolescents. *Journal of Consulting and Clinical Psychology, 63*(1), 154–157.

St. Lawrence, J. S., & Scott, C. P. (1996). Examination of the relationship between African American adolescents' condom use at sexual onset and later sexual behavior: Implications for condom distribution programs. *AIDS Education and Prevention, 8*(3), 258–266.

Stoil, M. J., Hill, G. A., Jansen, M. A., Sambrano, S., & Winn, F. J. (2000). Benefits of community-based demonstration efforts: Knowledge gained in substance abuse prevention. *Journal of Community Psychology, 28*(4), 375–389.

Stomfay-Stitz, A. (1993). *Peace education in America, 1828–1990.* Metuchen, NJ: Scarecrow.

Straus, M. A., Gelles, R. J., & Steinmetz, S. K. (1980). *Behind closed doors: Violence in the American family* (1st ed.). Garden City, NY: Anchor/Doubleday.

Substance Abuse and Mental Health Services Administration (SAMHSA). (2003). *Overview of findings from the 2002 National Survey on Drug Use and Health* (DHHS Publication No. SMA 03–3774, NHSDA Series H-21). Rockville, MD: SAMHSA Office of Applied Studies.

Sudermann, M., Jaffe, P. G., & Schieck, E. (1996). *A.S.A.P.: A School-based antiviolence program: Revised.* London, ON: London Family Court Clinic.

Sutherland, I., & Shephard, J. P. (2002). A personality based measure of adolescent violence. *British Journal of Criminology, 42*(2), 433–441.

Taffel, R., & Blau, M. (2001). *The second family: Dealing with peer power, pop culture, the wall of silence—and other challenges of raising today's teens.* New York: St. Martin's Griffin.

Tannen, D. (1991). *You just don't understand: Women and men in conversation.* New York: Ballantine.

Tapert, S. F., Granholm, E., Leedy, N. G., & Brown, S. A. (2002). Substance use and withdrawal: Neuropsychological functioning over 8 years in youth. *Journal of the International Neuropsychological Society, 8*(7), 873–883.

Thorne, B. (1993). *Gender play: Girls and boys in school.* New Brunswick, NJ: Rutgers University Press.

Thorne, B., & Luria, Z. (1986). Sexuality and gender in children's daily worlds. *Social Problems, 33*(3), 187–190.

Tobler, N. S., & Stratton, H. (1997). Effectiveness of school-based drug prevention programs: A meta-analysis of the research. *Journal of Primary Prevention, 18,* 71–128.

Totten, M. D. (2000). *Guys, gangs, and girlfriend abuse.* Orchard Park, NY: Broadview.

Travis, J. W. (1988). *Wellness workbook.* Berkeley, CA: Ten Speed.

Troiden, R. R. (1989). The formation of homosexual identities. *Journal of Homosexuality, 17*(1–2), 43–73.

Tutty, L., Bradshaw, C., Thurston, W. E., Tunstall, L., Dewar, M. E., Toy-Pries, D., et al. (2002). *School based violence prevention programs: A resource manual to prevent violence against girls and young women.* Calgary, AB: RESOLVE Alberta.

U.S. Department of Health and Human Services. (1996). *Physical activity and health: A report of the surgeon general.* Atlanta: U.S. Department of Health and Human Services, Centers for Disease Control and Prevention, National Center for Chronic Disease Prevention and Health Promotion.

U.S. Public Health Service & Office of the Surgeon General. (2000). *Youth violence: A report of the Surgeon General.* Washington, DC: Department of Health and Human Services.

U.S. Surgeon General (2004). *The health consequences of smoking: A report of the Surgeon General.* Washington, DC: Author.

Walker, E. (2002). Adolescent neurodevelopment and psychopathology. *Current Directions in Psychological Science, 11*(1), 24–28.

Walker, E., & Bollini, A. M. (2002). Pubertal neurodevelopment and the emergence of psychotic symptoms. *Schizophrenia Research, 54*(1–2), 17–23.

Walker, M. L., Schmidt, L. M., & Lunghofer, L. (1993). Youth gangs. In M. I.

Singer & L. T. Singer (Eds.), *Handbook for screening adolescents at psychosocial risk* (pp. 400–422). New York: Lexington.

Wallace, J. M., Brown, T. N., Bachman, J. G., & Laveist, T. A. (2003). The influence of race and religion on abstinence from alcohol, cigarettes, and marijuana among adolescents. *Journal of Studies on Alcohol, 64*(6), 843–848.

Wang, A. Y. (1994). Pride and prejudice in high school gang members. *Adolescence, 29*(114), 279–292.

Wang, L. Y., Davis, M., Robin, L., Collins, J., Coyle, K., & Baumler, E. (2000). Economic evaluation of Safer Choices: A school-based human immunodeficiency virus, other sexually transmitted diseases, and pregnancy prevention program. *Archives of Pediatrics & Adolescent Medicine, 154*(10), 1017–1024.

Waters, E., Merrick, S., Treboux, D., Crowell, J., & Albersheim, L. (2000). Attachment security in infancy and early adulthood: A twenty-year longitudinal study. *Child Development, 71*(3), 684–689.

Watson, J. M., Cascardi, M., Avery-Leaf, S., & O'Leary, K. D. (2001). High school students' responses to dating aggression. *Violence & Victims, 16*(3), 339–348.

Weissberg, R. P. (2003). *Long term trends in the well-being of children and youth.* Washington, DC: CWLA.

Wekerle, C., Wolfe, D. A., Hawkins, D. L., Pittman, A.-L., Glickman, A., & Lovald, B. E. (2001). Childhood maltreatment, posttraumatic stress symptomatology, and adolescent dating violence: Considering the value of adolescent perceptions of abuse and a trauma mediational model. *Development & Psychopathology, 13*(4), 847–871.

Whitaker, D., & Miller, K. (2000). Parent-adolescent discussions about sex and condoms: Impact on peer influences of sexual risk behavior. *Journal of Adolescent Research, 15*(2), 251–273.

White, H. R., Bates, M., & Labouvie, E. (1998). Adult outcomes of adolescent drug use: A comparison of process-oriented and incremental analyses. In R. Jessor (Ed.), *New perspectives on adolescent risk behavior.* New York: Cambridge University Press.

Whiting, B. B., & Edwards, C. P. (1988). *Children of different worlds.* Cambridge, MA: Harvard University Press.

Wiley, D. C. (2002). The ethics of abstinence-only and abstinence-plus sexuality education. *Journal of School Health, 72*(4), 164–167.

Williams, P. G., Holmbeck, G. N., & Greenley, R. N. (2002). Adolescent health psychology. *Journal of Consulting & Clinical Psychology, 70*(3), 828–842.

Wills, T. A., & Dishion, T. J. (2004). Temperament and adolescent substance use: A transactional analysis of emerging self-control. *Journal of Clinical Child and Adolescent Psychology, 33*(1), 69–81.

Wolfe, D. A. (1985). Child-abusive parents: An empirical review and analysis. *Psychological Bulletin, 97*(3), 462–482.

Wolfe, D. A. (1999). *Child abuse: Implications for child development and psychopathology* (2nd ed.). Thousand Oaks, CA: Sage.

Wolfe, D. A., Crooks, C. V., Lee, V., McIntyre-Smith, A., & Jaffe, P. G. (2003). The effects of children's exposure to domestic violence: A meta-analysis and critique. *Clinical Child and Family Psychology Review, 6*(3), 171–187.

Wolfe, D. A., & Jaffe, P. G. (2001). Prevention of domestic violence: Emerging initiatives. In S. A. Graham-Bermann & J. L. Edleson (Eds.), *Domestic violence in the lives of children: the future of research, intervention, and social policy* (pp. 283–298). Washington, DC: American Psychological Association.

Wolfe, D. A., Scott, K., & Crooks, C. V. (2005). Dating relationship violence among adolescent girls. In D. Bell-Dolan, E. J. Mash, & S. Foster (Eds.), *Handbook of emotional and behavioral problems in girls* (pp. 381–414). New York: Kluwer Academic.

Wolfe, D. A., Scott, K., Wekerle, C., & Pittman, A.-L. (2001). Child maltreatment: Risk of adjustment problems and dating violence in adolescence. *Journal of the American Academy of Child and Adolescent Psychiatry, 40*(3), 282–289.

Wolfe, D. A., Wekerle, C., Gough, R., Reitzel-Jaffe, D., Grasley, C., Pittman, A., et al. (1996). *The youth relationships manual: A group approach with adolescents for the prevention of woman abuse and the promotion of healthy relationships.* Thousand Oaks, CA: Sage.

Wolfe, D. A., Wekerle, C., Reitzel-Jaffe, D., & Lefebvre, L. (1998). Factors associated with abusive relationships among maltreated and nonmaltreated youth. *Development and Psychopathology, 10*(1), 61–85.

Wolfe, D. A., Wekerle, C., & Scott, K. (1997). *Alternatives to violence: Empowering youth to develop healthy relationships.* Thousand Oaks, CA: Sage.

Wolfe, D. A., Wekerle, C., Scott, K., Straatman, A. L., & Grasley, C. (2004). Predicting abuse in adolescent dating relationships over 1 year. *Journal of Abnormal Psychology, 113*(3), 406–415.

Wolfe, D. A., Wekerle, C., Scott, K., Straatman, A. L., Grasley, C., & Reitzel-Jaffe, D. (2003). Dating violence prevention with at-risk youth: A controlled outcome evaluation. *Journal of Consulting and Clinical Psychology, 71*(2), 279–291.

Ybarra, M. L., & Mitchell, K. J. (2004). Youth engaging in online harassment: Associations with caregiver-child relationships, Internet use, and personal characteristics. *Journal of Adolescence, 27*(3), 319–336.

Young, S. E., Corley, R. P., Stallings, M. C., Rhee, S. H., Crowley, T. J., & Hewitt, J. K. (2002). Substance use, abuse, and dependence in adolescence: Prevalence, symptom profiles, and correlates. *Drug and Alcohol Dependence, 68*(3), 309–322.

Younoszai, T. M., Lohrmann, D. K., Seefeldt, C. A., & Greene, R. (1999). Trends from 1987 to 1991 in alcohol, tobacco, and other drug (ATOD) use among adolescents exposed to a school district-wide prevention intervention. *Journal of Drug Education, 29*(1), 77–94.

Zapert, K., Snow, D. L., & Tebes, J. K. (2002). Patterns of substance use in early through late adolescence. *American Journal of Community Psychology, 30*(6), 835–852.

Zimmer-Gembeck, M. J., Siebenbruner, J., & Collins, W. A. (2001). Diverse aspects of adolescent dating: Associations with psychosocial functioning from early to middle adolescence. *Journal of Adolescence, 24*, 313–336.

Zins, J., Weissberg, R. P., Wang, M., & Walberg, H. J. (2004). *Building academic success on social and emotional learning: What does the research say?* New York: Teachers College.

Index

A

abortion, 84–85

abstinence-based programs: effectiveness, 80; harm reduction strategies, 165–167; sexual behavior, 143–146, 148, 151, 180, 231

abusive behaviors: adolescent behavior development, 15, 53–67, 72–73, 85–89; attention disorders, 123; causal influences, 100–109, 113–120, 229–230; change process, 208–217; child abuse, 1–10, 32–33, 116–118, 135; dating relationships, 54–61, 66–67, 72, 89–90, 109, 202; Forum Theatre, 185, 216; Fourth R curriculum, 176–178, 181, 184, 188, 190–192; gangs, 66–67; homophobia, 61–65, 72–73; mortality rates, 80–81; motivation, 59–60, 66; overlapping behaviors, 92–99, 101, 229; parenting styles and expectations, 113–120, 156; potential benefits, 186–187; prevention initiatives, 128–143, 150, 182–184; role models, 116, 186; role-play strategies, 184; school environment, 120–122, 200–203; stage-based prevention strategies, 209–217, 223; substance use and abuse, 15, 80–81, 85–90, 92–99, 101; zero tolerance programs, 204–205; See also gender differences; peer relationships

accountability, 201, 204–206, 212, 214, 216–217

adaptive behaviors, 3, 15, 22–23, 30

ADD Health Study, 205

adjustment issues, 5–7, 11

adolescent behavior development: abusive behaviors, 15, 53–67, 72–73, 85–89; age ranges, 29; attitudes and beliefs, 124–127, 187; brain development research, 24, 76–77, 89; causal influences, 100–109; community involvement, 16–17, 21–22, 25–27; conflict resolution skills, 12; dating relationships, 42–43, 47–52; decision-making skills, 9, 16, 19–22, 25–26, 77–79, 126–127; developmental issues, 13–15; early childhood development analogies, 17–19; experimentation, 234; mass media influences, 30, 51, 67, 140–142; premature behaviors, 75–76, 88, 90, 95–97; prevention initiatives, 16–17, 21–22, 224–227; relationship rules, 28–29, 50; sensation-seeking behaviors, 122–123; sexual behavior, 229; sexuality, 48–49, 51–52, 80–85; skills-building strategies, 197–198; social learning processes, 105–109; social skills training, 155–157, 161–165, 167–168, 172–179; status, 36–39, 43–47; substance use and abuse, 229; See also peer relationships; transition periods

adversity, reactions to, 160–161

advertisements, as influence on adolescent behavior, 30, 67–68, 111–112

affluent families, 118–119

African American youth: See ethnic differences

aggression: attitudes and beliefs, 131–132; child abuse, 10; conflict resolution skills, 117; dating relationships, 124–125; domestic violence, 6; family influences, 116–118; gender differences, 39–40, 59–60, 91–92; interpersonal violence, 91–92; mass media influences, 68–73; prevention initiatives, 128–136; relationship issues, 54–65; same-sex relationships, 38; sexual assault, 89–90

AIDS/HIV, 83–84, 93, 145, 148–149, 178

alcohol use: abstinence-based programs, 166; adolescent behavior development, 15, 76; attitudes and beliefs, 103–105, 109, 124–126, 141; causal influences, 102, 111–112, 114; community/cultural influences, 111–112; harm reduction strategies, 165–167; mass media influences, 111–112; mortality rates, 80–81; overlapping behaviors, 92–93, 94–96, 98, 229; parenting styles and expecta-